STREETWISE FOR BOOK SMARTS

Streetwise for Book Smarts

Grassroots Organizing and
Education Reform in the Bronx

CELINA SU

Cornell University Press
Ithaca and London

First published 2009 by Cornell University Press
First printing, Cornell Paperbacks, 2009

Printed in the United States of America

Library of Congress Cataloging-in-Publication Data

Su, Celina, 1977–
    Streetwise for book smarts : grassroots organizing and education reform in the Bronx / Celina Su.
        p. cm.
    Includes bibliographical references and index.
    ISBN 978-0-8014-4725-9 (cloth : alk. paper)—
    ISBN 978-0-8014-7558-0 (pbk. : alk. paper)
    1. School improvement programs—New York (State)—
New York—Case studies.   2. Educational change—New York
(State)—New York—Case studies.   3. Community organization—
New York (State)—New York—Case studies.   4. Nonprofit
organizations—New York (State)—New York—Case studies.
5. Social movements—New York (State)—New York—
Case studies.   6. Community and school—New York (State)—
New York.   7. Bronx (New York, N.Y.)—Social conditions.
I. Title.

    LB2822.83.N7S82   2009
    371.2'0709747275—dc22   2008049127

Cloth printing   10 9 8 7 6 5 4 3 2 1
Paperback printing   10 9 8 7 6 5 4 3 2 1

Contents

Acknowledgments

I want to thank the organizers and leaders at the case study social change organizations who so generously welcomed me into their world. In basement offices or fancy conference auditoriums, in the middle of a hailstorm or under highway overpasses on steaming hot black asphalt, I came to more fully appreciate the difficulty of their work: the long hours and last-minute summits, not to mention the flexibility, enthusiasm, and common sense required of someone who is not just akin to one person's personal digital assistant, but the personal organic enabler of dozens, if not hundreds, of people. These thoughtful organizers and leaders indulged me in answering thousands of questions and allowed me to mill around as they worked to mount campaigns for education reform. They also engaged me in hours of thought-provoking conversation about New York politics and schools, political strategies, and the current state of social change organizations and grassroots organizing. The depth of their analyses, personal experiences, and passion continue to move me. If I do not list them all by name or construct large banners to publicize their work, it is not because I wish to withhold credit where it is due but because I wish to treat their identities, aspirations, and concerns with the same sensitivity with which they treated me.

This book began as a doctoral dissertation, and from the beginning, the members of my committee—Archon Fung, Ceasar McDowell, Paul

Osterman, and J. Phillip Thompson—challenged me to articulate practical assertions as well as theoretical extrapolations about the importance of tool kits in social change organizations. Because of them, I remained cognizant of what led me to the Bronx in the first place—the promise of education reform via democratic participation.

I was fortunate to engage in pertinent conversations with numerous others who have thus informed the present study, either during fieldwork or the many stages of revision, including the Community Involvement Program staff at the Annenberg Institute for School Reform (who were at the Institute of Education and Social Policy at New York University when I first solicited feedback on and considered critical questions about working in the Bronx), as well as workshop colleagues or audience members at the *Journal of Planning Education and Research* New Scholars workshop, the Wagner Education and Policy Studies Association at NYU, and conferences of the Association for Research on Nonprofit Organizations and Voluntary Action and the World Planning Congress.

The intensive fieldwork that laid the foundation for *Streetwise for Book Smarts,* taking place over both days and nights for many continuous months, would not have been possible without the Jacob K. Javits Fellowship from the U.S. Department of Education. The Whiting Award for Excellence in Teaching and a Professional Staff Congress at the City University of New York grant enabled me to carve out time for intensive revisions to the book manuscript. Terri Bennett and Sofia Mussa provided excellent research assistance.

The support of my colleagues in the Department of Political Science at Brooklyn College, especially Sally Bermanzohn, was also essential to the book. It was a joy to work with Gaston Alonso, Noel Anderson, and Jeanne Theoharis on *Our Schools Suck,* a related project that allowed me to appreciate the Sistas and Brothas United case study from a new perspective and situate it in public debates about inner-city youth.

I cannot thank Carolina Bank Muñoz and Karen Miller enough for welcoming me into their academic writing group and providing encouragement and careful, detailed feedback on multiple iterations of the book manuscript. Without them, I would not have been able to transform my thesis into a book.

I thank Peter Wissoker, my editor at Cornell University Press, for his wonderful guidance and advice in making this book a reality. I also want to acknowledge superb editorial work by Brian Bendlin, Susan Specter, and Emily Zoss.

Barbara Green, Jane Kim, Jeanne Theoharis, and Joy Wang read portions of the manuscript with acuity and wit. Two reviewers also gave constructive criticisms that compelled me to flesh out the implications of the Bronx case studies, and that made this a stronger book. I especially want to thank Dennis Shirley for making expert suggestions and asking incisive questions that helped me to add precision and complexity to key arguments.

I am indebted to all friends and family who supported me along the way, including many of those named above, as well as Tiwonge Gondwe, Shubhada Kambli, Alexandre Su, Caleb Su, and Christina Su. Ann Brian Murphy, Kath Phelan, and Damon Rich were integral to the beginnings of the Bronx study, and Alex Bleecker and Felise Nguyen have been instrumental to all of my writing pursuits. I dedicate this book to those mentors whose skill and kindness have left an indelible impression on my work—Marta Heise, Joyce Jacobsen, Mike Markot, Alice Rivlin, Kate Rushin, Jen-Ming Tseng, Linda Virtue, and Dorothy Wang. Everyone deserves such mentors, but few of us are so lucky.

A fierce scholar and epistemological whiz kid, Peter Muennig's interdisciplinary research pinpoints the ways in which inequality poisons not just the most marginalized but our society as a whole. I am grateful for his compassion, clarity of vision, and, in times of hardship, bizarrely plentiful fountains of equanimity and laughter.

The reflections and feedback shared by leaders, organizers, colleagues, mentors, and committee members were so consistently well considered and astute that I sometimes found myself pulled in disparate directions. Mondros and Wilson wrote that "when you write a book about organizing, you can make many enemies. To them, our thanks for providing some of the recent examples included herein" (1994, xx). Never was anyone's passion for social justice, nor the struggles along the way, in doubt. This book reflects my interpretation of and views on the riches of data collected along the way. While its limitations remain my own, its insights could not have been developed without the collective help of so many others.

With the exception of public officials, all names throughout the book have been changed to ensure confidentiality. See appendix A for a more thorough overview of the study's methods.

Portions of chapter 5 have previously appeared in different form, as "Cracking Silent Codes: Critical Race Theory and Education Organizing," *Discourse: Studies in the Cultural Politics of Education* 28, no. 4 (2007): 531–48.

STREETWISE FOR BOOK SMARTS

CHAPTER ONE

A KALEIDOSCOPE OF PEOPLE POWER

In the 2003–2004 school year, Bronx, New York, high schools reeled from a series of stabbings and violent attacks. A number of schools were labeled dangerous. In these schools, students waited in long lines to pass through metal detectors each morning, facing quite a few police officers along the way. Several Bronx-based social change organizations (SCOs), grassroots organizations embedded in local communities and working toward systemic social change, contemplated appropriate responses to the situation.[1]

Some SCOs cited the need for additional safety patrols. A group of parents from one school spoke of how they had previously protested until they got extra officers—a fairly scarce resource in New York City public schools—at their local elementary school. Again and again, they argued, New York State has underfunded New York City schools, and New York City consistently gives the South Bronx the short shrift in necessary services— school safety officers, more classroom seats, and speed bumps in front of the school. Some of the parents, however, were doubtful that adding another officer would make a difference. As long as the children lived in a neighborhood with severe poverty and few economic opportunities, nearby drug dealing was likely to persist, and children would continue to grow up ("too quickly," one added) in unsafe environments.

In response to the same events, another SCO asserted that not all existing safety patrol officers were treating students humanely, thus exacerbating tensions within the schools. At first, they wanted to hold a press conference detailing students' grievances, but they eventually created and implemented an innovative alternative—they drew maps of their schools from a student's perspective, detailing all of the secret hiding places of drug dealers, bullies, and students cutting classes. Many of these spots had not been on the safety officers' patrol routes. They then invited the officers to join them in a workshop they constructed in which the students and officers scripted and acted in skits playing out their perceptions of one another. They asserted that concrete services like school safety officers mattered, but that how these officers behaved *within* schools also mattered. These leaders got a new safety protocol implemented in their schools.

In effect, the organizations and school officials battled over who was to blame for the school violence—the violence-perpetrating students, the overbearing police, or systemic forces like the poverty pervading dangerous shelters and housing projects. Were police a solution to the problem, or exacerbating the schools' violence-prone conditions? Depending on how groups framed the incidents, members mobilized to propose very different political campaigns. These different responses to the same challenges can shed light on the ways in which social change is not scripted, inevitable, or completely determined by circumstances; the choices made by each organization make a difference. By investigating case studies of different education organizing groups and campaigns in the South Bronx, policy makers, academics, and activists can better understand the efforts that ultimately lead to better and safer schools.

Although the different social change organizations were all working on the same issues of local school reform—namely, public safety and teacher quality–some organizations were staging fairly confrontational protests while others were hoping for backroom negotiations if not dealings per se. Some stormed City Hall, others tried to gain a seat with the politicians at the big oak table inside, and yet others claimed to storm City Hall but secretly hoped to negotiate themselves to the big oak table.

Given the similarities among larger goals of the case study organizations, the diversity of their tactics is puzzling. Why were their campaigns so different? How, then, were these campaigns shaped, and what is their impact?

Because these groups started off with similar language about their missions, their differences cannot be explained by their driving visions of what good schools look like. Rather, underlying cultural practices *inside* the organizations led to different political strategies. It was not just what they did but *how* they did it that mattered.

Two of these groups worked with what I call an *Alinskyite tool kit*, meaning that their organizational cultures are filled with practices originally associated with Saul Alinsky. Alinsky, whose work started to become famous in the late 1940s and early 1950s, was known for an irreverent, confrontational, and pragmatic style of organizing. Although the faith-based group he founded, the Industrial Areas Foundation (IAF), has changed quite a bit under new leadership, it remains quite influential. Alinskyite groups pursue strategies that help constituents to win referenda of existing policy proposals or elections, engage in confrontational strategies, and build broad-based coalitions in the name of "color-blind" equality; generally, racial or ethnic background is not formally considered in decision making.[2]

Meanwhile, two other groups worked with a *Freirean tool kit*, filled with practices originally associated with Paulo Freire, a Brazilian educator who first became famous in the 1960s and 1970s. At first, Freire was not known as an organizer per se since he primarily advocated for and designed programs for popular education, trying to bring adult literacy to the masses. His work has remained quite influential worldwide, primarily because Freire also argued that all good education includes a large participatory component for students. In this way, students and teachers engage in "consciousness-raising" together, and this critical thinking will, in turn, help them organize themselves to work for social change.

These Freirean groups in the Bronx pursued contrasting political strategies: they focused on constructing new policy proposals or implementing them rather than winning approval of existing ones, they engaged in primarily collaborative strategies, and they were adept at addressing issues of race, even if these issues disproportionately affected only one racial group.

The different political strategies pursued by these groups were not simply better or worse than one another; they led to radically different notions of what constitutes education reform and social change in the Bronx. The Alinskyite groups ultimately tried to help their constituents obtain a larger slice of the social, political, and economic pie while the Freirean ones tried to make the school system a whole new kind of bigger, better pie altogether.

Campaigns pursued by groups using the Alinskyite tool kit, such as increased state funding for New York City schools, will definitely help to alleviate the poor state of these schools. Nevertheless, to get to the root of the problems plaguing Bronx schools, financing formulae will need to be rewritten from scratch. Groups adopting the Freirean tool kits are more likely to tackle structural inequalities within the school system, as well as truly radical and sustainable social change. Such social change takes patience, but it is most truly satisfying in the long run.

Examining several case studies in a small geographical area allowed each group's choices to stand out. Over 18 months of intensive fieldwork, I attended meetings, workshops, rallies, and summits with policy makers within each of the SCOs. I also spent a lot of time hanging out in their offices, learning about their practices and the ways in which they interacted with one another. Over the course of months, leaders who eyed nonmembers (like me) with suspicion let their guard down, and they talked frankly about what they really thought about their SCOs. Thus, I got to see a whole lot more than what they were officially working on, and what they usually present to journalists, visiting researchers, curious outsiders, or even casual members. What these leaders and organizers did was hard work, and their strained struggles deserved no less respect than their "official" campaign wins. It is only by examining their cultural practices and their actions, as well as their words, that these SCO organizers and leaders will truly be given full credit for the creativity and innovation in their tool kits and subsequent political strategies.

The lessons learned by these groups can be applied to social change organizations around the country. These lessons are particularly striking because these SCOs aim for education reform, a notoriously difficult policy issue to tackle. Unlike campaigns against slumlords who make no repairs or employers who pay no wages, in education there are no obvious villains. Activists' relationships to teachers and schools are far more complicated: even if one child has a bad teacher, the parent may not want to complain if that might lead to antagonism from that teacher, or if the child might pay the price in some way. The lessons here are helpful for all SCOs trying to navigate thorny political and policy arenas, even those outside of education, where there are no clear good guys and bad guys. Should one pursue collaborative or confrontational strategies? Should one work on changing policy, or instead on making sure that it is properly implemented? By tending to their tool kits, SCOs can improve upon their current practices in order to work more effectively toward social change and policy reform.

These SCOs also matter because they stand as potential models for democratic participation, especially in contexts where formal, institutionalized channels of public input are scarce. New York City, for example, used to have school boards, where parents could get elected and represent the will of the larger public in the school system. These school boards had a contentious and fraught history of their own, however, and were dismantled in

2002. While community advocates largely felt that the school boards were structured in a way that sabotaged any chances of success, they had hoped that these boards would be replaced by a more meaningful system of democratic governance.[3]

Instead, New York's parents and students were left with no guaranteed way to relay their concerns to the city administration, even though the schools were supposedly there to serve them. Education councils for parents did not develop until a couple of years after Mayor Bloomberg's new Children First governance initiative went into effect, after the present study's fieldwork period ended. These education councils are themselves considered dysfunctional, as many of their positions remain unfilled and parents continue to struggle to wield decision-making powers at the school level.[4] According to the city's Department of Education, these councils are meant to be advisory. Social change organizations fill the gaps in such situations, and prove vital to American democracy.

The issue of education reform is especially appropriate for a study on democratic participation via collective action because public schools remain incredibly important spaces for public discourse for most Americans across class, race, and gender lines. Because the percentage of children being homeschooled or attending private schools is fairly small, most American parents go to schools, meet other adults, and engage in conversations about local policy, politics, and the future of the country's children. At schools around the country, everyday citizens talk about public education as the Great Equalizer, the means via which poor kids can make their way up the socioeconomic ladder and succeed in American society, so that everyone operates on a level playing field. They chat about how their schools are doing, and whether they are living up to the notions of the Great Equalizer.

The case study SCOs I present here are "laboratories of democracy," filled with parents and students like these, working to bring this vision a bit closer to reality, struggling to give the South Bronx well-funded schools with adequate space and facilities, good teachers, and substantive curricula. As Eliasoph notes, "Discussion, debate, disagreement: public life is hard work, not something for which every society or individual comes naturally equipped" (1998, 10). Whereas research demonstrates that Americans are not getting involved in public affairs the way they used to, and that those who have little money to give away and little time after work to attend meetings are even less likely to do so, these SCOs suggest that there are still ways to not only engage everyday citizens but to help those from marginalized communities work toward a better world.[5]

The Puzzle of Tactics and Strategies

On April 1, 2004, Sistas and Brothas United (SBU) led New York City Council members on a tour of Bronx high schools, pointing out details like overcrowded classrooms, floor-to-ceiling windows without bars or closing mechanisms, and bathrooms without stall doors or locks. This group of activist students had carefully planned their demonstration to draw attention to the need for more construction funding; they timed the tour so that the council members were caught in the hallways when the school bell rang, so that they could see and feel firsthand the pushing and shoving of throngs of teenagers between classes.

SBU's students then rode buses downtown to join other members of the Northwest Bronx Clergy and Community Coalition (NWBCCC), their umbrella organization, on the steps of City Hall. They arrived for a press conference marking the State Legislature's official deadline for its approval of the New York State budget. "April Fool's Day," quipped a key NWBCCC leader. "They haven't passed the state budget on time in over two decades, and they won't this year." SBU and NWBCCC members unfurled banners and held placards arguing for more state funding for New York City schools. Later in the day, Joel Rivera, the City Council majority leader from the Bronx, decided that since SBU members had already taken the day off from school, they might as well stay downtown and watch a City Council session firsthand.

A glance at the few days preceding SBU's tour and press conference demonstrate that other Bronx organizations concerned with school reform were equally industrious that week. For example, on the Sunday before, a few hundred members of NWBCCC had performed a surprise protest at Governor George Pataki's home in Garrison, New York. On Wednesday, members from another group, Mothers on the Move (MOM), had visited Albany to lobby for more New York City funding and to exhibit support for a lawsuit against the current state funding formula. Finally, members of the NWBCCC and the Bronx chapter of the Association of Community Organizations for Reform Now (ACORN), along with members of three other groups with similar missions, had just wrapped up a month's worth of collecting signatures for a petition asking the city to fund a lead teacher campaign, placing experienced mentor teachers in each of their partner schools.

Why were these social change organizations pursuing such different strategies when they all wanted the same thing—namely, better schools in the Bronx? If one group was really having that much more success than the others, and there were one most efficient strategy, then one would also expect the others to try to follow the successful group's lead, but no clear role model emerged. That said, neither was the striking variety of real, sustained campaigns being pursued by the education organizing groups completely unpredictable. What was the key piece in the puzzle of these groups' tactics and political strategies?[6]

In the situation just described in the South Bronx, the education campaigns at the book's four case study organizations—ACORN Bronx, the NWBCCC, SBU, and MOM—all held similar levels of resources, and were trying to get reactions from the same schools and government. This is important because usually, differences between collaborative and confrontational tactics and strategies are partly shaped by structural factors such as variations in political context or in resources.

For example, when an SCO pursues campaigns for policy changes, it might try to take advantage of political opportunities, such as the inauguration of a friendlier governmental administration, a landmark court decision, or significant shifts in the demographics of a population. The degree of repression imposed by the government, for example, helps to shape the responding political strategies pursued by SCOs.[7] Certainly, the Bronx education reform SCOs I studied all paid attention to Mayor Michael Bloomberg and New York City Schools Chancellor Joel Klein's every move, especially when it came down to schools in the Bronx. The fact that they were all hoping to garner wins from the same Bronx borough president, city administration, mayor, and governor and still reacted differently to all the same moves, however, meant that there was also something else going on.

Differences in political strategies can also be explained by variations in resources, such as money, means of communication, and social networks, as well as how these resources are mobilized.[8] It matters whether an SCO has just three full-time staff workers or thirty, across four offices in New York City, and whether it has a budget of $100,000 or $1 million. Further, it matters how the organization got the money—through direct mail appeals, by applying to foundations or other sources, via independent or coalition-based fundraising, and so on. This is especially important when SCOs attempt to access funds from external sources like prestigious foundations.[9] One can imagine the case study SCOs pursuing more collaborative political strategies, for example, if foundations proclaimed that confrontational strategies were too "militant" or "not constructive." Because these SCOs are working with low-income constituents, they are unlikely to raise enough money to pay for the organizers' and directors' salaries without external funds.

For the SCOs analyzed in this book, concerns over funding certainly mattered, but they did not necessarily dictate political strategies. While the amount of funding for education organizing in New York was hardly copious, it expanded during the book's fieldwork period. The SCOs all raised funds via a combination of grants from foundations and dues from members, and several different SCOs received grants from the same foundations. They were each staffed by a similarly small number of organizers, with two to three paid staff members focusing on education campaigns. They were all in similar boats, if not in exactly the same one. Once again, there was something else helping the leaders and organizers to make decisions in their campaigns and political strategies.

Further, in spending time with these SCOs, I saw that there was often a discrepancy between what the organizers said they did when writing grant proposals and what they actually did in real life. They never lied about their work, but as experienced grant writers they framed their work in ways that they knew foundation officers would look upon favorably, and they made sure to include buzzwords used by the foundations themselves. The SCOs' internal cultural practices were loosely coupled with the funding trends that swirled around them.[10] During my fieldwork period in the Bronx, funding was plentiful enough so that, for the most part, organizers looked for appropriate funding sources after they had already decided upon overall campaigns.

Structural explanations emphasizing resources and political opportunities did help me to make some sense of the SCOs' political strategies. They emphasized the ways in which SCOs think deliberately about where their money comes from, what they should do next, and whether they can win a certain campaign. The fact that these pragmatic considerations are so important suggests that SCOs are not bunches of crazed activists or groups subject to mob mentality. They are organizations with well-honed mission statements, bylaws, and goals.

Still, I wanted to focus on how these social change organizations were operating in such different ways, despite these constraints. It was not as if some of the organizations served well-organized, well-resourced, middle- or upper-class white constituents while the rest of them were poor, heavily Latino and African American groups of newbies. This indicates that the grassroots base building of SCOs is affected but not wholly predetermined by their circumstances. Of course, the state can make things harder or easier, or try to steer debates or campaigns into certain directions, but some of the steering can be done by the organizations themselves.

In this book, I focus on just this sort of steering, the kind of work performed by SCOs even when they are caught between a rock and a hard place. What made the SCOs steer themselves in such different directions?

A key piece of our puzzle of strategies and tactics remained missing, and a clue lay in how some researchers have used the concept of "culture" to examine what happens *inside* SCOs. After all, the leaders making these collective decisions are still humans, not automatons. Theories that emphasize cultural practices and how organizers and leaders perceive and react to each other and their environment explain situations in which the behavior of SCOs cannot be entirely predicted by structural variables such as resources and the political context. Well-organized people power can make a difference. The groups' different political strategies were not products of pure rational calculus, and they cannot be predicted solely from adding up the expectations of individuals or by examining the political contexts and resources available to them.

On the other hand, culture is not everything. The choices made by individuals and organizations are largely circumscribed by the actions of those around them, especially if these individuals are powerful or have more resources. There is little choice in being forced to do something, or just making do and going through the motions.

Further, "culture" is a slippery term, bandied about a bit recklessly these days. In the realm of education policy reform, for instance, comedian Bill Cosby received heaps of media attention (and for the most part, public acclaim) when he lambasted African Americans' dearth of "values" at a gala celebrating the fiftieth anniversary of the U.S. Supreme Court's *Brown v. Board of Education of Topeka* decision to desegregate public schools. He declared, "These people [low-income African Americans] are fighting hard to be ignorant.…What the hell good is *Brown v. the Board of Education* if nobody wants it?" (Cosby, quoted in Dyson 2005, 58). Meanwhile, Puerto Rican–born Congressman Herman Badillo cried that a five-hundred-year-old "cultural siesta" has led Latinos to devalue education (2006, 32). These laments over the "culture of failure" among low-income African Americans and Latinos in inner cities pay surprisingly little attention to the voices of real-life students and parents in urban centers.[11]

Sloppy discussions of culture often make it seem like an ill-defined blob of essentialist characteristics of groups of people rather than historically embedded practices, implicit and explicit values, and behavioral responses to structural constraints and specific situations. Thus, I also do not want to give the impression that grassroots groups can choose their "cultures" with abandon, nor that the organizations' tool kits are simply extensions of the individuals who use them. This study pays attention to all the ways in which African Americans and Latinos in the Bronx, the very inner-city folks Cosby and Badillo lament as lacking values, take matters into their own hands. It behooves us to pay attention to the key factors that may be within our control in order to ascertain how education organizing groups might take advantage of them.

This study operates with the assumption that SCOs can matter, and in believing that the notion of "social change" and policy changes exist it refuses to dismiss agency by saying that we are all mere reflections of our socially constructed realities. It is true that people sometimes "go through the motions" instead of actively thinking about every action. Still, leaders, organizers, and organizations do have some genuine choices to make, even if many of these choices are often quite constrained. Frankly, activists might need to think this way to maintain a sense of hope, to maintain the notion that social change organizations can make a difference. Otherwise, leaders and organizers might be tempted to stop fighting, and succumb to their respective fates.

Without trivializing the power of constraints, it remains important to answer the question, "Where's the agency?"[12] In other words, in what ways do decisions and actions made by the members, leaders, organizers, and organizations matter? The case study organizations did not espouse different missions or ideologies. None of them rejected confrontational or collaborative strategies outright, for example. If neither pure rational calculus nor wholesale ideology explains how leaders in these organizations tended to collectively make their decisions and choices, then what does?

In the South Bronx case studies, the groups' cultural practices made a big difference in political strategies. Among the South Bronx groups, repertoires of the rituals, activities, language, and symbols adopted, as well as the rules of interaction, helped to shape political strategies that eventually are developed in each of the organizations. These cultural practices are important because they help organizers and leaders to transform "intuitive visions into explicit...proposals" (Goodwin, Jasper, and Polletta 2001, 19). They help SCOs to retain and energize their constituents, and then help these members in "connecting ideas to motivations for action" (Ferree and Merrill 2000, 457).[13]

To really see *how* these cultural practices matter we need to dig deep into the organizations' cultures.[14] Culture consists of the shared behavior and views within a community, "including beliefs, ritual practices, art forms, and ceremonies, as well as informal cultural practices such as language, gossip, stories, and rituals of daily life" (Swidler 1986, 273).[15] Here, *culture* does not refer to ethnic- or race-delineated culture. In this context I am not talking about dance, food, or the customs of groups of specific racial or ethnic backgrounds.

I focus on organizational culture as the crux of my analysis. This might include how organizers talk to and relate to leaders and members, how meetings are conducted, and how decisions about campaigns are made. Do members feel invested in the organizations because they feel emotionally tied to the organizers, because they put a lot of time into the work, or because they put a lot of money into the organization via dues? Do they stick to it because they love it, or because they are close friends with their coleaders, or do they just feel obligated to keep going? All of the above? When they get upset, do leaders talk it out, do they make a decision with a majority vote, do they yell at the others in the group, or do they often quit instead, forcing the organizers to find new members? Do organizers coordinate all of the activities and basically delegate tasks to individuals, or do the members decide on what to do themselves, and then ask the organizers for help with a few tasks?

Such cultural practices might all look similar right now, but the differences among them will become apparent as soon as we start to take a look at specific case studies. Such contrasts will also become more clear than they might seem at first glance because, once we spend time with the case study organizations in the South Bronx, we see that their cultural practices are not random. In real-life cultures, these stories and rituals might be varied and even contradictory; handbooks to action might include some passages emphasizing nonviolence and others emphasizing confrontation. Bibles of social change organizations, from the Holy Bible to Alinsky's *Rules for Radicals,* usually leave enough ambiguity between the lines and give enough contextualized advice so that a SCO can pick out a line to support a range of actions, even if others disagree with the thrust of that SCO's strategic interpretation. Each organization also has its own activities and rituals, which tend to acquire a tenor of their own. In this way, cultures are not monolithic but more akin to tool kits, "public practices infused with power" (Swidler 1995, 38).

More specifically, Swidler (1986) critiques ends- and value-oriented analyses of culture, noting, "If culture influences action through end values, people in changing circumstances should hold on to their preferred ends while altering their strategies for attaining them. But if culture provides the tools with which persons construct lines of action, then styles or strategies of action will be more persistent than the ends people seek to attain" (Swidler 1986, 277).

In other words, it is important to investigate the real-life habits of SCO participants as well as their ideals, goals, missions, and "end values" such as "education reform" or "social change." Not every single practice, habit, or declaration is necessarily shared; nor do individuals' behaviors necessarily reflect articulated values. The Alinskyite or Freirean tool kit used by each case study organization is simultaneously informed by larger organizational cultures, the idiosyncrasies of individual leaders, and the conditions of specific situations. By measuring actions and silences as well as words, researchers can dig deeper into how four SCOs, all claiming to be working toward education reform and social justice in the Bronx, in fact pursued divergent political strategies.

Tool Kits, Prototypes of Power

Each organization subscribed to a *tool kit,* a set of cultural practices regularly used by its leaders and organizers. Recording each SCO's tool kit could result in a massive compendium of parables, instructions, songs, chants, agenda, oral histories, and artifacts, as if each organization could have an authoritative bible, apocrypha included. Compiling and presenting these compendia would not be especially helpful for researchers, however, if all of the case studies were presented as unique and exceptional. However, from these compendia, we can analyze the tools that stand out, the themes that arise, and the ways in which these tools and themes might help to shape different political strategies with external actors. Articulating tool kits then facilitates a comparative analysis of SCOs and their respective political strategies.

In investigating each case study SCO's tool kit, we also see that they were collectively reused and reinforced by all participants: members, leaders, organizers, and even third-party observers. While they may have been instrumental when they were first created, the cultural practices then become entrenched in their own right. Neither completely instrumental nor meaningless scripts, these tool kits gave meaning to and were in turn given meaning by SCO campaigns. In this way, each participant had an important role to play and several important tools to use, but the tool kits were less likely to be active, self-conscious constructions created by any single participant.

What does a powerful tool kit look like? First, it might be useful to see if models or examples of tool kits already exist in the literature. Most books on contemporary community organizing have focused on housing or worker campaigns, which have a longer recent history.[16] Such works are quite helpful, but not all of their lessons are relevant for the Bronx case studies because education demands a different set of strategies than other issues do. An actual policy change is perhaps even more dependent on implementation and everyday practice in the classroom than on favorable budgeting and legislation. Getting a landlord to make repairs on a leaking roof is different from getting a teacher to dote on and challenge your child every day. Further, both researchers and practitioners have suggested that education might require more collaboration, or maybe a more difficult balance between confrontation and collaboration, than a lot of community organizers are used to.

Public education reform may be the most decentralized, and yet galvanizing, public priority and social movement today. Several prominent books that specifically address organizing on education issues, such as Warren (2001) and Shirley (1997), focus on case studies in the Southwest. These have focused on the strengths and weaknesses of the strategies in those cases, the ways in which social capital can be developed and utilized for social justice, and the implications of a model based on congregation-based organizing. Osterman (2002, 2007) also focuses on the Texas IAF, specifically on how certain rituals and training styles in the organization help to develop member leadership that questions and challenges the top and prevents the organization from becoming oligarchical. These works have raised the flag on education organizing nationwide, and they have articulated many of the key ways in which grassroots work can make a difference in local education policy.

Still, it remains useful to look at comparisons, to see what characteristics are unique to one education organizing group and what characteristics or tool kit components might be shared by all similar groups operating in a given political context. Only via such comparative analyses can we discern which cultural practices, and which political strategies, stand out and make a difference. If these groups pursue strategies based on Alinskyite tool kits, for instance, might groups with Freirean tool kits succeed even more?

Comparative analyses are fairly rare; those that do exist usually include organizations that subscribe to very different ideologies, or operate in different political contexts. For example, a recent edited volume (Orr 2007) collects case studies from across the nation; the book highlights some potential overarching challenges and promises of community organizing, focusing on larger organizations and success stories such as the IAF.

In a book on case studies clustered in Portland, Oregon, and Chicago, Smock (2003) compares the five "models" of power-based, women-centered, transformative, civic, and community development organizing. The book critically analyzes key assumptions, strengths, and weaknesses in each of these five models. Notably, Smock's power-based model organizations draw from the works of Alinsky, and her transformative models draw from the works of Freire, exactly the inspirations of the two tool kits I discuss.

In Smock's conceptualization, "while proponents of the power-based model assert that the political system basically works as long as residents are sufficiently organized to participate in it, the transformative models proponents believe the system itself is part of the problem ... [that] the public decision-making process is shaped ... by our society's underlying power dynamics ... [therefore,] urban problems can be solved only through a radical restructuring of dominant political, social, and economic institutions" (29). In turn, transformative model organizations excel in building alternative institutions and view much of mainstream participation as an inevitable co-optation of dominant interests.

Smock's power-based and transformative models are starkly different and serve very different missions. Some of the transformative model organizations were outside the purview of traditional community organizing, for instance, and would bristle at any notion of "fighting city hall." Such organizations might focus squarely on cooperative arrangements and mutual aid without any goals for explicit policy changes on the part of the government.

The differences between the SCOs in the Bronx are more subtle—they all believe in the power of mainstream political participation and collective action, but their practices are different enough so that some are more likely to lead to real social transformation than others.

All of the South Bronx case studies attempt to influence policy making by gathering residents to work on a single education campaign. Further, the reach of Alinsky's shadow in community organizing is such that all four case studies follow some of the basic practices described in Smock's power model. Once again, I do not wish to contrast completely different kinds of organizations, but to compare and analyze the differing cultural practices, choices, and consequences of similar ones.

Further, existing comparative studies usually examine organizations from more than one city. This makes it difficult to attribute differences among the groups to just their cultural practices; these groups could have been facing very different circumstances in different urban contexts.

This book offers a unique opportunity to see how four education organizing groups developed different internal cultures of participation. Still, it took me a while to adequately describe the two categories of tool kits that best captured what I observed in the South Bronx. At first I assumed that the four groups would have organizational cultures that largely flowed out of how they described their constituency pools. For example, the ones who described themselves as neighborhood organizers only knocked on doors located in certain, well-bounded neighborhoods.[17] Other groups, especially the ones that offered social services like free general equivalency diploma (GED) classes or day care, might draw on the people who used their services as constituents. Finally, there were groups that worked with Christian, Catholic, Jewish, and Muslim congregations, so these were faith-based groups; their main constituents were those who showed up for religious services. Even though the constituents for all of these groups would be mostly working-class or poor, primarily Latino or African American, South Bronx residents, they would largely be divided into categories as residents, social services clients, or congregation members. This kind of categorizing would be similar to the one adopted by Wood (2002), who compared two groups based in Oakland, California. The rationale is that the organizing groups might have different organizational cultures according to how they reached out to constituents.

I was inspired by Wood's book, and thought that it would be interesting to see if the NWBCCC, which is affiliated with several congregations, had the same strengths and weaknesses at Wood's faith-based groups. Could I replicate his typology, and if so, would I get the same results? Wood examined Oakland Community Organizations (OCO), a faith-based Pacific Institute for Community Organizing (PICO)–affiliated group alongside a race-based, Center for Third World Organizing (CTWO)–affiliated group and drew conclusions about their cultural strategies. He concluded that ultimately, OCO was less radical but more successful in its campaigns.[18] It could be argued, however, that these conclusions were quite dependent upon one's definition of "success." For instance, Mumm (2003) argues that Wood does not "grasp the depth of cultural transformation that PUEBLO [People United for a Better Life in Oakland] is capable of generating in its leadership." Likewise, in the present study, the Freirean tool kit might seem more labor-intensive and time-consuming, but the SCOs that used it worked toward more substantive social change and social transformation.

Ultimately, Wood's race- and faith-based case studies are not wholly analogous to those I got to know in the Bronx. None of the case studies here holds onto any ideology, class-based or otherwise, as steadfastly as the CTWO-affiliated group. Further, it is easy to imagine how a single individual might be a public housing resident in a certain neighborhood, a client of a social services agency or nonprofit organization, and a congregation member at the same time.

After spending a lot of time with the organizations, I began to see that among my case studies, faith-based rituals were not the crux of any organization's tool kit. Unlike the organizing described in books on faith-based national networks like PICO and IAF, faith-explicit practices, like prayer, were much less common at the NWBCCC.[19] Second, all of the organizations, whether they were ostensibly faith-based organizations or deliverers of services, were in fact very much rooted in neighborhoods. Organizers worked with individual members, not congregations. While the original categorizations were helpful and not completely irrelevant, they failed to capture the meaningful variations among the different groups.

I then attempted to pick up on the language used by community organizers themselves, trying to see if the main characteristics of different tool kits lay there. Some of the education organizers and key leaders kept talking about issue-based, versus relational, organizing. In issue-based organizing, an organizer already has an issue such as education reform in mind, and she perhaps uses a potential campaign as the starting point for rallying members and leaders. In relational organizing, an organizer builds a one-on-one relationship with individuals, trying to get to know everything about these leaders and members—even things about them that might at first seem to be irrelevant to education reform. The ideas for campaigns come about more slowly that way, but some argue that groups engaging in relational organizing can be more successful in the long term.

It was quite difficult for me to place the four case study organizations into these categories, though, for several reasons. First, while some of the organizers debated these terms all the time, other organizers had never heard of them. According to those organizers, they just did what they did. More substantively, what *all* of the organizers did was actually a combination of the two, even if some of the organizers were closer to members than others. They all engaged in iterations of outreach, the refining of campaign issues, and reorganization. In addition, even if I could find a pattern of discernible differences, I was not sure if the issue-versus-relational organizing debate was the crux of it. I did not want to succumb to the very pitfall I had set out to avoid—namely, that of a typology that ignored other, equally important, more nuanced parts of the organizations' tool kits.

After spending some time with the SCOs I noticed that half of them did seem to operate within a framework I understood to be Alinskyite. Because of this, I looked back on a study of the Alinsky and women-centered models of community organizing—particularly that presented by Stall and Stoecker (1998).[20] This study described the two models in well-rounded ways, and it included their conceptual differences, such as their respective definitions of leadership and power, as well as variations in their organizing processes. Still, the real-life case studies in my research did not quite fit these models. In my case studies, theories of human nature, ethics, public versus private space, and conflict were not articulated or consistent enough to serve as driving principles.

Finally, I classified groups according to their Alinskyite or Freirean tool kits. These categories felt satisfying, as they reflected many facets of the organizations' collective practices, rhetoric, and the relationships between their leaders and organizers. At the same time, the categories were distinct enough as to capture patterns in the case studies' organizational cultures.

Alinsky is considered the father of contemporary American community organizing, so it seems intuitive to name one of the two categories after him. But why Freire, a South American educator whose most famous works focused more on theory than on-the-ground practice? In fact, some of the activists themselves mentioned these points about Freire. They felt that Freire's emphasis on becoming "more fully human," however abstract that concept may seem, helped them to reach beyond mainstream politics, to dream a little more, and to reach a bit farther in their visions for radical social change. Although a few of the activists also referred to organizers like Ella Baker, they generally did not define themselves as inheritors of the civil rights movement. Instead, they invoked Freire much more often. Thus, my decision to call the second tool kit Freirean has both empirical and theoretical reasons: I paid attention to how the grassroots leaders themselves described their work; further, emphasizing the organizations' Freirean emphasis on radical, imaginative, and personal transformation made theoretical sense to me.

At the SCOs, all of the staff organizers had heard of Saul Alinsky and most of them had also heard of Paulo Freire. Some consciously tried to follow the principles of one or the other, but inevitably, their real-life practices turned out to belie their ideal forms. Because of this, I felt confident that I had made a good choice in focusing on and trying to describe complex practices rather than goals or ideals. I was relieved that the Alinksy and Freire categories adequately captured the case study organizations' tool kits, since these categories helped me to streamline the key points of my comparative analysis.

Each of the two tool kits has three key components. These components mean that members in the SCOs become leaders in certain ways, that there are patterns in how they interact with paid organizers, and that paid organizers spend most of their time and energy on certain activities.

Here, the Alinskyite tool kit is marked by an emphasis on the organization rather than the individual member or leader, an organizer-leader relationship with the organizer as guide, and recruitment and campaigns as the focus of organizational activities. An emphasis on organizational development means that leaders are treated in fairly uniform ways, and that their participation is structured in ways that directly help to further the SCO's reputation or add to its resources.

Freire's attention to pedagogy makes a tool kit based on his work especially apropos for the SCOs in the present study, since they are fighting for social change in the field of education. However, I want to differentiate the SCOs in this book from those that seek to replicate Freire's work via popular education programs. All of my case study SCOs worked foremost on political school-reform campaigns, pressuring elected officials and civil servants to heed their goals through organized meetings, petitions, rallies, and protests. Thus, the bulk of their activities lay not in research and formal classes per se but in interacting with policy makers.

In this book I examine three key cultural practices in the Freirean category: a focus on the individual member (rather than the organization itself), leadership development with the organizer as partner, and emotional or cultural exchange as the focus of organizational activities. A focus on individual development means that in these SCOs leaders are encouraged to pursue personal interests even if they differ from those of other members and do not seem to directly contribute to the SCO's campaign work.

The final typology of case studies, then, looks like this:

Table 1. List of Education Organizing SCOs in This Study

	Primarily Alinskyite	Primarily Freirean
ACORN Bronx	X	
NWBCCC	X	
SBU		X
MOM		X

Perhaps because they are both inspired by influential organizers, the two categories discussed here are by no means distinct in practice, and it should not come as a surprise that the tool kits manifest themselves in slightly different ways among the groups. Nevertheless, differences in emphases can be clearly drawn, and the categories resonated. One organizer, for instance, reflected upon the two categories I use here by stating, "I think we experienced…different 'cultures' without always labeling them as Freirean or

Alinskyite...but we *knew* what we were referring to in ACORN's culture and NWBCCC's culture that distinguished their work from ours."

While Freire and Alinsky are often cited as inspirations for the same contemporary SCOs, this might be because they are both associated with progressive causes.[21] Still, the two influential thinkers make different assumptions about what SCOs should look like—what leadership development should be, what organizers should focus their efforts on, and what the role of member-leaders should be. This, in turn, makes a difference in the kinds of political strategies chosen by these social change organizations. These differences will become more apparent in later chapters, when we examine the tool kits in action. In the meantime, the three key characteristics of these categories are summarized in the following table.

Table 2. Key Characteristics of Tool Kits

Key Practices	Alinskyite Tool Kit	Freirean Tool Kit
Emphasis of organization activities	Recruitment and campaigns	Emotional or cultural exchange (through services or "hanging out")
Focus of typical activity agenda	Organizational development	Individual development
Nature of organizer-leader relationship	Leadership development with organizer as teacher	Leadership development with organizer as partner

Tool Kits in the Field

In addition to developing the Alinskyite and Freirean tool kits framework, I concentrate on how these tool kits shape SCOs' political strategies in three key ways.

First, tool kits help SCOs to pick the specific issues they ultimately pursue in their campaigns. Within the larger mission of education reform in the Bronx, for instance, the NWBCCC and ACORN Bronx focused on issues best remedied via concrete, fairly easily defined public policies such as increased funding or school construction. These groups pursued signature campaigns to address the severe underfunding and overcrowding of New York City schools in general and Bronx schools in particular. Parts of their Alinskyite tool kit—especially the strong focus on organizational identity and recruitment—encouraged them to build broad-based alliances and campaigns that all constituents could immediately support. Along the way, Alinskyite groups also placed greater emphasis on campaigns that were readily winnable, even in the short or medium term.

Groups with Freirean tool kits supported campaigns for increased funding and school construction, but their signature campaigns focused instead on discriminatory practices by school safety agents and counselors, inequities in the quality of education within the New York City school system and within Bronx schools, animosity between staff and parents, and the creation of new small schools with social justice curricula. In short, MOM and SBU pursued campaigns that demanded not just new official public policies but new dynamics and relations within the schools, as well as behavioral changes on the behalf of all actors involved—teachers, parents, and counselors in addition to policy makers.

These campaigns were also significantly different from those inspired by the Alinskyite category in that they overtly addressed issues of race within New York City schools, including issues that disproportionately affected members of one minority group. For example, police harassment sometimes disproportionately affects African American males in one school and Latinos in another. Groups with the Alinskyite tool kit focused on color-blind issues and stated that issues of racial inequality are often divisive, but critics contend that color-blind policies perpetuate decidedly unequal protection of rights and privileges in American society.[22] Meanwhile, SBU and MOM highlighted ways in which cultural practices inside the organizations can lead constituents to nevertheless unite and broach issues of race without alienating one another. Their campaigns suggested that it is possible for education organizing groups to construct visions of equality other than color blindness, and to be "color conscious" without being racist.

Second, different tool kits build capacities for different political strategies. In turn, Alinskyite and Freirean groups often aim their efforts at different points of the policy cycle—Alinskyite ones at the policy or program adoption stages and Freirean ones at the formulation and implementation/ monitoring stages, before and after the adoption stage. At Alinskyite groups like the NWBCCC and ACORN Bronx, cultural practices that focused on recruitment better lent themselves to political strategies dependent upon intensive outreach and turnout, like an election. These practices often acted as the clincher that ultimately "won" policy adoption or additional program funding rather than the formulation of new policies from scratch. At SBU and MOM, cooking communal meals for organizational meetings and sleepover retreats compelled SCO members to know one other relatively well, to form rapport, and to jointly develop game plans and agreements on the division of labor. Such cultural tools developed trust that, combined with critical reflection exercises, enabled members to take on risky political strategies, where SCO members developed their own policy proposals.

Practices such as careful documentation of all meetings did more than in-
form members of what had been going on and who had been there. They
also formed different expectations in members and translated into political
strategies that required data analysis. Some tools in the kit became stronger
than others, and so strategies were chosen to befit the confrontational ham-
mer, even if another organization might have reached for its manipulative
monkey wrench instead.

Third, SCO members develop embedded preferences for certain tactics
and strategies. Books often describe how SCO members change through
their participation, usually focusing on how such members become less shy
or become politically awakened.[23] In addition, SCO members usually at-
tach certain emotions to these changes.[24] Many people feel sympathetic to
several causes and think that several political strategies have potential, but
ultimately pursue those that are, to them, fun and fulfilling. The delight of
seeing a powerful person in a setting where the tables are turned, if only
figuratively, can lead SCO members to seek such a strategy even when they
expect the event to be unsuccessful in terms of official, expected campaign
outcomes. For instance, ACORN Bronx and NWBCCC members felt the
thrill of confrontational strategies, of large, adrenaline-driven crowds gathering and significantly outnumbering the politicians they wished to support or denounce. For once they felt more powerful than the elites. They
could also yield large turnouts at elections, know that their votes would
be counted, bask in the guarantee that they would make some sort of impact, and hopefully defeat their opponents. At the next critical juncture of
their campaigns one can imagine that the first tactical or strategic ideas to
pop into mind would also involve confrontational strategies and strength
in numbers.

Likewise, members of groups who subscribed to Freirean tool kits also
developed some attachment to certain tactics and strategies. A teenager at
SBU or a mother at MOM who learned basic statistical analysis did not
just know it, she probably felt proud of it, and may even have gone out of
her way to find occasions to utilize her skills. In such cases a collaborative
meeting with which to impress the target with her adept use of numbers and
evidence sometimes seemed more appealing than a confrontational, electoral strategy.

Sometimes an SCO pursues a political strategy because it fits well with
the subtle, embedded preferences that have been developed in the SCO.
A norm does not have to be explicitly articulated to make a difference; by
concluding meetings without summarizing the points of agreement, for
example, an SCO's culture can lead to incremental or isolationist political

strategies. Even if no one said anything about how individuality or partial success is valued, it is understood to be the case. Cultural practices—infused with rituals, beliefs, and symbols—form not only capacities but also expectations.

Only by knowing what is possible given a political context can we pinpoint the strengths and weaknesses of individual tool kits and organizations. Thus, Alinskyite groups can address some of their weaknesses in generating long-standing commitment among their members and Freirean groups can increase their recruitment and scale up their labor-intensive, substantive campaigns. SCOs can then reevaluate their missions and calibrate tool kits so that political strategies befit them.

By analyzing how tool kits help to shape political strategies, we can investigate how structure and agency interact in a more nuanced way. With my apologies for briefly borrowing a metaphor other than the tool kit, "If the choice of tactics is like deciding to take a car rather than a bus or train, strategic decisions include how fast to drive, when to switch lanes, and whether to use the horn" (Jasper, 1997, 234). By extending this political-strategy-as-travel metaphor, we can contemplate all the ways of getting from point A to point B. This is partly determined by what we can or cannot afford, and how we travel might also reflect our fundraising approaches. Our travels also depend on the availability of public transportation like buses and subways. This book in no way attempts to refute the importance of such structural factors in explaining SCO behavior, but to add to them, to explore the effects of agency in the mix. These approaches, after all, are hardly mutually exclusive. Our perceptions of travel opportunities cannot be completely divorced from what we think is possible.

With our own tool kits we also develop preferences depending on whether we are strong enough to walk, whether we like carpooling or find scheduling conflicts with potential partners to be too troublesome, or whether we have a taste for adventure and would like to hitchhike like Jack Kerouac. We also form preferences as to whether we like to get people's attention by honking, cutting them off, or surprising them at point B. Sometimes, we alter our transportation lifestyles not only when the subway fare goes up or bus routes change, but when we spend more time with a new partner who turns out be a bicycling fanatic, when a heart attack tells us we need more exercise and we decide to walk everywhere no matter how long it takes, or when our environmental concerns about the greater world tell us that we need to buy a more fuel-efficient car or stay away from automobiles altogether.

Tool kits pay due attention to the consequences of practices and actions of members within the organization. By reconsidering their tool kits, SCOs as a whole can work to encourage civic capacity among their constituents, ignite social transformation, and attain policy-making legitimacy. By pinpointing the tensions among different goals, SCOs can examine whether such goals are, in fact, mutually exclusive. Ultimately, it is within the power of SCOs to change themselves, and their political strategies, in their struggles for education reform and social justice. They can shape their vision of social change as well as what sort of better world they will help to create.

Setting the Scene

The NWBCCC, MOM, SBU, and ACORN Bronx all work with the same overwhelmingly poor, predominantly Latino, African American, and African populations in the Bronx. They are all fairly small, and have all been engaging in grassroots political campaigns for similar goals in local school reform and funding increases in the South Bronx. Together, these groups have garnered millions of dollars in new program funding and construction, voted in politicians and forced public officials to resign, received quite a bit of attention in the news, and struggled to maintain campaigns. They are also part of a burgeoning social movement of grassroots organizing for school reform. In the South Bronx alone, the number of such education organizing groups has tripled to more than a dozen in the last fifteen years. Over half of these groups started as or were sponsored by social service organizations.[25]

Perhaps because their work is so rich and complex, the case study organizations can be legitimately categorized in several slightly different ways. They are all education organizing groups in that they all aim to make the public school system more accountable to parents—namely, the overwhelmingly low-income communities of color that serve as the organizations' core constituents. They do this via community organizing, by forwarding or supporting specific public policy proposals, and by pressuring elected officials and civil servants to heed these proposals through organized meetings, petitions, rallies, and protests.[26]

ACORN Bronx, the NWBCCC, MOM, and SBU are also social change organizations in that they "aim not only to serve those who have been disadvantaged, but to address systemic problems in a way that will increase the power of marginalized groups, communities or interests" (Chetkovich and Kunreuther 2006, 2). They do so by engaging in community organizing around education issues; along the way, they help to empower members to see themselves as stakeholders in the policy-making process, with political and leadership skills to boot. These groups also have established entities, with 501(c)3 tax-exempt status from the Internal Revenue Service, as nonprofit and nongovernmental groups.

I chose to place these education organizing groups in the larger category of social change organizations to emphasize how their struggles are relevant not just to other community organizing groups but to a significant portion of nonprofit, grassroots organizations around the country. One can imagine activist service-delivery organizations, such as harm reduction and intravenous needle exchange centers, and advocacy groups facing the same tensions and struggles as the ones investigated here. Further, the division among categories such as service delivery, organizing, and advocacy is sometimes an artificially imposed, nominal one. Even as the case studies here claim to all primarily engage in community organizing, for instance, one interviewee spoke about how "they call me a funny organizer" explicitly because she integrates advocacy and social services into her organizing practices.

The efforts of SCOs are largely absent from the academic literature, which often places them in the same broad category as social movement organizations.[27] My research was greatly informed by research on social movements and their organizations, and I originally attempted to couch this study in that literature. This did not work out, however, for two key of reasons.

I had thought that by relating my case studies to the struggles of social movement organizations, I could emphasize the ways in which grassroots organizations perform the grunt work of movement building—speaking to students and parents at schools and apartments, convincing already overstretched folks to attend meetings and cultivate vision statements, and keeping them mobilized so that they do more than move from crisis to crisis. Since education organizing has been gaining momentum nationwide, some argue that they are also part of a growing social movement while others contend that this is currently still wishful thinking.[28] I do have a sense that a movement is brewing, but it is still quite difficult to articulate its unifying traits.

The literatures on social movements and social change organizations do address similar themes, but at their cores lie different levels and units of analysis. In the social movements literature, "organizations are understood in relationship to larger movements, which are themselves the engines of change" (Chetkovich and Kunreuther 2006, 4). By contrast, SCOs often work for social justice independently, and several of the Bronx leaders I interviewed bristled at the notion of identifying with a movement.[29] In turn, the literatures examine different phenomena; the threat of explicit countermovements, for example, was not very relevant to SCOs. The organizers in the Bronx case study groups focused on a different horizon than movement activists might, and they spent almost all of their energy on members, rarely considering the opinions of nonaffiliate activists or independently acting supporters.

There is also empirical evidence suggesting that SCOs tend to be structured differently than most contemporary social movement organizations. Trends among social movement organizations suggest that many of them are now professionalized nonprofits working in mainstream politics, and sometimes have top-down decision-making structures. By contrast, SCOs are all grassroots, meaning that the main participants are ordinary people from a community, folks like regular parents and students, rather than the elected officials or lobbyists we typically see trying to change public policy.[30] In this book, each of these organizations has a few paid organizers, and active, unpaid members called "leaders."

While the case studies here speak to different literatures in community organizing, social change, and social movements, they nonetheless overlap. What remains beyond doubt is the fact that the national landscape of SCOs is dynamic and diverse. By peeking into a small slice of this landscape in the South Bronx, this study aims to articulate the causes and consequences of this kaleidoscope of people power.

An Overview of the Book

This chapter has presented the puzzle of strategies and tactics for social change organizations all facing the same political context and working toward similar goals of social change. It has thus ended with a brief sketch of how cultural practices form tool kits in SCOs and how these tool kits, in turn, shape the organizations' capacities and embedded preferences for political strategies.

Chapter 2 shows why the book's case studies matter, via a quick snapshot of public education in New York City and, in particular, the Bronx. Class and race inequalities pervade the recent history of New York City schools. The students currently attending public schools in the Bronx are disproportionately from low-income and African American or Latino families, and the schools they attend are relatively poor by any standard. In response, the amount of community organizing in the Bronx, especially around education issues, has increased dramatically in the past fifteen years. Because the struggles of these social change organizations are emblematic of those faced by American SCOs overall, so too are their lessons.

The rest of the book delves into the organizations themselves, as well as the practices of their organizers, leaders, and members. Chapters 3 and 4 are full of fine-grained accounts of events, retold stories, and other data to give readers a rich sense of the neighborhoods, leaders, teachers, and target city administrators involved, as well as what participating in these organizations is like.

In chapter 3, the practices at ACORN Bronx and the NWBCCC illustrate key themes of the Alinskyite tool kit, which helps leaders to participate in structured group activities and work toward specific goals. The tool kit excels in assisting the SCOs achieve breadth and scale in their campaigns, but leadership development is sometimes not as comprehensive as it should be.

Chapter 4 explores the Freirean tool kit via the case studies of SBU and MOM. The assumptions embedded in the Freirean tool kit throw the Alinskyite tool kit's features into sharp relief. The Freirean-based SCOs were especially strong in triggering personal transformation in their leaders, but they sometimes struggled to achieve the scale associated with Alinskyite SCOs.

The next three chapters analyze specific tensions in the relationship between tool kits and political strategies. Chapter 5 illustrates how issues of race figure prominently in the organizations' respective tool kits, albeit in hushed tones. A consistent theme is whether an issue that disproportionately affects a specific racial or ethnic population is automatically labeled as a "divisive issue," one that is in danger of pitting some members against others. Should campaigns only address nondivisive, winnable, "color-blind" issues? The Alinskyite and Freirean tool kits encourage very different responses to the subtext of race and rank within the organizations, whether issues of race are raised in decision-making processes, and whether color blindness is contested in antiracism campaigns.

Chapter 6 addresses the ways in which the Alinskyite and Freirean tool kits help the organizations to build very different skills and tools for their school reform campaigns. While the Alinskyite tool kit helps organizations in electoral campaigns, large rallies, and support of well-articulated, prepared policy proposals and legislative bills, the Freirean tool kit helps organizations to design their own policy proposals and to implement policies in nuanced ways. Because both sets of capacities are integral to successful campaigns, the organizations have attempted to hone both, and the chapter ends with how they might successfully do so.

As chapter 7 reveals, the Alinskyite and Freirean tool kits do not just lead to different strengths and weaknesses; they lead to distinctly different embedded preferences in political strategies. This is most apparent in the case study organizations' choices between collaborative and confrontational strategies. The repertoires of strategies were self-reinforcing. While Alinskyite leaders told of the adrenaline associated with their big rallies, Freirean leaders were rightfully proud of the large repertoires of knowledge and expertise they had amassed on school policy. Since all of the case study groups attempted to work with power brokers only when appropriate, preferences in strategies sometimes prevented leaders from being as deliberate as they should have been.

Chapter 8 discusses how, overall, the case studies show that what leaders and organizers do make a big difference in political strategies, and it is possible to change and refine tool kits along the way. With complementary strengths and weaknesses, the trick lies in developing an organic tool kit that mixes elements of both the Alinskyite and Freirean tool kits. Some of the key weaknesses of the Freirean tool kit—namely, that of depth at the expense of size—might be sufficiently addressed via the growing use of networks and alliances. Ultimately, tool kits also help leaders to envision a very different notion of justice and transformation—one of making the system give some room to the less privileged versus revamping the system altogether.

CHAPTER TWO

PUBLIC EDUCATION AND
ORGANIZING IN THE BRONX

A look at the social, political, and economic landscape in which the present study takes place helps to explain why the case study organizations have launched campaigns against racial and economic inequalities, for access to decent schooling and basic social services, and for more democratic governance. Further, since the struggles of these organizations are emblematic of those faced by American social change organizations (SCOs) overall, this study provides a magnifying glass for an examination of larger tensions in the country.

The South Bronx provides a uniquely rich opportunity for a comparative analysis of SCOs. There is a remarkable amount of activity in a very small geographical area, and at first glance, the SCOs all look pretty similar. A very short historical walk or, more truthfully, a historical jaunt, through the most recent changes in New York City school governance and education organizing demonstrates that although social change organizations have a long history in New York City, democratic participation was never institutionalized. Thus, civic participation in social change organizations remains important today. Further, the incredibly poor state of Bronx schools, especially when compared to wealthier schools in neighboring Manhattan and Westchester County, suggests that this area is ripe for social change.

A Crossroads of Accountability and Democracy

During my eighteen months of fieldwork in the Bronx, parents and students in education organizing SCOs tried to make sense of a number of policy changes at New York City schools. Recent, key legislation and policy debates at the city, state, and federal levels have left little room for formal democratic participation. In response, parents, students, educators, and activists have turned to SCOs as a means to voice their concerns and aspirations for education reform.

Some of the older activists interviewed for this book still remember the acrimony of the community control debates of the 1960s. They recalled how African American leaders, joined by leaders of the growing Puerto Rican community, had fought for racial desegregation and equality in the schools for decades, only to face deep-seated resistance and, in many cases, counterprotests.[1] A February 1964 boycott of segregated schools drew half a million students, for example, but failed to yield a substantive integration plan in response. Eventually, they advocated for a community control system of governance for the New York City schools, whereby local neighborhood residents and parents had a say in which teachers they hired, what curricula were ultimately implemented, and how discretionary budgets were spent.[2] At that time, education policy decisions in New York were made by borough- or citywide administrators. Activists in the black and Latino communities felt that these administrators rarely took their views into account, and that even when these administrators were well-meaning their "universal formula" for success was constructed with middle-class whites in mind, not low-income people of color.

Activists had hoped that community control would bring education policy making the flexibility it deserved and required, and that it would empower parents and students, the ultimate stakeholders in New York City schools. They could not garner empowerment simply by electing better representatives; they had to engage in governance themselves: "By involving the community in the educational process, we will be giving children the pride and hope that is a vital prerequisite for learning" (Gordon 1968, 35). It was only then, postempowerment, that school policies could become effective: "Compensatory programs in education have missed the mark precisely because they concentrate on the child's failure to learn rather than the school's failure to instruct and because they avoid a central devastating fact of life in the ghetto—'powerlessness'" (Gordon 1968, 32).

The community control debates were famous, or perhaps infamous, for the racially charged, highly contentious teachers' strike and the Ocean

Hill–Brownsville crisis.[3] In November 1967, the Mayor's Advisory Panel on Decentralization issued the Bundy Report, calling for a school system with thirty to sixty community school districts and elected school boards. On April 30, 1969, the decentralization bill passed in the State Assembly with a vote of 125 to 23, and with similar ratios in the State Senate (Ment 1995a, 121–22; Stafford 2000, 73). The compromise legislation in the end, however, did not give parents and community residents a majority of seats on the school boards. Instead, the United Federation of Teachers retained many of its previous powers and shaped the required compositions of the school boards. Therefore, most of the dissenting votes were cast by black, Puerto Rican, and liberal legislators who did not feel that the legislation gave local neighborhoods real community control or meaningful decentralization.

The different sides disagreed on both the shape and effectiveness of the resulting governance structures. While some have characterized the failure of the subsequent decentralization as proof of the need for renewed recentralization, some of the leaders in this book's case study organizations argue that the teacher's union retained control over the majority of school boards, that parents remained relatively powerless, and that media distorted the legitimate claims made by the impoverished neighborhoods. In subsequent years, activists and academics on all sides have accused others of being revisionist.[4]

In 1996, after almost three decades of teachers, parents, and politicians criticizing school boards for being ineffective and corrupt, state legislation transferred some of the key powers, such as that over the hiring and firing of superintendents, from the school boards to the chancellor.

In 2002, state legislation further centralized governance by placing the entire school system under the control of the mayor. Mayor Michael Bloomberg used this power to shut down the Board of Education and replace it with the Department of Education, located right next to City Hall, and to implement the Children First initiative, which imposed a uniform curriculum on most elementary schools. The community districts and their accompanying school boards were eliminated, replaced by regions with accompanying regions, parent coordinators that answer to the principal at each school, an appointed panel for education policy, and local education councils that were still under construction in late 2004. Further, parents argued that the mayor's plans for these councils gave them few substantive powers, and only superficial advisory roles. All in all, these changes gave the mayor the most control in 130 years of school governance.

On the state level, the Campaign for Fiscal Equity (CFE) campaigned to increase state funding to New York City schools.[5] In 1995, the Court of Appeals (the state's highest court) ruled that the CFE had a right to sue the state for not meeting its constitutional clause of providing all constituents with a "sound basic education." In 2001, a trial court judge ruled in the CFE's favor and asserted that the current state funding formula is unconstitutional because New York City residents are not receiving sufficient funds. The next year, the State Supreme Court stated that the state funding formula was adequate, since it provides the city with enough funds to provide the equivalent of an eighth or ninth grade education, fulfilling the "sound basic education" clause. One year later, however, the Court of Appeals overturned the Supreme Court's decision, and the courts then ordered the State Legislature to pass a bill adjusting the funding formula to give New York City its due by July 30, 2004.

Because of debates surrounding the education funding formula, the state budget not only failed to pass by its April 1 deadline for the twentieth year in a row but failed to meet the court-appointed summer deadline. A special master and panel were called upon to create a new timeline and plan. In August 2004, there were still three versions of the budget being debated, from Governor George Pataki, Republican Senate majority leader Joseph L. Bruno, and Assembly Speaker Sheldon Silver. Although exact opinions differ, the Assembly's proposal was considered the most generous toward New York City. In December 2004, the panel ordered the state to increase New York City funding by as much as $5.6 billion.[6] In his 2006 campaign platform for state governor, Eliot Spitzer promised to finally give NYC schools their due by increasing state funding by $4 billion per year. Just after his election, however, the state's highest court ultimately ruled that around $2 billion was "reasonable."[7]

Nationally, President George W. Bush signed No Child Left Behind (NCLB) in January 2002. The legislation emphasizes punitive and incentive mechanisms for school performance, measured primarily by standardized test scores. In addition, the bill aims to encourage school efficiency by mandating more "highly qualified teachers" and allowing parents to transfer their children out of failing schools and to sign them up for tutoring.[8] Since 2002, however, the bill has been criticized for punishing schools for underperformance without giving the resources and funds the schools require to meet standards.

Local implementation of measures has also been mired in controversy. Parents have complained that they did not receive notice of their rights to transfer or to tutoring in time, small percentages of eligible parents exercised these rights, and funding limitations forced the city to limit the number of transfers in 2004.[9] Furthermore, when Chancellor Joel Klein announced that third graders who failed standardized tests would be retained, critics accused that he did so only because the policy would 'cream' promoted fourth graders, thus garnering artificially inflated fourth grade standardized test scores. According to these critics, the city chose to do so because NCLB legislation judges a school district on its fourth grade and eighth grade test scores.

All of the organizations in the present study participated in campaigns aimed at both city and state policy; each organization's signature campaigns are presented in later chapters. Overall, the policy debates have centered on notions of accountability and democracy, with the two concepts sometimes portrayed as at odds with each other. Specifically, both the NCLB and Children First initiatives were explicitly written to increase "accountability" of schools, thus increasing performance. Mayor Bloomberg, for instance, has argued that centralization and appointed panels allow him to have a clear chain of command in the school system. In the meantime, social change organizations, including some of those in this study, argue that these policy changes were made at the expense of "democracy" since there were no elected policy-making bodies in the current governance structure. They contend that top-down accountability has not been accompanied by sufficient bottom-up accountability.[10]

These circumstances and debates render a volatile but fascinating context for organizing for education reform. At first glance, the centralization of New York City school governance and strict federal NCLB regulations make it seem as if there is little room for organizing activity or social movements; indeed, Fernando Ferrer, former Bronx borough president, suggested that the education councils would be the primary "window of opportunity" for organizing groups to work for social change. Still, the four case study organizations are doing more than participating in such councils or working on small projects. They are also protesting other policy changes or conditions, including safety, overcrowding, and poor parent-teacher relations. Several are also focusing on state funding, while others participate in these protests only peripherally.

There are no prescribed paths for civic participation or activism in the current political context, and circumstances do not look too friendly to SCOs. It almost seems peculiar, then, that so many SCOs are growing and campaigning in such an environment. To thrive in such a context, SCOs must be innovative, creative, and artful in their political strategies. They must wisely cultivate their tool kits, and they must use them well.

The Current Scene

Community Organizing for School Reform in the Bronx

The current crop of community organizing SCOs in the Bronx, including those organizing for school reform, began to proliferate after the 1960s school control debates.[11] At that time, in the 1970s and 1980s, New York City was suffering from a fiscal crisis, "white flight" from the inner city had been completed, and in the South Bronx, buildings with plunging property values and occupancy rates were set on fire by landlords, sometimes still with people in them, so that they could collect insurance money.[12] Several local organizations and parishes tried to prevent buildings in the area from burning down. Many people specifically credit the Northwest Bronx Clergy and Community Coalition (NWBCCC) for "saving" the Bronx.[13] Through a series of well-orchestrated protests and campaigns against these landlords, and the banks and government agencies that funded or subsidized them, the organization worked to stop the "South Bronxing" of the Northwest Bronx. By the time the arson crises abated in the 1980s, the NWBCCC was well known as a local hub of people power, especially on housing issues. It continued to target slumlords who refused to make mandatory repairs, and to fight for decent affordable housing in the Bronx.

In the mid-1980s, the Association of Community Organizations for Reform Now (ACORN) also decided to expand from the Midwest and Southwest to the East Coast. It began by organizing in Boston and opened an office in New York a couple of years later. At the same time, the Industrial Areas Foundation (IAF) resolved to plant a stake in New York, sending Jim Drake from Valley Interfaith to help a Texan named John Heinemeier open South Bronx Churches in 1987 (Rooney 1992, 109). South Bronx Churches, like the NWBCCC, primarily focused on housing issues.

By the late 1980s the housing situation in the Bronx was still grave, but it had calmed down and no longer constituted a crisis. Although there continued to be a dire need for low-income housing, the amount of housing stock available stabilized. Parents were ready to tackle another essential policy issue—namely, schools. Enough time had passed since the defeats of the community control movement, so that parents were again optimistic about working toward social change in the schools.

In response, ACORN and the IAF began to form parent groups at alternative sites such as Head Start offices and congregations, and to encourage parent participation outside of traditional institutions such as the Parent-Teacher Association and school boards. This is partly because many of the official parent organizations were known as corrupt, and portions of school board budgets sometimes went missing. Overall, however, this stage of community organizing for school reform in the Bronx consisted of small groups of parents, without larger networks or districtwide campaigns.

By the early 1990s, the trend of shifting interest from housing to education intensified around the country. The publication in 1983 of the National Commission on Excellence in Education's *A Nation at Risk* set off a fury of alarmist policy papers and editorials warning that the American school system was in decline.[14] Competition against the "Asian tigers" of Japan, Hong Kong, and Taiwan further fueled worries about the state of American schools. At the same time, the manufacturing sector began to shrink and union membership rates fell, but the newer computer- and information technology–based industries grew. These industry changes meant that there were fewer well-paying, low-skill jobs out there, and education was more important than ever. Schools were once again in the spotlight.

It therefore makes sense that another, more significant "wave" of education organizing in the Bronx, and in New York City as a whole, took place in the early 1990s.[15] Mothers on the Move (MOM), for example, started off as an adult literacy class. As the mothers learned more about the disparities between wealthier schools and the ones their children attended, they began to organize on multischool issues, such as systemwide facilities funding and district accountability. Concurrently, organizations in other parts of New York City were forming as well. Together, six local groups (including MOM, ACORN, and the NWBCCC) formed the citywide Parent Organizing Consortium (POC), so that they could pool efforts in overlapping campaigns. The POC still meets occasionally to share updates on campaigns and possible ideas for coordination.

Finally, the last noticeable "wave" occurred in the mid-1990s, after Ramon Cortines's term as schools chancellor ended in 1995. Community groups, who generally felt antagonism toward Cortines, were pleasantly surprised to see that their demands were more likely to be heeded by his successor, Rudy Crew. As a result, organizing groups grew during Chancellor Crew's four-year term, when traditionally social service–oriented organizations, such as United Parents of Highbridge, joined the organizing arena. At the same time, the New Settlements Apartments formed a parent action committee nearby, after working with the Institute for Education and Social Policy at New York University. The collaboration with NYU encouraged other agencies in the area to venture into community organizing as well. As a result, the Citizens Advice Bureau (CAB) and the Mid-Bronx Senior Citizens Council, which traditionally offered classes and services, also hired organizers. This wave in the Bronx was also accompanied by the founding of several similar groups in Brooklyn and Queens. At this time, the Edna McDonnell Clark Foundation created a new opportunity for organizations to specifically work with parents and form new groups holding schools, and the board of education, accountable.

Meanwhile, two other trends began to emerge: those of youth organizing and network building among education organizing groups. First, youth organizing increased. The NWBCCC began to work with high school students in the late 1990s, forming youth components of various neighborhood associations. In 2001, these youth advocated for their own, youth-specific seats on the NWBCCC board and formally formed Sistas and Brothas United (SBU), a separate association within the NWBCCC. In 2002, Organizing Asian Communities moved to the Bronx. Formerly headquartered near Chinatown, Organizing Asian Communities is still known by the acronym CAAAV because it began as the Committee against Anti-Asian Violence. The CAAAV first developed the Youth Leadership Project (YLP) with Cambodian and Vietnamese refugee youth in the Bronx in 1996, but most of its education campaigns really took off after the office move. While most of the YLP's campaigns have focused on welfare benefits, which affect 70% of Southeast Asians living in the Bronx, it has also pushed for language- and culture-appropriate interpreters and additional resources in schools.

In addition, another organization called Youth Force began organizing in the southeast region of the Bronx. Youth Force focused specifically on racial and school discipline issues, such as racial disparities in suspension rates in the schools. The group recruited many students who were formerly in juvenile detention and released reports on race, violence, and the media. For example, one report compiled all *New York Times* articles about school violence in a four-year period and noted that white youth defendants were quoted an average of four or five times in news reports and articles while black or Latino youth were quoted an average of once, or not at all.

The other recent trend is that of networking among the different organizations. Specifically, the statewide Alliance for Quality Education has been working with community organizations, lobbyists, unions, and others to increase the amount of funding the state bestows upon New York City schools. Similarly, several organizations have collaborated informally with the Center for Fiscal Equity (CFE). The CFE sued New York State because, it argues, the state has violated constitutional provisions mandating that all New York City public school students be provided with an "adequate" education. During Governor Pataki's administration, the state and the CFE disputed each other's definitions of what such an "adequate" education means, and social change organizations provided organizing support during key moments of the court case. Finally, researchers and associates at the NYU Institute for Education and Social Policy (who have since moved to the Annenberg Institute for School Reform), Fordham University, and other institutions provided numerous resources to the organizations, from data collection and analysis to space for meetings. Fairly easy participation in these campaigns, technical and research support by NYU and Fordham, and additional funding by key social change foundations helped to encourage coalition building among Bronx and New York City SCOs. Whether the coalitions are strong enough to outlast or span beyond these specific campaigns, however, remains debatable.

When Harold Levy took over in 1999, most community groups felt ambivalent toward him because they viewed him as a transitional schools chancellor; they knew that the subsequent mayor would probably hire a new one. This is exactly what happened when Mayor Bloomberg took office and appointed Joel Klein. During this study's fieldwork period, Klein, who is noted for his service at the Department of Justice under President Bill Clinton, was known as a technocrat rather than a politician. For the most part, he maintained this technocratic image by paying more attention to policy reports and pedagogical experts than to parents, teachers, or community members. While many SCOs believe his intentions are well-meaning, they argue that his intransigence regarding exactly what constitutes "good policy" may sabotage even well-designed plans by failing to secure public and political support, especially during the implementation stage. At the beginning, Klein did not cement antagonistic or collaborative relationships with community groups as a whole. After two years or so, however, community groups began to consistently protest the lack of community input and democratic participation in the city's education policy making.

Accompanying Chancellor Klein's appointment was a sweeping overhaul of the school system in New York City, with thirty-two community districts being replaced by nine regions, and school boards being replaced by advisory councils. Some of the changes had yet to be implemented in 2005, but by 2007, there were more plans to replace the nine regions with informal networks facilitated by private contractors.[16] Community groups viewed each of these changes with a mixture of resignation and hope. They hoped to help shape the new institutions to their liking, and felt frustrated when their expertise was not used and their advice went unheeded.

Finally, interviews with community activists and policy makers show that the Ocean Hill–Brownsville experience of community control debates continued to be salient to Brooklyn activists, but that fewer Bronx residents and community organizations remained embittered toward the New York City Department of Education because of the memory. This is partly because none of three experimental districts sponsored by the Ford Foundation was located in the Bronx, and because there has been a substantial amount of teacher turnover in the past three decades. This means that many of the teachers who experienced the community control movement firsthand have since retired, and leaders and organizers of SCOs felt that, during the book's fieldwork period, at least, community and school relations could be remolded from scratch. (Overall, they have become a bit less optimistic, but also more galvanized, since then.)

Thus, in a relatively short period of time, the South Bronx sprouted a new crop of education organizing groups. These came about as the housing crisis abated and the national spotlight shifted to schools. Similar developments have taken place in Brooklyn and Queens, and indeed, in other cities around the country. Still, the magnitude and breadth of education organizing in the Bronx, from the past decade alone, is quite remarkable.

The Bronx therefore provides a good study of a larger national trend in education organizing in similar communities at this historical moment. It is important to remember these common origins when we see in later chapters how the case study organizations, working in a small area, exhibit such vastly different tool kits and political strategies.

The State of Public Education in the Bronx and New York City

In the American popular media, the South Bronx is portrayed as the quintessential ghetto, full of drugs, blight, and violence. Jimmy Carter and Ronald Reagan both chose the South Bronx for their symbolic "troubled-inner-city" campaign stops during their respective presidential runs.[17] Although the area is not quite as dangerous as it used to be, it still suffers from severely underfunded and overcrowded schools, lack of affordable housing, and concentrated poverty. By all measures, unemployment and dropout rates in the South Bronx remain high.

Because of its relatively large size and severe poverty, the state of public education in the Bronx remains an important issue to the borough's residents and a symbol of larger racial and economic inequalities in the United States. The struggles of education organizing groups there serve as potential models for larger struggles for access to a decent education in the United States, especially for underprivileged racial minorities such as African Americans and Latinos. To fully appreciate the efforts of SCOs in the Bronx, it is imperative to consider their context and constituency during my fieldwork period there, from April 2003 to October 2004. Although I have written much of what follows in the past tense, conditions have not changed considerably since 2004.

New York City is the largest of the nation's approximately 15,000 districts and serves over 1.1 million children.[18] The Bronx, which houses more black, Latino, and low-income residents than any other borough, also houses a disproportionate percentage of the city's worst schools. This is true despite the fact that, out of the five boroughs, the Bronx reported the highest percentage of children, as well as households with children. In the year 2000, over 230,000 children attended public primary and secondary schools in the borough.[19]

Many of the high schools in the Bronx reported occupation rates as high as 300% of capacity. This means that schools meant for 1,200 students instead enrolled 3,000 students. Students showed up to school only to wait in long lines to get through metal detectors, thus arriving late to classes. There were windows missing glass panes and safety bars in upper-floor classrooms, and in these classrooms, students froze through the winters. Others rooms felt hot and stuffy because there were too many classmates crammed in them and the windows could not be opened. At John F. Kennedy High School there were so many students that five lunch sessions were held each day so that the cafeteria could accommodate them all; the first lunch period began at 9:21 in the morning.[20]

The challenges faced by Bronx public schools continue to be illustrative of weaknesses in schools throughout the nation: overcrowding, poorly qualified teachers, inadequate funding, and populations segregated by race and income. Persistent test scores and dropout rates show patterns of inequality to exist along racial and economic lines.

South Bronx neighborhoods are also among the poorest in New York City, and in the nation as a whole.[21] In tables 3, 4, and 5, lines in bold are those for larger, composite areas.

Table 3. Population and Income by Borough and Sub-Borough (Aggregated Community Districts)

Area Name	Population	Per Capita Income, 1999 ($)	% Poor
New York City (five boroughs)	8,008,278	22,402	21
Bronx	1,332,650	13,959	30
Brooklyn	2,465,326	16,775	25
Manhattan	1,537,195	42,922	19
Queens	2,229,379	19,222	14
Staten Island	443,728	23,905	10
South Bronx	**682,725**	**10,148**	**40**
North Bronx	**637,143**	**18,108**	**19**

The table above illustrates how the Bronx has the lowest per capita income in New York City, around one-third of that in neighboring Manhattan. Because North Bronx neighborhoods are much wealthier than those in the South Bronx, numbers for the Bronx as a whole conceals pervasive segregation within the borough. The per-capita income in the South Bronx is only one-quarter of that of Manhattan.

New York City's Department of Education has traditionally released statistical data sorted by school district. However, school districts, as currently drawn, mask many of the income and educational disparities within the Bronx. District 8, for example, reports a 27% poverty rate, when almost half of all MOM member area residents in that district are poor.

Map 1, which uses smaller, more helpful community districts as geographical units, clearly shows that the Bronx has large tracts of high poverty, and that these tracts lie in the southern part of the borough. The only other community districts with 40% or more poor persons lie in Harlem, and on the western tip of the Brooklyn-Queens border.

Data also show that the South Bronx did not benefit from the booming late-1990s economy. Even as the rest of the city, and the rest of the country as a whole, thrived economically, poverty and public assistance rates in the South Bronx remained steady. Again, this highlights the immense need for social change in the South Bronx.

While the number of public assistance recipients declined from 1992 to 2002 throughout New York City, they did so less dramatically in the Bronx, and the numbers of New York City public assistance recipients living in the Bronx increased from 27% in 1992 to 34% in 2002; the Bronx thus carried a disproportionate burden of public assistance recipients within the city. While its overall population constituted only 17% of the city, its share of public assistance was double that. The numbers for the South Bronx, the geographical area for my fieldwork, were even more extreme: Its population constituted just 8.5% of the city's population, but 25.9% of the city's persons on public assistance lived there.

When we turn from statistics on poverty to those on racial demographics, we see in the following table that most residents of the Bronx, especially the South Bronx, are black and/or Latino.[22] As compared to New York City overall, the South Bronx reports much lower percentages of white and Asian persons. Almost two-thirds of South Bronx residents are Latino.

Separate data by country of birth (not included here) show that Puerto Ricans and Dominicans account for the largest numbers of foreign-born persons in the Bronx. While Africans constitute 2% of black persons in New York City, they constitute 10% of African Americans in the South Bronx,

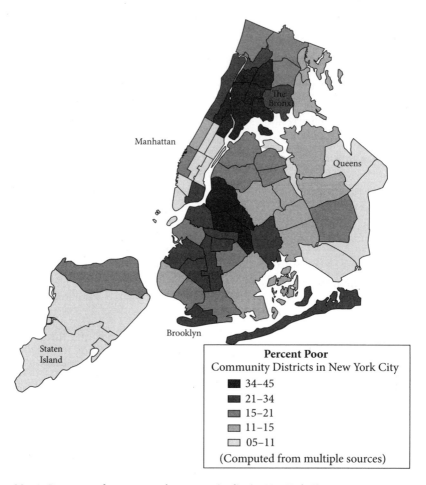

Map 1. Percentage of poor persons by community district, New York City.

Table 4. Income, Poverty Status, and Public Assistance in New York City, the Bronx, and the South Bronx

	New York City		Bronx		South Bronx	
	Number	%	Number	%	Number	%
Persons with income below $15,000	699,727	8.7	149,178	11.2	**92,956**	13.6
Persons with income below poverty level	1,668,938	20.8	395,263	29.7	**273,723**	40.1
Persons with income 200% and above poverty level	4,729,636	59.1	622,310	46.7	**233,166**	34.2
Total persons on public assistance, 2002	449,691	5.6	153,637	11.5	**116,367**	17.0
Area's share of New York City's general population	—	100.0	—	16.6	—	8.5
Area's share of New York City's public assistance population	—	100.0	—	34.2	—	25.9
Area's share of Bronx general population	—	—	—	100.0	—	51.2
Area's share of Bronx public assistance population	—	—	—	100.0	—	75.7
Total persons on public assistance, 1992	859,024	—	233,286	—	**177,563**	—

Table 5. Race and Hispanic Ethnicity in New York City, the Bronx, and the South Bronx

	New York City		Bronx		South Bronx	
Race	Number	%	Number	%	Number	%
White	3,577,052	44.7	398,530	29.9	**146,751**	21.5
Black	2,116,379	26.4	473,407	35.5	**236,634**	34.7
Native American	36,657	0.5	10,429	0.8	**7,208**	0.0
Asian/Pacific Islander	792,980	9.9	40,175	3.0	**16,358**	2.4
Other race	1,485,210	18.5	410,109	30.8	**275,774**	40.4
Ethnicity						
Hispanic/Latino	2,161,530	27.0	645,222	48.4	**421,698**	61.8
Total	8,008,278	100.0	1,332,650	100.0	**682,725**	100.0

and they are especially visible in the Highbridge, Fordham, and Kings-bridge Heights neighborhoods. The Bronx population shows how racial demographics in New York, and the United States as a whole, are changing. Those seen as black cannot be assumed to be traditional African Americans.

Nevertheless, racial minorities in New York, including African immigrants, continue to live in disproportionately poor neighborhoods. The Bronx remains a focal point of larger patterns racial and economic residential segregation in the metropolitan area.

As my fieldwork period in the Bronx began, partly in response to such data, the Bill and Melinda Gates Foundation gave a $51 million grant to New York City nonprofit organizations that help large high schools break down into smaller, ideally more intimate and nurturing, themed schools. New Visions is the largest nonprofit doing this work, and it alone received almost $30 million to open thirty "small schools" (New York City Department of Education, 2003). This is a large enough trend so that three of the four case studies in this book have relationships with specific New Visions or otherwise Gates-funded small schools. Even the SCOs that work on small schools sometimes feel ambivalent about them, however, as activists fear that policy makers will abandon the bulk of existing schools that are not also a foundation's pet project. Thus, the Bronx is ripe for social change, and foundations, politicians, and SCOs are debating just what this social change will look like.

Finally, the Bronx context for education organizing is partly defined by what it is not. Much literature discusses Chicago as a democratic model of education reform and participatory policy making. There, mass protests and negotiations by SCOs forced the Illinois State Legislature to decentralize Chicago school governance in the late 1980s.[23] In some ways, the Chicago decentralization reforms looked like what New York community control activists in the 1960s had originally aimed for. Chicago local school councils, with elected parents and neighborhood residents, teachers, and principals, oversee most school issues, including budget allocations and approval and administration employment.[24] They have substantive policy-making power, are not advisory, and allot the majority of their seats to parents. In Chicago, then, bottom-up participation has been institutionalized.

In contrast, New York has decided to standardize curricula and recentralize school boards. Other cities may follow a New York model, where SCOs play an especially significant role in both challenging and buttressing expert-driven and politician-harnessed reform. Indeed, just a few years after local school councils were formed in Chicago, that city's mayor regained greater powers over the public schools.

When parents do not have official channels through which to make their voices heard, they organize themselves via SCOs. It is therefore important to investigate what strategies organizations employ where bottom-up participation is not institutionalized, and how these organizations respond to political contexts in flux.[25]

An Overview of the Case Study Organizations

A quick look at the case study organizations suggests that they not only share the same mission of school reform and operate in the same political and demographic context but are also similar in size, shape, and overall structure. Of the Bronx education organizing groups mentioned earlier in this chapter, this book's four case study organizations are the only ones that did not have ideologically prescribed political strategies dictating that they always or never work with the government, had been operating for at least seven years, pursued education reform campaigns during the book's fieldwork period, and exhibited fairly stable tool kits. (The research that led to this book originally focused on five organizations, but after data were gathered, one organization was omitted as a case study because it did not meet the final criteria. Its cultural practices were still in a rather dramatic flux when the fieldwork took place.)

The following table presents some basic characteristics of the four social change organizations and the communities they serve within the South Bronx. While the overall organizational budgets vary, the primary cost of education organizing is staffing, and all of the case study organizations have similar levels of staffing and salary scales. Therefore, budget components pertinent to the SCOs education campaigns are comparable. Descriptions of each case study organization and their tool kits are presented in chapters 3 and 4.

While the NWBCCC and ACORN appear to have much greater numbers of base members, they pursue housing and environmental justice

Table 6. Basic Characteristics and Constituencies of Case Study SCOs

Organizational Characteristics/Constituencies	ACORN	NWBCCC	SBU	MOM
Number of education organizers	2–3	2–4	2–4	2–3
Number of full-time education organizers	1	1	2	1
Constituencies by race[a]				
Black (%)	44	37	35	32
Hispanic/Latino (%)	61	56	59	72
Non-Hispanic white (%)	1	6	5	1
Constituencies by income				
At or below poverty level (%)	44	38	39	44
Leadership and membership				
Core leaders	10	20	20	15
Estimate of base membership	7,000	2,000	300	450
Estimate of education campaign membership	unknown	150	100	150

[a]Note: Percentages for black and Hispanic/Latino populations add up to more than 100% because black constituents are calculated by race, Hispanic constituents are calculated by ethnicity, and many constituents report as black Hispanics (e.g., Black Puerto Ricans).

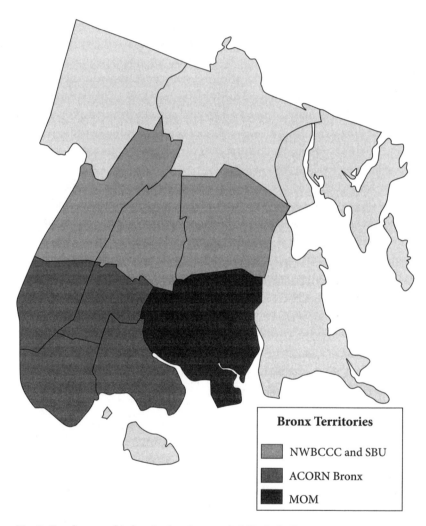

Bronx Territories

NWBCCC and SBU

ACORN Bronx

MOM

Map 2. Rough geographical territories of case study SCOs in the Bronx.

campaigns alongside education campaigns. For the remainder of the case study SCOs, education campaigns continue to constitute either the sole or primary use of resources. Therefore, the estimates of education campaign membership, like the education campaign budgets, are considerably more comparable than aggregate SCO numbers. When I interviewed them, organizers earned salaries that ranged from $22,000 to $30,000, and estimates of the annual education organizing budgets for all four organizations covered were around $50,000 to $60,000.

As stated earlier, participants in all of the case study SCOs share the same goals and code words of building *power* in a *movement for justice* and working toward good schools and school reform for the people of the Bronx; among the different SCOs and participants, these code words do not hold any obvious differences in their use or definition. Education campaign organizers at all the SCOs faced a few hundred members who were interested in education issues. At each of the organizations, leaders and organizers did not get to create cultural practices from scratch to fit their needs but did get to participate in, and help to perpetuate, divergent cultural practices that speak to the explanatory power of culture in shaping political strategies.

Finally, map 2 shows geographical boundaries of the neighborhoods served by the four case study social change organizations within the South Bronx.

The map is shown with caveats. Some of these boundaries were far from set in stone; they especially changed when SCOs chose to "expand their territory," engage in disputes over territory with other SCOs, or draw constituents from a large geographical area, partly because their cultural practices formed organizational identities around principles *other than* neighborhood. Borders between MOM and ACORN Bronx, as well as those between MOM and SBU, were especially porous. For example, as MOM expanded into youth organizing, constituents that might have earlier joined Youth Force or SBU may have joined MOM instead. It should also be noted that because the SCOs sometimes organized by school or by building, SCOs often "claimed" constituents on certain blocks or in large apartment buildings in one another's territories. Finally, it should also be noted that a good chunk of MOM's territory, especially in the southeast corner or Hunt's Point, was largely unpopulated and composed of industrial parks.

These organizations were chosen precisely because their political strategies could not be predicted just by looking at their overt characteristics. One must dig deeper and investigate their tool kits to see where the real differences lie.

CHAPTER THREE

ORGANIZING THE ORGANIZATIONS

The Alinskyite Tool Kit

This chapter focuses on the nuts and bolts, or the tool kit, inspired by Saul Alinsky. Contemporary Alinsky-inspired social change organizations, such as the Industrial Areas and Gamaliel (a Chicago-based network of congregation-based community organizing groups) foundations, have developed practices and frameworks quite different from those espoused by Alinsky in the 1950s and 1960s.[1] Further, even when social change organizations agree on what Alinsky principles or "rules of organizing" are, they can implement these principles in varying ways. Still, it remains possible to articulate what an archetypal Alinskyite tool kit looks like. There are also much greater differences between the Alinskyite and Freirean tool kits than among variations of them. Such categories are necessary in order to develop a framework of cultural practices in action so that such practices do not simply exist in the abstract, and so that there is evidence for the link between tool kits and political strategies in my later analysis.

The case studies in this chapter suggest that the Alinskyite tool kit helps education organizing groups to build strong organizations and large bases of support, often in short periods of time. While the Bronx chapter of the Association of Community Organizations for Reform Now (ACORN) accomplished this with a narrative of martyrdom and sacrifice, the Northwest Bronx Clergy and Community Coalition (NWBCCC) did it with intensive, hands-on leadership apprenticeships. These organizations excelled in breadth and speed. However, they suffered a bit when it came to depth and sustainability in their leadership development, with this tradeoff being much more apparent in ACORN Bronx than in the NWBCCC. Further, their tool kits fostered quite a bit of interaction between organizers and leaders, but less interaction among leaders themselves.

The Alinskyite Category

In the present study, the Alinskyite category is defined by its emphasis on three factors: (1) activities and protocols that relate directly to organization campaigns, especially recruitment of new members to the social change organization (SCO); (2) a focus on developing the organization as a whole, especially its coffers and reputation as an SCO, rather than the varying interests and skills of individuals within them; and (3) leadership development with the organizer as a guide.

In two books (1946, 1971), Alinsky outlined a specific set of rules for community organizing. These rules include "The first step in community organization is community disorganization" (1971, 116), disrupting existing patterns of interaction to mobilize neighborhood residents into citizen participation, and focusing on winnable issues. The rules emphasize practical organization building rather than social movement building per se. At least in the popular imagination, one would hazard to guess that the reigning images of social movements are those of the 1960s civil rights bus boycotts or more recent lesbian, gay, bisexual and transgendered pride parades, where individuals join, and sometimes exit, a group of people united by a specific goal or cause. By contrast, the Alinsky-founded Industrial Areas Foundation (IAF) is officially a federation of dues-paying religious congregations and community organizations with their own organizers. Although the IAF has changed considerably since Alinsky's time, this characteristic fits well within the Alinskyite category. Other community organizations following the Alinsky model, which tend to mobilize individuals rather than existing institutions, still tend to have dues systems, as well as well-defined bylaws, and official nonprofit organizational status filed with the Internal Revenue Service.

Further along these pragmatic lines, the category's organizational political ideology is conspicuous via its determined absence. Alinsky urged organizers to stay away from political ideologies (though that might strike some as itself ideological).[2] He was careful to criticize liberals as well as conservatives and "cited as his intellectual forerunners Jefferson, Paine,

Lincoln, and Gandhi, as well as Hannibal and Machiavelli" (Delgado 1986, 21). In keeping with Alinsky's refusal to identify with a specified political ideology, no particular issue is guaranteed to be addressed by an Alinsky-descendant community organization. Instead, local constituents choose issues, and the respective campaigns focus on aims from housing repairs from slumlords to minimum wage increases. Since 1983, there have also been more campaigns on education reform; such campaigns accelerated in the mid-1990s.

Still, Alinsky's writings also show that education and leadership development remain important aspects of organizing as a whole. For instance, "A People's Organization is constantly searching and feeling for methods and approaches to make the community climate receptive to learning and education. In most cases the actual procedures used to further popular education will not be independent projects but simply a phase of every single project which the (organization) undertakes" (Alinsky 1946, 159).

The Alinskyite tool kit makes good use of the concept of self-interest, and a focus on delineating concrete self-interests as a source of motivation and mobilization. Potential participants are often recruited with an explicit explanation of what they will win in return for their support. Examples of these incentives might include new bathrooms in the schools, the legislation of new parent-friendly or Bronx-friendly bills, or the construction of a local playground. Texas IAF organizer Ernie Cortes and others have greatly elaborated on self-interest as more than narrowly focused, selfish interest and drawn upon the word's etymological roots as meaning that which is *between* as well as *in* individual actors.[3] This concept of self-interest links organizational activities to the needs and desires of individual members, drawing upon experiences and interests to which members can immediately relate. This aspect of the Alinskyite category will become much clearer when it is contrasted with, and thrown into sharp relief by, activities of the Freirean category in the next chapter.

ACORN Bronx: Building the Organization

ACORN, which was founded in 1970, is the oldest organization among the four case study SCOs I spent time with. ACORN Bronx's cultural practices are incredibly consistent, meaning that there is little variation in how different organizers and leaders act or talk about the organization or its chapter. Its tool kit, then, reflects the strengths and weaknesses of the Alinskyite tool kit quite well.

At first glance, ACORN's roots make its Bronx chapter a peculiar example of an Alinskyite tool kit. After all, Alinsky worked to build federations of existing institutions in his community organizing, and ACORN nationally sees itself as a giant organization of individuals and families. ACORN claims to be "the largest organization of lower income and working families in the United States" and was started by Wade Rathke, who remains chief organizer of the entire organization, in Little Rock, Arkansas (Russell 2003). At the time, Rathke had just worked as an organizer in the short-lived National Welfare Rights Organization, described as a case study in Piven and Cloward (1977).

Upon closer examination, however, ACORN Bronx's cultural practices fit well in the Alinskyite category. Alinsky's focus on federations is not a part of my definition of the tool kit inspired by him, but his emphasis on organizations is. Actually, the fact that ACORN Bronx's tool kit belies its parent organization's roots fit well with the present study's thesis—that members and organizers within an SCO have the power to change their practices in order to improve their work for social change. It also makes sense that ACORN Bronx's tool kit is not that of ACORN as a whole.

Still, some of the basic structures found at ACORN Bronx reflect those of the larger national entity. Its financing structure, and its emphasis on "people power" and large membership bases, fit well with both the Alinskyite tool kit and ACORN's overall image. Nationally, about 85% of funding is internal, and about half of this internal funding comes from members (Delgado 1986, 204). With more than 120,000 dues-paying members nationwide, this alone ideally amounts to $14.5 million each year, since each member pays $10 per month. Each family is only allowed to have one member, which also means that the number of people easily tapped for actions and rallies is that much larger. The remainder of the funding comes primarily from foundation grants.

New York is clearly an important hub for ACORN. Although the national organization claimed to have staffed offices in the more than fifty cities across the nation during my fieldwork period in the Bronx, organizers told me that more than one-fifth of the nation's members resided in New York City. In addition, the relatively new international offices, based in Peru and the Dominican Republic, were based on networks established by New York members.

The academic literature on ACORN also applauds its organization building, but it is somewhat more hesitant about its ability to contribute to sustainable social change. The main book specifically about ACORN is *Organizing the Movement* by Gary Delgado (1986), who previously worked with the organization and traces its roots and the first fifteen years of its development. This book lauds the organization's successes but warns that the original ACORN model was not truly member-driven and neglected race- and gender-delineated issues. This was partly because its organizers were primarily middle-class white progressives working in low-income minority neighborhoods, and because it avoided such issues in order to attract people via socioeconomic status. Later, Delgado founded the Applied Research Center, affiliated with the Center for Third World Organizing. The other book that focuses on ACORN, Dan Russell's *Political Organizing in Grassroots Politics* (1990), also emerged from the author's experience working with ACORN. While this study comes to some of the same conclusions that Delgado's does, it should be noted that Russell continues to be affiliated with ACORN, authoring its history and accomplishments for its website and archives. More recently, a conference on ACORN's legacy thus far discussed the organization's role in American progressive politics, deeming it at the forefront of certain trends, such as that of "community reinvestment" (Dreier 2005).

A look at ACORN Bronx itself suggests that it embodies the Alinskyite tool kit's focus on organization building, recruitment, and hierarchical organizer-as-guide leadership development models especially well. Unlike the other case study organizations, ACORN Bronx was part of an obvious organizational hierarchy, and it engages in city, state, and national campaigns on a regular basis. Mothers on the Move (MOM) and the NWBCCC have attended national conferences or actions, and all of the organizations in the study have participated in a statewide campaign sponsored by the Alliance for Quality Education and the Center for Fiscal Equity, demanding more educational funding for New York City at the state capital in Albany. Still, ACORN is unique in the study because it went much further in institutionalizing the organization as well as its activities. It not only organized residents around social justice issues but also worked with the Working Families Party and electoral politics, was involved with union organizing via the Service Employees International Union, operated radio stations in Texas and Arkansas, and actually developed and owned housing, sometimes through the U.S. Department of Housing and Urban Development.

It is significant that, unlike the other case study organizations, ACORN worked with an electoral party and a union. First, its affiliation with these well-established, hierarchical institutions (in that they have well-defined levels of leadership, with representatives at the top levels coordinating decisions) further supported ACORN's emphasis on organization building. ACORN members would argue that these strategic alliances with progressive institutions were smart, pragmatic moves toward solidifying its own "people power." Second, although the organization's nonprofit tax status meant that it was officially not allowed to engage in overtly partisan activities itself, its affiliation with the Working Families Party was well-known. The Working Families Party, in turn, claimed to be an independent third party representing low-income families, but it often endorsed Democratic Party candidates. ACORN's affiliations, then, reflected larger tensions in its attempt to both speak truth to power and, when useful, engage with the powers that be.

ACORN's recent history in New York suggests that it excelled in campaigns that required large turnouts of its members. ACORN began organizing in New York City in the late 1980s. Nationally, ACORN admittedly had a hard time in that decade; as "the movement spirit" of the 1960s and '70s died off ACORN had trouble hiring organizers, and there were an increasing number of policies to fight under the administration of President Ronald Reagan (Russell 2003). At that time, the ACORN Schools Office consisted of representatives discussing issues throughout the city. ACORN began to gain attention for its education work with the report *Secret Apartheid* (1996), which used test audits to document the city schools' tracking students of color away from gifted and talented programs from kindergarten on. In 1998, ACORN Bronx released a report detailing underfunding and persistent problems in three South Bronx school districts. Then, in 2001, ACORN joined the United Federation of Teachers to lead a voting campaign to defeat a city proposal handing the Edison Corporation control of five schools.

Finally, a quick glance at ACORN Bronx's own staffing suggests that its size was similar to those of other case study organizations. While ACORN Bronx is located in the Mott Haven section of the Bronx, it also operated in the sections of Concourse and Morrisania. Furthermore, it shared an office with Manhattan ACORN, which primarily operated in East and Upper Harlem.

However, ACORN Bronx experienced higher staff turnover than the others. During the eighteen-month fieldwork period of this study, the official duties of one ACORN Bronx organizer changed several times. While ACORN Bronx employed approximately six organizers, there were long stretches without any education organizer, despite ACORN Bronx's participation in education coalition campaigns with other groups.

Recruitment and Campaign Activities

The main activities at ACORN Bronx clearly reflect the Alinskyite tool kit's emphasis on recruitment and campaign activities. (This starkly contrasts with the organizational activities presented in chapter 4, which include book clubs, support services, and a whole lot of hanging out.) This was most evident in the organizers' schedules. Organizers worked under quite a bit of pressure to recruit as many members as possible, so that New York ACORN might have the "people power" to stage sizable rallies or hold elected officials accountable as well as to bring in membership money to finance successful campaigns.

Organizers' official work hours were 11 a.m. to 10 p.m. each weekday, plus a half day on Saturdays. They showed up at the office around 11 a.m. and made phone calls; those that had e-mail addresses also checked the Internet. Once a week, around 12 noon, there was a staff meeting, and organizers prepared to go out door-knocking. Otherwise, general paperwork, designing flyers, and other administrative work was done at this time.

Generally, organizers went out door-knocking from 2 or 3 p.m. to 7 p.m. each day. One day I accompanied Melissa,[4] then the sole full-time education organizer, who was paid approximately $21,000 a year, on a door-knocking trip in a large apartment building in the Morrisania/Concourse Village neighborhood, a fifteen- to twenty-minute bus ride away from the office. Melissa knocked on each door, primarily introducing herself in Spanish. There had been an introductory meeting in the building lobby a few weeks earlier, and a few of the tenants recognized her. Other than on one occasion, however, she did not stop to speak with those tenants, because they had already signed up as ACORN members. She focused on new potential members, telling them that she was with ACORN, an organization that "builds power" and "wins victories" on issues that concern them, such as building and school repairs. Most residents who opened their doors said politely that they were not interested; if they stated a specific reason, Melissa responded. For example, to those who said that they did not have dues money on them, Melissa stated that ACORN has a bank draft program, so that members did not have to hand in a $10 check or cash each month. To those who declared that such efforts were futile, Melissa listed specific victories from ACORN history.

The outreach at ACORN Bronx was widespread and not necessarily targeted. On that day, for example, Melissa knocked on over eighty doors, spoke to about twenty people, and had conversations of longer than five minutes with perhaps six or seven of them. At two apartments, the tenants spoke extensively about poor building conditions, and they gave Melissa and me a tour of their apartments. When the meeting approached fifteen minutes in length, however, Melissa politely ended the conversation if they did not agree to sign membership forms. On that day, no new official members were recruited.

The official target for ACORN organizers was to sign up two new members per day, but realistically, Melissa wanted to recruit between five and eight a week. Based on observations made on door-knocking in several case studies, even this "realistic" goal was rather ambitious. Melissa expressed some concern about the high demands of the work, stating, "I don't know if [another organizer] thinks we just door-knock without taking a break for lunch or dinner." With a wry smile, she added, "I think maybe she does."

Around 7 p.m. organizers returned to the office. For the remaining three hours of the workday organizers called existing or lapsed members from phone lists, asking them to renew their memberships. They also used this time to call certain members to remind them of upcoming meetings and events. Some organizers noted, however, that most households rarely answered telephone calls after 9 p.m., so that the last hour felt like a "waste."

Members, too, were consistently encouraged to recruit as many others as possible, and many leaders were first introduced to ACORN Bronx by friends. Angela, an ACORN member for eleven years, said that she first joined "by accident. [Another leader] was already involved with ACORN and constantly inviting me. I always said no—'I have to take care of my kids,' or 'I have classes,' 'I don't have time'—you know, the typical excuses. But then I came here, and I really liked it! So then I kept coming."

That said, not all of ACORN's members were recruited via door-knocking or through friends. Sylvia, for example, became interested when she stumbled into ACORN because, as she explained, "My daughter, she's not a good student, but it's not because she doesn't want to.... And when I started going to meetings, to try to do something, I went to the PTA meetings and saw that they were just the same people every time, drinking coffee and talking about nothing. Drinking coffee and gossiping. And at the PTA meetings, they had no Spanish. I found out through ACORN that I had a right to an interpreter." Here, Sylvia's reasoning fit well with the Alinskyite notion of self-interest, where the returns to organizing were readily apparent.

Sylvia's story also fit well with the fact that meetings and activities were not scheduled regularly; rather, they were arranged around existing campaigns. This left little room for individual leaders, especially new ones, to change the course of campaigns, develop in-depth skills at a leisurely pace, or work on new ideas. For instance, ACORN Bronx organizers and leaders conducted outreach on several occasions for large rallies and petitions as part of the Community Collaborative to Improve District 9 Schools (CC9) with five other SCOs (including the NWBCCC). They also hosted some CC9 meetings, and conducted a neighborhood tour with approximately ten teachers in October 2003. At several of the CC9-wide meetings, including a leadership development and planning retreat as well as a planning meeting for family-school partnerships at local schools, the organizer was the only ACORN affiliate to attend. At the latter event, school principals and teachers had been prepared to meet with parents to set agenda for the family-school partnerships. During such events, the organizer usually joined other working groups hosted by other SCOs; each of those usually had approximately eight to twelve members in attendance.

ACORN Bronx was better at participating in larger campaigns than in implementing the sort of local work that other CC9 SCOs conducted. For instance, a subsequent meeting with one of ACORN's two partner schools did yield a significant number of issues to be explored by the partnership there. After months of attempts, a meeting at the other school had yet to occur. (By contrast, the other CC9 SCOs conducted frequent, regular meetings with parents from individual schools. Further, they held regular meetings at least once a month, and special meetings more frequently, sometimes twice a week, during campaigns.)

Finally, a peek inside a general leadership meeting succinctly illustrates ACORN Bronx's emphasis on recruitment and existing campaigns. General leadership meetings were held sporadically, usually four times a year, in addition to meetings and one-on-one conferences with specific campaign agendas. These meetings allowed new ideas for issue campaigns to be aired and discussed. This particular meeting was advertised as a "leadership-building" workshop, but in reality, it primarily served as a recruitment and campaign meeting. Little time was devoted to ACORN's mission, members' personal struggles or neighborhood concerns, skills building among leaders, or lively debate.

Four men and eleven women attended the general leadership meeting. Although this was a decent number of attendees for a regular meeting, quarterly leadership meetings at the other case study SCOs would have attracted three or four times as many people. No child care was provided, and this may have been one factor in the relatively low attendance.

The first two activities underlined the importance and honor of being ACORN members. The meeting began with the members stating their names and how long they had belonged to ACORN (in years and months). Sylvia, a leader, chaired the meeting, handing out "network forms," sheets of paper with lines for ten people—relatives, friends, and neighbors—whose phone numbers attendees should list for recruitment to ACORN. The agenda stated that the next item was "rebuilding the base...why/how," but this was not discussed. Instead, the chair gave instructions about filling out the network forms, and a few people in the room immediately began to do so. In the meantime, Sylvia addressed the next agenda item, a discussion of new, key issues in the community. Few people spoke; one stated that she had been having a lot of trouble with a specific bus route, and another spoke of witnessing a man get mugged and beaten a few nights earlier. At that moment, Jack, an elected officer in the SCO and the first non–Spanish speaker to attend the meeting, arrived. The chair announced his official position, and attendees clapped in response.

Although translation equipment was available, it was not used until Jack arrived. A young woman assumed the role of translator, but remarks were only translated sporadically, with her own commentary of agreement or disagreement interspersed. Jack listened as the two stories about neighborhood issues were repeated. Sylvia cited the summer heat as a factor in crime waves, and Jack noted, "There are muggings in every neighborhood, so we can't do anything about that. At night, when the restaurants close, is when these kinds of people come out and follow you." He gave a series of tips, including commonsense ones such as "Don't walk alone. To the store, to the subway. Walk in groups," as well as "Carry a whistle and mace. It's illegal. The cops catch you, they'll arrest you for it." Other members nodded their heads, and he continued, "Use a chain with an old-fashioned can opener, the kind with a point at the end, and swing it. It can take an eye out. Trust me, I did it already." Some members laughed. The talk emphasized their group solidarity and gave pragmatic tips, but solicited little input from the members themselves and did not ask them to consider the reasons or systemic forces that have led to higher crime rates in their neighborhood in the first place.

Sylvia asked if there were additional issues to be addressed, and Jack asked, "Do people know about the shelters that are going to be built?" People shook their heads, and he listed information for three shelters, including their street intersections, the numbers of beds, and the demographic characteristics of the clients: "At Cypress and 141, there's going to be a shelter for two hundred single men coming out of prison and drug programs across the street from the public school. At 142 and Jackson, there will four hundred beds for single men.... And at 146th street and St. Ann's, there will be one hundred men who are [*sic*] AIDS."

Murmurs of dismay sprang from other meeting attendees, and someone asked Jack, "What can we do?"

"You can protest," he declared. "The mayor's office said that there would be no more shelters of that type anywhere built." Someone asked if the mayor had made that promise before these proposals were made, and Jack announced that he had. Later in the meeting, he stated, "Instead of giving the building to the community, they gave it to the drug program.... It becomes a big problem for schools." Jack's objections to the proposed shelters were vociferous: "Not even families! Coming out of prison! People from the South Bronx just eat shit and don't fight.... Our asthma rates are the highest! This is the worst place in the world to bring up children! And it's only going to get worse! We don't have nothing here." Sylvia concurred, murmuring, "Trash and drugs...." Since the neighborhood already housed three shelters within a five-block radius, meeting attendees nodded in agreement to most of what Jack said during the meeting. Still, he and Sylvia were the primary speakers; no one else spoke except to meekly ask for one or two more details about a certain situation. It was decided that ACORN would arrange a meeting with the local police precinct in order to ask for more surveillance in the neighborhood and to look at shelter options. It was getting late by then, and the meeting adjourned.

As illustrated by meetings such as this one, ACORN Bronx's focus on recruitment and campaign activities helped members to quickly learn about the organization's work and about the roles they could play in assisting the organization to grow and secure campaign wins. It did not, however, necessarily give them much room to carve out new roles for themselves, or to explore this work in great detail. It also dovetailed nicely with the second key component of its tool kit, a focus on organizational development—that is, the majority of its activities directly built the organization's reputation or assets in concrete ways.

Organizational Development

The bulk of activities at ACORN Bronx furthered the organization's power base in a way that helped ACORN to attain scale and breadth in its campaigns. For example, activities that did not relate directly to existing campaigns were rare. Instead, members primarily showed their loyalty to ACORN via dues that had been imbued with feelings of ownership and sacrifice. ACORN Bronx organizers' comparison of the SCO to a labor union was especially appropriate, since both have traditionally sought social change by building strong organizations and via consolidation of "people power."

Outside of the events mentioned above, a handful of meetings were held during the school year. On more than one occasion, this researcher was the only person, besides the organizer, who showed up at the hosting ACORN member's apartment for a local education meeting. During one meeting, the organizer called several members to inquire about their promised attendance; these members cited emergencies and lack of child care as reasons for their absences. Although they did not explicitly say so, Melissa also hazarded to guess that a World Series Yankees game discouraged some members from attending the ACORN meeting. On other occasions, the attendance was not necessarily nil, but remained strikingly low.

Even during one-on-one meetings, organizers maintained their unspoken focus on campaigns. These organizers occasionally held such meetings in members' apartments, and they usually concerned plans for specific, already existent campaigns. In one instance, Tara, an organizer, updated the member on a recent campaign and asked if she was interested in upcoming events and if she could be relied upon for her attendance. In this case, the member had been watching Spanish-language television, and commercials for Mel Gibson's *The Passion* aired repeatedly during the meeting as the TV set was still on. The member started to speak about the upcoming Easter holiday, and Tara quickly changed the subject before leaving. Once outside the apartment, Tara noted, "She's Pentecostal, and I'm Jewish," by means of explaining her avoidance of speaking about religion. To Tara, such discussions might have brought up potential differences in opinion, and they would have detracted the member from the campaigns at hand. Even during one-on-one meetings, unspoken protocols at ACORN Bronx dictated that organizers focus the conversation on topics that relate to the campaigns at hand, so that leaders did not become distracted and large numbers of people were ready for upcoming events.

The bulk of ACORN Bronx's nonrecruitment activities were, in fact, not Bronx-based; they were citywide or sometimes national in scope. The SCO's members and organizers explicitly worked to help build their chapter's parent organization. They helped ACORN to coordinate efforts, flex its muscles, and work toward large-scale efforts. A major portion of regular meetings was associated with the elected boards. Citywide board meetings took place once a month, and statewide ones quarterly.

Tara, who held management-level positions among organizers at ACORN, commented that she was "not a big fan of school-by-school organizing. There's a lot of petty relationships and gossip and things that you can get sucked into." In this view, to be involved in local education politics was to be mired in them, and activities were accordingly structured. Instead, Tara asserted that ACORN had been more successful with school improvement zones and citywide campaigns. Therefore, meetings were more likely to take place in Brooklyn, ACORN's New York headquarters, than they were in the Bronx.

The importance of organizational development at ACORN Bronx was also reflected in its organizers' comments about labor unions. In some social change organizations, organizers and leaders distanced themselves from the hierarchical structure at some labor unions, even if they agreed with the unions' progressive goals. They feared that some unions strayed too far from the individual members' wishes to maintain democratic legitimacy. At ACORN Bronx, however, Tara mused about forming a large parent union as a laudable goal. This reflected ACORN Bronx's institutionalized hierarchies, large citywide and national networks, and organizationwide rather than locally or individually based activities.

Edgar, another organizer, echoed Tara's comparison of ACORN to a union, stating that, "We organize kind of like a union. There's a lot of similarities. We talk to folks just like union leaders talk to the workers in a shop and get together to put pressure on the owner and the contract for better wages, better vacation time. We do the same thing with the schools." To the extent that unions have clear institutional practices, dues, well-defined tiers of leadership, and work to build powerful organizations, ACORN does hold striking similarities.

ACORN Bronx's strong institutional practices included the dues system, which instills a sense of ownership and sacrifice in its members. According to both members and organizers, the dues of $10 per month rendered the organization accountable to members rather than external forces, such as foundations. The dues were fairly hefty for poor or working families, many of whom lived off a few hundred dollars each month. (By means of comparison, the other case study SCOs asked for $10 to $30 per year, with sliding-scale options.) This feature of ACORN has been emphasized since its inception; Delgado writes that although they were simply political rhetoric at first, dues did become the primary source of organizational funding within a few years (1986, 48–49).

Furthermore, dues were portrayed as a necessary and natural sacrifice. Several leaders quipped some variation of the phrase, "You can't have something for nothing." Sylvia, for instance, mentioned the dues system as one reason members would be comfortable asking to see ACORN budgets. She noted, "If you're paying, you're paying for power. It all depends on the people. If my parents give me everything, why should I do anything?" That said, not one member during my eighteen months of fieldwork asked to see ACORN budgets. ACORN Bronx organizers effectively promoted transparency as an explicit organizational value, but this transparency was not always tested.

According to Edgar, dues also lent members a sense of entitlement in holding the organizers accountable: "Dues are a commitment. It's coming out of your pocket. You're paying my salary [so that] in essence, I need to bust my ass for you. There has to be an understanding that neither one of us can do this work alone." He anticipated an argument that the dues were too steep for the working poor by continuing, "Yeah, dues can be a problem for some members; that's why we have the bank draft account system, because you don't feel $10 coming out of your bank as much as putting it on my hand, you know? Listen, it's $2.50. Anyone can do that—If you can put up $7 for a pack of cigarettes, six bucks for a six-pack of beer, you can also put $2.50 a week away. So that we can make your life a little better." Edgar's use of pronouns is telling; to him, members lent people power with their support, but it was mostly up to the organizers to perform the daily work of organizing. In this way, ACORN Bronx's organizing culture was more organizer-dependent than that at the other case study SCOs. By emphasizing dues-paying membership rather than in-depth participation or the pursuit of various individual interests, the SCO's tool kit generally emphasized capacity building at the organizational level more than at the individual level.

Thus, ACORN Bronx's subscription to the Alinskyite tool kit helped it to coordinate the efforts and resources of an impressively large number of people. When their efforts were combined with those from other ACORN chapters, this SCO managed to achieve great scale in its campaigns, as well as breadth in the variety of issues tackled. The last key component of ACORN Bronx's tool kit helped the group's paid organizers to manage campaign activities and dictate the responsibilities and rights of leaders.

Leadership Development with Organizer as Teacher-Guide

Members helped ACORN Bronx to show off its people power, but organizers performed the majority of behind-the-scenes work—meeting with other organizations and crafting campaigns, outlining goals for short- and medium-term work, and coordinating events. While leadership development for its members existed, a fairly small percentage of members participated in this aspect of ACORN Bronx's work.

Overall, the roles of "organizer" and "leader" were strictly defined so that the relationship between them was like that of a teacher and student. By this I mean that organizers were imparting concrete knowledge and skills to the leaders, rather than exchanging knowledge and information as peers.

Substantial leadership development existed, but because workshops and training were inconsistent, organizers could not rely on all, or most, members as leaders. Rather, a fairly small percentage of members became high-level leaders. These cultural practices instilled deep commitment among some leaders and organizers but wore out others.

ACORN Bronx's members were involved in all types of organizational activities, but recruitment-oriented ones were most prominent. Angela, for one, did hold considerable decision-making power, for she was a member of ACORN's national board. Because of that, she noted that she had less time to pay attention to local issues. Instead, she made decisions on issues like the national wage structure for organizers—who, according to her, were due for a raise—and agendas for national meetings.

That said, organizers and members were careful to note that ideas for local campaigns came from members, rebutting a common criticism of many unions. Edgar, at least, avowed, "We don't say, 'You need to say this'; we say, 'What do you think?'" and Melissa, who was in many ways critical of ACORN, maintained even after she quit as organizer that, "Leaders do make decision locally, and citywide via representatives." It may be the case, then, that organizers and key leaders recognized persistent problems and relayed prioritized concerns to the official decision-making boards. Indeed, on an everyday basis, one encountered many instances in which organizers wrote down specific grievances by members calling in or just showing up. These grievances usually dealt with emergency repairs, heat or electricity being suddenly cut off, or instances of harassment. In many cases, organizers helped members to address these problems fairly quickly. The origins of larger campaigns were more difficult to discern, especially since ACORN Bronx did not hold as many general, issue-generating meetings as other organizations.

In addition, active members could receive a significant amount of attention from organizers for what was in effect hands-on leadership development. After attending a number of meetings and rallies, members became familiar with what such activities looked like. They also became familiar with public administration, and the decision makers they might contact regarding common neighborhood problems. For example, leaders knew that the Department of Transportation, rather than the Department of Education, should be contacted for a safety guard or speed bump in front of schools. As with the organizers, however, the primary way in which members asserted their leadership was via recruitment of additional members. Sylvia, for example, was working on establishing an ACORN group among grocery store workers in Westchester County, where she worked every day.

On the whole, the amount of leadership development workshops and training available varied greatly by organizer and member. During my eighteen months of direct observation in the Bronx, such workshops were repeatedly postponed, and to my knowledge, none occurred, despite repeated inquiries. Helen, a leader who was often the only person representing ACORN Bronx at CC9 meetings, stated that she had not met with an education organizer more than twice during the entire school year, even though ACORN Bronx ostensibly participated in three or four CC9 meetings per month.

Still, when training did occur, it could be substantive. Angela attended leadership school after three or four years as a member. (For the other case study SCOs in this book, three years was a long time to wait for leadership training.) In addition to learning public speaking skills, she "also went to legislative training in D.C., over five days...[and] spoke with politicians," learning about various issues along the way. According to organizer Edgar, most of these workshops consisted of mock role-playing with landlords, politicians, and other authority figures.

There were exceptions from these patterns of institution- and recruitment-heavy activities. Helen solely attended the frequently scheduled CC9 meetings, and her intense involvement in ACORN Bronx included little or no recruitment and outreach. Her case was an exception, however, and her lack of communication with organizers and other ACORN members was indicative of her isolation from the organization as a whole. Those members who did not participate in recruitment-oriented activities tended to abstain from ACORN-specific activities overall.

In short, organizers and members held distinct roles at ACORN Bronx. Leadership development existed, and it was sometimes substantial, but it varied greatly. When it did exist, members viewed organizers as teacher-guides rather than partners. Meetings were more likely to pertain to specific campaigns and events than serve as regularly scheduled gatherings, and they were more likely to be part of city- and nationwide activities than stand on their own. The notion and importance of official membership permeated all of the activities and rhetoric at the organization. Organizers' time revolved around members, newsletters emphasized the number of members locally and nationwide, and other documents emphasized the organization's uniqueness in its reliance on membership dues.

ACORN Bronx was exceptionally adept at building a strong organizational identity, one in which each member felt a part of a much greater force in politics, thus making a difference in local education reform. Further, the cultural practices built a specific brand of ownership and sacrifice. Both organizers and leaders spoke of expectations to do more with less in the organization. Those committed to ACORN Bronx stated that the high dues (for members) and low pay (for organizers) were worth it because of the mission and almost spoke of themselves as martyrs, stating that they must sacrifice and work on behalf of everyone else. Not everyone agreed, however, as exhibited by high turnover among both members and organizers.

The Northwest Bronx Community and Clergy Coalition: Strength in Unity

Although cultural practices at the Northwest Community and Clergy Coalition (NWBCCC) fit well within the Alinsky category, they were quite different from those at ACORN Bronx. By looking at the NWBCCC and ACORN Bronx in the same chapter, we see how the Alinskyite tool kit is actually a prototype, and that real-life iterations always vary. This also indicates that SCOs have some power to fine-tune the tool kits in their work.

At first, NWBCCC's full name sounds like a misnomer, since this study focuses on the South Bronx. The name hints at the powerful changes that swept through the Bronx in the past few decades. As "white flight" and concentrated poverty took their toll and spread from southern to northern neighborhoods in the Bronx in the 1970s, the "South Bronx" label came "to signify a syndrome of social ills, an era even, but not exactly a place" (Fernandez 2006). When adjacent neighborhoods in the Bronx began to report deteriorating housing stock and rising crime rates, they became "South Bronxed."[5] When Catholic clergy founded the NWBCCC in 1974, images of burning buildings in the borough raged on the evening news. Working on housing issues to hold landlords (and the banks and government agencies who funded them) accountable, the organization wanted to stop the "South Bronxing" of the Northwest Bronx (Jonnes 2002). While the NWBCCC's community remains on the borderline, its colloquial inclusion in the South Bronx points to the organization's struggles for safe neighborhoods and racial and economic equity.

Officially, the Northwest Bronx consists of all neighborhoods west of the Bronx River and north of the Cross-Bronx Expressway. The NWBCCC's neighborhoods included Norwood, Bedford Park, University Heights, Mount Hope, Crotona, Mosholu–Woodlawn South, and Fordham. Together, their population was similar to but slightly more diverse than that of the other case studies in this book. While African Americans and Latinos constituted the bulk of the local demographic, there was also a large number of Korean, African, and to the wealthier northwest, primarily white, Jewish residents. In the organization itself, 20% of the membership was white and 10% was Asian (Mediratta 2001). The group's education campaigns, however, were most concentrated in the southern, and more African American and Latino, neighborhoods.

Like ACORN, the NWBCCC is actually a coalition. It comprises ten neighborhood associations, including social action committees from religious congregations, and Sistas and Brothas United. Unlike ACORN and like MOM, however, the NWBCCC is decidedly local. It has by far the largest staff of any group in the Bronx, with over fifteen organizers. One organizer serves the Education Committee exclusively, and at any given time, several neighborhood association organizers work on education campaigns part-time as well.

With a well-established structure and a large, solid budget, the NWBCCC is quite successful in its organization building. During this book's fieldwork period, the organization had just implemented a new dues system, which worked on a sliding scale, included partial-year memberships, and suggested a top tier of $30 per family per year.

The NWBCCC was the only case study organization with explicitly faith-based organizing activities. It is relatively unique nationally in that it does not work primarily with Catholic, Methodist, and Episcopal churches.[6] One teacher working with the Texas IAF, for instance, even quipped, "Are there any Protestant churches in Valley Interfaith? As far as I can tell, the folks in charge seem to be pretty much one nun after another" (Shirley 2002, 61). Over the years, however, the clergy in the NWBCCC relinquished leadership positions and decision-making power to the neighborhood associations.

Then the growing number of immigrants (many of whom viewed their respective congregations as the main connection to their new city of residence) and religious diversity in the NWBCCC's neighborhoods prompted the SCO to not only work more closely with Jewish and Muslim congregations but to reconsider its faith-based organizing. A new organizer was hired to resolidify the relationship between congregations and other parts of the organization. This organizer left within the next two years, for reasons not pertaining to her work at the NWBCCC. Unfortunately, the SCO did not find an immediate replacement for her, even though she gave the group notice a long time before her departure. She noted that it was incredibly difficult to find an activist who spoke at least one foreign language, was well versed in theology and held a graduate degree in religious studies, and had experience in community organizing.

The NWBCCC began to organize around education issues in 1995. Parents were angry about overcrowding in schools. First the organization campaigned to open schools on time, and then later to increase the amount of classroom space in the district—a major, long-term struggle considering the fact that New York City School Construction Authority budgets school construction only once every five years. It also worked to gain staff changes at an underperforming school. These campaigns helped the NWBCCC to create additional neighborhood associations in its network, and to unite all member associations in tackling a single issue.

During this study's fieldwork period, the NWBCCC continued its work on convincing the city to turn the Kingsbridge Armory into a school and community center, fighting a water filtration plant in the area, and numerous education issues. The issue of overcrowding continued to be salient, and 2004 marked another capital plan year in the five-year physical plant budget cycle. One of its schools also joined the CC9 network, though the other NWBCCC schools remained independent.

The NWBCCC and its Alinskyite tool kit also excelled in breadth and scale, though because the NWBCCC was a Bronx-specific organization it did not have the national reach that ACORN did. Its cultural practices were also a bit more varied than those at ACORN Bronx, so that both organizers and member leaders engaged in a wider range of activities. This, in turn, helped the NWBCCC to mitigate some of the weaknesses associated with the Alinskyite tool kit—namely, a lack of depth in leadership development.

Recruitment and Campaign Activities

Outreach was considered a keystone activity at the NWBCCC, even if it was not an agenda highlight at meetings in the way it was for ACORN Bronx. In fact, it was considered so important before large events like rallies and the annual meeting that Daniel, a leader and former organizer, resented it, because it cut into time usually reserved for other activities. For the most part, however, recruitment was well integrated into overall campaign activities and leadership development rather than serving as a separate activity of its own. For most of the year, organizers spent little time door-knocking per se. Rather, they recruited new leaders by working on campaigns, collecting signatures, and talking to people at campaign-specific locations such as schools.

While activities at the NWBCCC were almost all campaign-related, they were conducted in ways that allowed for behind-the-scenes participation by members as well as organizers. There were regularly scheduled meetings for every major campaign, along with more activities before a big event, such as a major protest or the annual meeting. For the overall education campaign, for example, meetings were held on the first Thursday of each month. A typical meeting opened with introductions, where members would state their names and concerns for the meeting, either as people with particular roles (e.g., teachers, parents, students, etc.) or with particular passions (e.g., teacher training, fighting overcrowded schools, etc.). The first item on the agenda was usually a reflection on a quotation; examples included, "It's better to light a candle than to curse the darkness," from Eleanor Roosevelt as well as quotes by Martin Luther King Jr. and other civil rights leaders. These were always available in both Spanish and English. Once in a while the reflection was not a quote but a short discussion on a specific topic; for example, after one meeting grew heated, the next meeting's icebreaker centered on the meaning of respect as manifested in meetings and negotiations, and the ground rules that were necessary to make all participants feel respected.

During the NWBCCC annual meeting, banners from individual neighborhood groups hung around the school gymnasium walls, but the actual speeches emphasized how individual contributions formed a *collective* record of achievement. After the actual meeting, members piled onto school buses and performed a surprise hit against Governor George Pataki at his home, protesting his stance on the education budget. Later, the membership split into two; half the members proceeded to conduct a hit on "problem landlord" Frank Palazzolo (where a local police officer approached the crowd and exclaimed, "You can't protest here! This is a *rich* neighborhood!"), while the other half went to an action against a proposed local water filtration plant. However, when at first it appeared that more people wanted to visit Palazzolo, two head NWBCCC staff requested that some members volunteer to attend the antifiltration action instead. This incident indicates that, to a certain extent, all members of the NWBCCC were presumed to be in the same boat, and all activities served each member's interest. Together, the annual meeting activities echoed the organization's themes of "strength in unity" and emphasized the overarching vision of a whole organization and campaigns that impact all of its members.

The NWBCCC also boasted of significant non-campaign-related activities, to which all were welcome. This stood in contrast to ACORN Bronx meetings, which only paying members could attend. One interesting ritual was the annual Interfaith Thanksgiving Service, which included sermons by a Korean Presbyterian minister, a Muslim imam, a Jewish rabbi, a Catholic bishop, and several other priests and deacons. In 2003, its third year, the service included sermons from different traditions, several songs, spoken word by members of the congregation, and a large dinner afterward, with both kosher and halal food available. The overriding theme was again "strength in unity," and this was displayed by both the content and the format of the event. For example, a homily on the Tower of Babel by the participating rabbi underscored the moral that great achievement and tall structures are self-defeating if other members of the population are left behind; the chorus in the gospel finale emphasized the importance of joining forces and forgiveness; and dinner tables were set up to facilitate intermingling. Translation was provided throughout the service.

The faith-based activities, which were fairly rare, were also structured to accompany current campaign goals rather than the other way around. Sermons during the Thanksgiving Service were still NWBCCC-specific and often spoke about school reform; in another instance, a Catholic priest, in speeches at each stop of the Passion of the Christ procession over Easter weekend, explicitly linked the struggle for environmental justice to Jesus's struggle for social justice. An interfaith vigil and action for civil rights, celebrating the fiftieth anniversary of *Brown v. Board of Education of Topeka*, also explicitly included protests on the steps of the state capitol in Albany, demanding more New York City funding per the *Campaign for Fiscal Equity v. State of New York* decision of 2003. While the NWBCCC's practices included faith-based activities, the congregations were not official members, as they are in the IAF and Gamaliel networks.

On the whole, the NWBCCC boasted of a wider range of activities than did ACORN Bronx, all of which still meshed well with the Alinskyite category described earlier in this chapter. Although membership itself was not the basis of most organizational rituals, other practices—such as an opening reflection, research, and organizationwide leadership development—were also important ways of capacity building at the organizational level, and all related to campaign issues, such as overcrowding in Bronx schools.

Organizational Development

Maintaining a unified vision of the NWBCCC was sometimes made difficult by the SCO's willingness to emphasize diversity as well as likenesses among its constituents. As some interviewees cited "mission" and others "victory" as their primary reason for continued commitment to the organization, the NWBCCC worked to accommodate different membership narratives by providing cultural practices that formed a sort of social glue, without cementing leaders in place. NWBCCC worked hard to establish elastic definitions of solidarity and membership via its cultural practices. To a certain extent, it succeeded in making "strength in unity," for all the diversity, a driving force.

The NWBCCC's activities emphasized organizational development, but in a way that almost foiled those at ACORN Bronx. They were generally compendia of activities put together by individual neighborhood groups rather than local activities following the agenda of citywide and national networks. As a result, some members felt loyalty to individual groups and little affinity to the NWBCCC as a whole. The fact that the NWBCCC had several neighborhood offices, and that many members rarely set foot into the main headquarters, exacerbated this. Furthermore, the board was known as more of a rubber-stamping authority than a decision-making group, and most substantive activities were based in issue- or neighborhood-specific committees. These are some of the reasons why the NWBCCC focused so heavily on organizationwide institution building during the present study's fieldwork period, formulating new dues systems and bylaws.

Member leaders' investment in the NWBCCC lay mainly in time and labor, not money. The local work was often intensive, and as leaders learned more about the issues and how to coordinate their efforts they became more committed to the organization. As Monica, an education organizer, noted, "We had to be interchangeable in our knowledge." That is, all of the leaders had to receive enough training as to assume responsibilities in emergencies. Although this example drew from her work on the environment rather than education, it is indicative of the activities that surrounded new potential campaigns: "So we kind of divvied up the issue. Part of it was research into the actual nitty-gritty scientific details of exactly what [water] filtration does and whether we need it, another was the political structure and how we can use it, or for us, or how it was being used against us, past instances of filtration. And then we came together and exchange[d] information constantly." In the realm of education, such division of labor occurred in campaigns against overcrowding, regarding research on school construction codes, local zoning, and vacant lots that serve as potential construction space, the political power structures to be pressured in campaigns, student population projections, and the views of local principals and teachers.

In education campaigns, there were leaders designated to research the situation on one issue, another to stake out a specific politician, and so on. Meetings were more likely to be comprised of discussions around potential campaign plans than outreach, which often happened in less formal ways.

Leadership Development with Organizer as Teacher-Guide

Leadership development at the NWBCCC was substantive and consistent, with a combination of well-developed workshops and hands-on training by the organizers. As leaders spent time with the organization they were made to assume more responsibilities and work on different campaigns, building expertise in both content and transferable organizing skills. It was no surprise, then, that quite a few of them later became paid organizers.

Mark's introduction to the organization illustrates some of the NWBCCC's key cultural practices. He joked that when he was younger, he was a "detriment" to society, and that he was never involved in community organizations. In fact, "I actually lived there on the corner for two years, and used to go to this store [next door], and never knew what this building did; I never cared." He suddenly became involved in 1996, when he discovered that the kindergarten his daughter was supposed to attend, a couple of blocks away from his home, was full. Instead, she was to be bused over four miles away. Since she was prone to motion sickness, he thought this was outrageous. "There's no way," he said.

He wanted to do something about this, but he did not know what. He spoke to a reporter from the *Norwood News,* a local newspaper, who suggested that he approach the NWBCCC. He found Sam, an organizer in the group. Sam told Mark that a good starting point might be a petition, and that he should collect signatures from aggrieved parents and neighbors. Sam helped Mark to formulate such a petition.

In many ways, Mark demonstrated leadership potential from the beginning. He claimed to have been nicknamed the "Mayor of Norwood," was born in the Bronx and had lived there all his life, and was clearly embedded in local social life. "I didn't know anything about community organizing," he said, "but I was pissed off." After the meeting, Mark and a friend "stood on street corners, by the supermarket, by the school, and collected fifteen hundred signatures over three days. We showed it to Sam, who was floored." More than sixty parents showed up at a subsequent meeting, spilling into the hallways, but most appeared resigned to the busing situation. Sam told Mark that the NWBCCC had formed an education committee the year before, and though those parents were from a different neighborhood Mark saw that they shared interest in many of the same issues, so he got involved in the organization.

A rally soon thereafter at the Kingsbridge Armory, an enormous building nearby, managed to gather media attention, especially since the Reverend Al Sharpton and Ruth Messinger, both then running for mayor, attended.

Mark spoke to the *New York Post* and *New York Times*, stating that he had already bought *Hooked on Phonics* to keep his daughter at home rather than bus her away. Concurrently, parents were signing up on waiting lists for kindergarten placements at another school, only three blocks in the other direction. Mark, however, received a phone call from the school saying that a spot for his daughter had opened up. "It turns out there was no real waiting list, and the other parents complained…, 'Why he should cut in line?' But you know, the squeaky wheel gets the grease, and this should serve as an illustration of when organizing makes a difference."

This episode suggests that at the NWBCCC, organizers' criteria for campaigns and leadership development were clear from the beginning. Here, for instance, they used the petition partly to consider whether an issue was winnable and had ready public support as a criterion for potential campaigns. As a contrast to ACORN, it was also noticeable that the first activity was campaign-related, and discussions about membership did not come until much later. In fact, the NWBCCC had not instituted a dues-paying structure until fairly recently, and in comparison to ACORN's, it was nominal.

That said, the newer dues system was fairly elaborate and closely linked to new, clear delineations of the leadership structure. Although leaders did not have to be on the board to carry significant responsibilities in an official capacity, such as assigned "expert" roles in campaigns, the NWBCCC had clear bylaws about what constituted a member, a leader, a key leader, and so on.[7] Each category was accompanied by certain expectations, such as the number of campaigns with which the member was familiar and could speak upon, the responsibilities held by the member, and, to a lesser extent, the length of time she had been involved.

The NWBCCC certainly offered extensive leadership development, with Organizing 101 and 102 sessions at least a few times a year, research groups, some training during regular meetings, and special sessions and longer retreats facilitated by hired consultant organizers from other groups and foundations.

In the NWBCCC's extensive leadership development, the organizer generally acted as a guide to the budding leader. Sam gave Mark quite a bit of hands-on intensive training, from which Mark drew great personal satisfaction. As he points out, "I spent a lot of time with Sam after breaking my back. [Soon after joining the NWBCCC campaigns, Mark had suffered an injury.] And a lot of other parents. Since I had nothing else to do and couldn't go to work, this was like therapy. And it gave me a chance to talk to adults, which, you know, when you have three kids, is just great." Still, his mentor was another NWBCCC organizer, one who gave him "so many opportunities to learn how to be a leader, to follow her lead." According to Mark, much of this dealt with learning to allow others to speak, to do research, read documents, and become well-versed in policy. At least at first, preparation for frequent activities like distributing flyers, door-knocking, speech writing, and meeting with politicians was performed under the guidance of organizers.

Monica described leadership development this way: the NWBCCC "give[s] the parents the tools...to be able to see a problem, not view it as just a problem but as a campaign—if the school lunch is not nutritious, in their minds, they can see we need to bring in a group that does nutrition, maybe get the support of a local hospital that works with children. These questions pop into their heads automatically. They see all the steps they have to go after. We've enabled them to do so."

To a certain extent, NWBCCC organizers looked for ready-made leaders to further develop. (In the contrasting Freirean SCOs, the personal transformation of leaders is, in some ways, even more dramatic.) Some of the skills traditionally emphasized in leadership development, like public speaking, appeared to have come naturally to Mark. He himself admitted to being a "ham," adding, "I think I had some of these abilities before; I just didn't make use of them. Like speaking, I've always been into it....But if you ask my ex-wife today, she said that the coalition was my mistress" since he was spending so much time attending meetings. The constant activity tapped into interests and capacities that were perhaps not fully realized before. Eventually, being a leader developed into a career for Mark: "After chairing an education committee meeting, the woman who would become my boss asked, 'Would you like a job?' I said, 'Doing what?' and she said, 'What you're doing, organizing parents,' and I said, 'You're going to *pay* me to do what I'm already doing for free?' She said, 'Sure, it pays $12.50 an hour, are you interested?' So I went down there!"

Mark, who had up until then worked as an office manager and had dropped out of high school years before in order to get a job, was hired as an organizer around literacy issues for a separate local services organization, separate from the NWBCCC.

Monica, a longtime leader and then an organizer, also received both formal and hands-on leadership training. Monica recounted a rally as her "initiation" in front of over four hundred people at St. Nicholas Church: "The translator hadn't really done a meeting that size, and she got involved in the issues and forgot to translate, and Louisa came up to me and said, 'Could you translate for the rest of the meeting up in the front?'...I had a very small role, because I really wasn't very confident. But someone needed to do that, and I was fluent in both languages. And it was difficult at the beginning, but then it just flowed, including the questions and answers in Spanish and English. And at the end, I said, 'Wow! I didn't know I could do that!'"

While some key leaders faced steeper learning curves than others, all of them expressed sentiments similar to Monica's, at least in terms of recognizing a sense of power and participation in the political system. One commented on the importance of "[b]eing able to see myself as someone who did have a voice and who did have power," adding, "[Leaders] will not blink if they believe something needs to be done. They roll up their sleeves and do it. But that's because they were given the tools, they weren't just given the part."

Finally, both the NWBCCC's mission statement and its actual activities tended to emphasize the input of leaders rather than organizers, but the organizer remained an important, guiding force. For example, according to several organizers and leaders, the top staff ultimately determined the final copy of flyers and announcements, if only by means of vetoing several drafts before approval.

Perhaps partly because organizationwide activities tended to be more focused in Alinskyite category SCOs, the education organizing activities were also campaign focused rather than free-ranging, and they tended to mirror overall organizational practices. Agendas were fairly straightforward or, in some cases, so standardized as to be easily predicted or assumed.

Moving Forward

At the same time that these organizations maintained grassroots credibility only so long as they threatened, challenged, and protested those who were then in power, the leaders and organizers also went out of their way to make assertions of their militancy. What might seem like a contradiction in fact fit well with the Alinskyite focus on building institutions that act as real power brokers. These groups felt that they needed to gain legitimacy in order to forcefully criticize individual players within the mainstream political system—that is, currently elected officials and administrators.

As embodied in ACORN Bronx and the NWBCCC, cultural practices in the Alinskyite category were pragmatic. They excelled in helping the SCOs to quickly tackle a wide range of campaign issues and in achieving an impressive scale in membership. In order to achieve this, members and leaders formed the base of the organizations, and organizers remained the glue. Activities were structured to emphasize collective identity by emphasizing the leaders' shared membership within each SCO; this then increased organizational capacity (by increasing the SCOs' ability to execute large-scale, well-organized efforts) and moved campaigns forward. Leaders in both organizations learned public speaking and outreach skills, and some campaign-design skills, and those in the NWBCCC were more likely to also learn research skills.

The potential drawbacks of the Alinskyite tool kit were more apparent in ACORN Bronx's iteration than in the NWBCCC's. ACORN Bronx was so recruitment-driven that this came at the expense of in-depth leadership development, individual transformation, and experimentation and innovation in social change work. For organizers of other SCOs, one-on-one meetings with potential leaders were worthwhile even if they lasted more than fifteen minutes without official membership, even if these leaders were not dues-paying members, and even if conversations went "off topic" and addressed personal or family issues as well as those related to campaigns. (In fact, SCOs that subscribed to the Freirean tool kit would not consider family issues to be off topic at all.) One could see the effects of ACORN Bronx's tool kit in the high turnover of its staff and membership.

When similar trade-offs existed in the NWBCCC tool kit, they were much more subtle. The NWBCCC also excelled in breadth and scale, but for the most part, however, it prevented organizational identity from overwhelming individual interests. It did so by giving all members a good road map for leadership development, allowing neighborhood and faith-based associations to pursue campaigns as they saw fit, and implementing a wider range of activities in addition to recruitment, all under the "strength in unity" umbrella.

How do these two iterations of the Alinskyite tool kit compare with that of Oakland Community Organizations (OCO), the faith-based group in Oakland, or those of IAF affiliates, direct inheritors of the Alinsky legacy, like Texas Valley Interfaith (TVI)? OCO and TVI do seem to be even more successful than ACORN Bronx and the NWBCCC in quickly building large constituencies. This is partly because they are organizations of organizations—that is, coalitions of congregations. ACORN Bronx and the NWBCCC could not rely upon imams, pastors, and rabbis to act as organizers quite in the same way as IAF affiliates demand. Nor did religious leaders in the Bronx SCOs have the authority to veto divisive issues. In these significant ways, the OCO and TVI tool kit is dramatically different—all of their activities and one-on-one conferences were performed with members of official congregations and infused with overt religious doctrine. In his study, Wood (2002) performed close hermeneutic analyses of homilies and texts at different OCO congregations.

By contrast, ACORN Bronx and the NWBCCC worked with individuals and loose social networks, many of whom did not identify with organized religion. As Fung argues, "the IAF and OCO do much more to *mobilize* and *politicize* social capital than to *build* it where it is absent....Individuals cannot join the IAF or OCO" (2003, section 2, para. 4, emphases in the original). This suggests that ACORN Bronx and the NWBCCC developed some leaders that the IAF or OCO would have left behind.

It is impossible to make strong conclusions without firsthand observation. Some time-intensive activities documented in earlier books, like personal visits by teachers, leaders, and organizers to parents' homes, can feed membership rolls but are more intensive than most of the activities practiced by ACORN Bronx. Further, each organizer probably helps leaders to frame and perceive their "self-interest" in different ways. Certainly it is difficult to imagine that every leader and organizer in *any* large organization could articulate the full breadth of "self-interest" as Cortes defines it, "'incorporat[ing] all of their concerns, values and desires, including the need for self-preservation, creativity, self-definition, power, money, love, and meaning in life'" (Cortes, quoted in Warren 2001, 224). These concerns suggest that truly replicable tool kits require intensive training and support. Indeed, even as Osterman has written that the IAF's cultural practices were consistent throughout the nation's different chapters, he also emphasized the paucity of well-trained, experienced organizers as a key obstacle to the IAF's continued growth (2007, 2002).

Still, the one-on-one meetings and accountability sessions described by Shirley (1997), Warren (2001), Gecan (2002), Wood (2002), and Osterman (2002, 2007) seem, for the most part, like cultural practices one could also witness at the NWBCCC. Further, the ways in which campaigns are developed—with an emphasis on recruitment for "people power," with research teams investigating both the power brokers and the issues that might seem winnable—also sound familiar. In fact, some of the organizers at the NWBCCC were trained via the IAF.

While the specifics vary, then, some of these other documented groups' strengths and weaknesses are also those of the Alinskyite case studies in this book. For instance, it may be that the Alinskyite leadership-development model helps to build leaders and organizers who are adept at running successful campaigns in the short run but who do not always stick around in the long run. The case of ACORN Bronx, especially, suggests that without adequate support, organizers and leaders can quickly burn out on education organizing.

Subsequent chapters address how an Alinskyite tool kit also shapes an SCO's campaign-issues selection process, its tactical strengths, and its embedded preferences in political strategies. Warren's analysis suggests that racial divisions remained a problem for TVI: After a white skinhead killed an African American, for instance, the SCO did not pursue a campaign against the brutality (2001). In less stark terms, the ACORN Bronx and NWBCCC case studies indicate that an Alinskyite focus on recruitment and organizational development created tensions when some leaders felt strongly about a political issue but others were not yet ready to launch a campaign. A pragmatic approach was quite useful when tackling clear-cut issues like school underfunding, but more complex ones, like police brutality, were sometimes deemed too controversial or "divisive."

A related concern about the pursuit of winnable campaigns is that even local organizing increasingly takes place in globalized and diverse contexts. Thus, there may be a need, as one former NWBCCC organizer observed, to "recognize...the connection between local and international organizing." She elaborated, noting that, especially in the Bronx,

> Diasporic issues and politics were very palpably felt by the people....At that time, the U.S. Navy's military exercises in Vieques...was a very hot issue in the neighborhoods and in the media—people [were] talking about it and getting passionate about it...even the Bronx politicians were getting involved. Yet...it was not a winnable issue according to the Alinsky model...that we posted on a chart—What is the most winnable? What builds the organization? etcetera....Well, Vieques would *not* fit on that chart—it is *not* local to the Bronx, and yet it *is* local in the way that it was very present in Puerto Ricans' hearts and minds at that time. So, certain issues may not be winnable, but they *move our people!*

Further, the Bronx case studies suggest that Alinskyite SCO members and leaders excelled in joining forces when they knew about a legislative bill to fight for or against. It was sometimes difficult for leaders to step out of their well-defined roles: They showed up and collectively shouted down "targets" at accountability sessions and rallies, but they could not necessarily negotiate close-up, give-and-take collaborations with policy makers.

Because organizing is so context-specific, it is difficult to glean how TVI's or OCO's political strategies would have developed in the South Bronx. The contours of ACORN Bronx and the NWBCCC's tool kits really become meaningful only when we place them next to tool kits of the Freirean variety.

Chapter Four

Friends Forever

The Freirean Tool Kit

Everyday activities are often unpredictable for any organizing group. Meetings are canceled at the last minute or simply fail to materialize for inexplicable reasons. At other times, constituents seem to appear out of nowhere, galvanized by a landlord's misstep or a politician's sudden announcement. In the context of community organizing, where little activity is predictable on a daily basis, routine activities at the Sistas and Brothas United (SBU) office in the Bronx were surprising. Every day, dozens of teenagers showed up to discuss local education politics, conduct orientation sessions without the supervision of organizers, carry out research, chair meetings, and strategize campaigns. Participation rates were high, and the work was consistent. As boys in baggy, knee-length shirts and girls in decidedly nonbaggy tank tops arrived, they gave one another kisses, and some of them even shouted, "I love you!" across the room as a greeting.

One girl sat alone, with a sullen look on her face. "Leila," another girl asked, "What's up?" Leila quickly slid a composition book across the main table and said, "Last page." The other girl quickly opened the composition book and read a poem to herself. She then nodded, walked over, and gave Leila a hug. The scene evoked images of support groups, therapy sessions, or conflict resolution meetings. It did not conform to traditional notions of community organizing in the United States. Yet these participants were empowering themselves in a way that belied traditional notions of service organizations, too. The Freirean case studies highlight the need for more research on social change organizations (SCOs) that challenge dominant systems of inequality but exhibit practices that fall outside the confines of categories like "community organizer" or "service provider."

One could not imagine such a scene in one of the Alinskyite SCOs from chapter 3, so it might be difficult to remember that all four case study SCOs are usually lumped together as progressive education organizing groups working in the Bronx. They have even worked together on campaigns sometimes. Yet one does not have to scratch far beneath the surface to see that Freirean SCOs do things very differently. As this scene suggests, SBU's daily activities were hardly limited to recruitment and work on existing campaigns. Quite the opposite, its strengths lay in the holistic, comprehensive approach it took in tackling issues faced by its constituents. The two case study organizations in this chapter suggest that the Freirean tool kit helps education organizing groups to elicit individual development and build deep, sustainable bases of support. This intensive process took time and effort, however, and the Freirean SCOs did not always achieve the scale exhibited by Alinskyite groups.

The Freirean Category

This study primarily draws from Paulo Freire's *The Politics of Education: Culture, Power, and Liberation* (1985) and, especially, *Pedagogy of the Oppressed* (1972), first published in 1968, for its description of the Freirean category. In its original context, the latter book describes a model with which Freire concurrently taught literacy and politically mobilized the uneducated poor. In exile in Bolivia, Chile, the United States, and Switzerland after the Brazilian military coup of 1964, he returned to his native country in 1980 and became its minister of education in 1988. Like Saul Alinsky's *Rules for Radicals*, Freire's books are products of lessons he learned through experience.

In the present study, the cultural practices of the Freirean category are marked by (1) activities that, at least initially, do not appear to be relevant to the content of campaigns or draw upon traditional notions of self-interest; (2) a focus on individual members rather than the organization itself; and (3) leadership development with the organizer as a partner. Perhaps even more so than in the Alinskyite tool kit, the three elements in the Freirean tool kit are clearly interlocking parts rather than separate elements.

First, Freire suggests that there are no ready-made campaigns or winnable issues ready to be pursued without critical reflection: "The insistence that the oppressed engage in reflection on their concrete situation is not a call to armchair revolution. On the contrary, reflection—true reflection—leads to action. On the other hand, when the situation calls for action" that action requires critical reflection whereby leaders draw connections among their personal experiences, the school reform issues they wish to address, and the social forces (laws, funding regulations, governmental and market institutions, etc.) that shape or affect these school reform issues (1972, 52).

To an organizer wed to the Alinskyite tool kit, putting aside a lot of time for such critical reflection might seem like a cop-out, an excuse to sit around and lick one's wounds, or worse, to engage in mental masturbation. Others, however, might argue that theorizing is hardly self-serving or problematic. Indeed, according to Freire, such critical reflection is necessary for radical change. Without it "the context of the...situation, that is, oppression, remains unchanged," and education organizing groups may inevitably perpetuate the very structures of inequality they are fighting against. "To surmount the situation of oppression, [people] must first critically recognize its causes, so that through transforming action they can create a new situation" (1972, 31–32). Organizers might also argue that critical reflection serves other pragmatic goals as well; for example, it helps us to learn from our mistakes and look at the issue at hand in new ways. Both insiders and outsiders must engage in critical reflection to glean patterns among SCOs on what works, how, and why.

In classic Freirean organizing, exercising critical reflection probably occurs most overtly in consciousness-raising workshops or classes, but at Mothers on the Move (MOM) and SBU, it was often embedded in socializing activities. Their Freirean tool kits included services and activities that served no immediate campaign purposes, such as meditation and yoga, fiction book trading, spoken word workshops, theater and musical events, talent shows, potluck dinners not accompanying meetings, and peer tutoring. What makes all of these activities Freirean is an essential element of dialogue. To Freire, "Only dialogue...is also capable of generating critical thinking" (1972, 81).

Second, these activities also contrast with the Alinskyite focus on recruitment. Groups with a Freirean tool kit do not focus solely on building the organization, as much of the social change that Freire advocates takes place within individuals: "At all stages of their liberation, the oppressed must see themselves as [people] engaged in the ontological and historical vocation of becoming more fully human" (1972, 52). In a way, the wide range of cultural practices has helped SBU and MOM leaders to articulate and realize goals, undergo transformation, and become "more fully human." Indeed, although Freire ultimately advocates for collective action, he argues this collective action will not be meaningful without personal transformation on the part of all participants; their participation in "the struggle...will be what it should be: not pseudo-participation, but committed involvement" (1972, 56).

Finally, neither Alinsky nor Freire suggests that organizers go into a community and immediately launch campaigns; nor do they advise organizers to come up with campaign ideas. Both advocate that organizers spend a long time learning about the pressures and goals of individual leaders before helping to develop any concrete campaigns. The Freirean tool kit, however, demands that organizers and leaders relate to each other in different ways.

At the heart of *Pedagogy of the Oppressed* Freire contrasts two categories of education: the "banking" and liberating methods. Put simply, the predominant "banking" method encourages a "culture of silence" whereby a teacher is accorded authoritarian status and "deposits" knowledge into the students, who are presumed to hold empty minds. Instead, Freire advocates a system of tackling illiteracy by teaching adults critical thinking skills as well as basic reading and writing. In the process, teachers and organizers are not simply relying upon students to become "enlightened" after accumulating a certain amount of information; nor are they assuming that "banking" is automatic. In this way, the students exchange information with the teacher and experience *conscientização* (consciousness-raising), which allows them to critically analyze the causal forces in society.

Organizers and leaders, like teachers and students, must work as partners. "A revolutionary leadership must accordingly practice co-intentional education. Teachers and students (leadership and people)," or, one might argue, organizers and member-leaders, "co-intent on reality, are both Subjects" (1972, 56). If organizers and leaders really act as partners, then there are also no universal formulae for leadership development. There are no *best* practices, only *good*, context-appropriate ones.

Two key points of contrast between Freirean and Alinskyite categories are (1) the relationship between means and ends, and (2) the primary categories into which societal actors are placed. First, Freire counts the means of organizing and education as important components of the struggle that should only be executed in certain ways; there is little distinction between means and ends (1972, 120–24). For SCOs in the Freirean category, it is not good enough just to be working toward progressive goals. SCOs must engage constituents in a way that leads to a radical new society. *How* responsibilities are assigned, leadership development occurs, and activities are carried out matters. Meanwhile, Alinsky (1971) is known for asserting that "in war the end justifies almost any means" (29) and "any effective means is automatically judged by the opposition as being unethical" (35). As a result, Facundo has deemed that "Freire's writings (perhaps because of the reasons we have stated) are in strong disagreement with what Alinsky presents as [rather cynical, hard] rules. I think Alinsky describes the way of things as they *are*, and Freire describes them as he thinks they *should* be" (1984, section 2, para. 29, emphasis in the original).

Second, Freire's writings express a more rigid dichotomy than do Alinsky's. More specifically, Alinsky writes that society is for the most part divided into the "haves," the "have-nots," and the "have some, want more[s]" (1971, 18–26). This third category, especially, has a built-in clause of self-interest (to "want more" of certain articulated self-interests), implying a potential for coalition building between middle-class and low-income individuals and populations. Although Freire also warns against doing nothing for the sake of avoiding co-optation, he primarily divides society into "oppressors" and the "oppressed," perhaps leaving less room for coalition building between the two groups (1972, 27–56). This element of Freire's writings was not readily apparent at SBU and MOM; they did not seem to subscribe to an ideology whereby those who work with the oppressors are deemed "suboppressors." Nevertheless, the division between the oppressors and the oppressed also suggests that ideas and intentions are as important as concrete situations and material interests, and MOM and SBU leaders might agree with the statement that both "haves" and "have-nots" could be oppressors or the oppressed, depending on their mind-sets, intentions, and actions.

Like Alinsky's, Freire's principles have been molded or changed in implementation over the last several decades.[1] Leaders in the Freirean case study SCOs did not appear predisposed to a Marxist lens in their conversations, as Freire did. Meanwhile, considerable amounts of research have used Freire's writing to discuss issues around race, when Freire himself (like Alinsky) focused mostly on issues of class.[2] Further, whereas Freire primarily worked in rural areas, his works have inspired quite a few organizing projects in contemporary American inner-city neighborhoods.[3] Specifically, a Freirean model may be promising in helping urban communities address complex, seemingly intractable problems like geographical concentrations of respiratory illness, where no single problem source or "target" exists (Romero González et al. 2007). The Freirean tool kit described above was carefully chosen to highlight important, consistent characteristics of cultural practices among the case studies here, and it serves as a good foil for the Alinskyite tool kit.

Sistas and Brothas United: "Couldn't Leave If I Wanted To"

SBU's story speaks to the power of cultural practices in building power among the disenfranchised. Despite its origins as a part of the Northwest Bronx Clergy and Community Coalition (NWBCCC), this SCO built an impressive constituency so quickly that it forced the NWBCCC to give its members their own seats on the board as well as their own bylaws. This is especially remarkable because SBU works with inner-city teenagers who are often dismissed by policy makers and who must prove, at every step of the way, that they are to be taken seriously.

In the mid-1990s, youth in the Mosholu–Woodlawn South and Kingsbridge Heights neighborhood associations of the NWBCCC began to actively participate in political organizing campaigns. One summer, the youth gathered to organize a campaign against city youth employment cuts. After months of work they decided to stick around, forming the Kingsbridge Heights Youth contingent of the NWBCCC. As the ranks began to grow, NWBCCC organizers and leaders learned that the youth would faithfully attend any rally if requested to do so, and by the accounts of several organizers and leaders, the NWBCCC came to rely upon the youth to add dozens, sometimes hundreds, of attendees to any event. As the numbers of youth increased dramatically and spanned beyond the Kingsbridge Heights neighborhood, these youth also became resentful of the fact that while they contributed greatly to political campaigns they did not have official voting power or board representation within the organization. In 1998, this changed, and the youth won not one but two seats on the NWBCCC board as the association called Sistas and Brothas United. Its membership also continued to grow far beyond the size of other NWBCCC neighborhood organizations.

Although SBU is officially part of the NWBCCC, it merited its own case study for several reasons. First, it boasted of its own bylaws and official leadership definitions, and even modified the NWBCCC dues system. Its staff members were NWBCCC employees, but it had its own floor in the main office and, during the present study's fieldwork period, was looking for a building of its own. The majority of its funding came from foundation grants that were SBU-specific. More substantively, its continued expansion had been accompanied by development of its own articulated values, cultural practices, campaigns, and political strategies. It carried its own reputation with public officials, and its political strategies sometimes contradicted those pursued by the NWBCCC as a whole. (Occasionally, SBU even garnered a coveted meeting with a policy maker by hiding its affiliation with the NWBCCC.)

From the beginning, SBU focused on education organizing. Its campaigns to transform vacant lots centered on adding classroom space to public schools and improving facilities, and its antiwar campaigns emerged from personal experiences with curricula and military recruiters in the high schools. Although campaigns focused on more than one Bronx neighborhood, they primarily dealt with the neighborhoods surrounding the three main public high schools attended by members, if not the schools themselves.

SBU's cultural practices clearly exemplified those of the Freirean tool kit. The bulk of its activities eventually contributed to campaigns, but more immediately, they facilitated trust-building and socializing among leaders. Member leaders were given the safe space, freedom, and resources to brainstorm and expand upon their critiques of the school system in a way that often led to new campaigns. Other activities built friendships and relationships between leaders and organizers, and contributed to the deep sense of commitment among all participants. As a result, leaders worked on campaigns even when they themselves were unlikely to benefit from them.

SBU's staffing alone suggested that its cultural practices did not revolve around campaigns or recruitment alone. One of its organizers, Elena, and several leaders had been with the organization since its inception. In addition, SBU staff included a second full-time organizer, a full-time tutor coordinator and in-house education expert, and, at various times, additional part-time organizers. SBU also had a political educational coordinator, a position unlikely to exist at "nonideological" Alinskyite organizations. Unlike the NWBCCC, then, SBU provided services to its members and overtly incorporated cultural and critical analysis into its leadership development curriculum. The other obvious characteristic that made SBU unique was its focus on youth, though there was also a new but growing youth component at Mothers on the Move.

Although SBU leaders and organizers cared quite a bit about the SCO's reputation, they attempted to build upon it with collaborations as well as displays of "people power" at rallies and protests. Unlike the Bronx chapter of the Association of Community Organizations for Reform Now (ACORN), it did not have its own team of lawyers; rather, SBU had strong ties to Fordham and New York Universities, teaming up with researchers on several projects.

During this study's fieldwork period, SBU worked on large campaigns on new school facilities, school safety, and overcrowding. This last issue was especially salient in an area where many of the high schools are at 200% capacity, with two students to a desk in some classrooms and some classes being conducted in hallways. These details were well known to teenagers in the Bronx, and SBU leaders rallied around such issues of educational inadequacy and inequality.

Peer Tutoring, Hanging Out, and Other Activities

Most of SBU's meetings had agendas specific to one of its education campaigns—the Student-Teacher Alliance to Reform Schools, or STARS (originally an alliance to "Better Schools," the campaign's name was ultimately changed to avoid the unfortunate acronym STABS); Cross-City Alliance New York, a youth-based alliance with the youth component of Mothers on the Move in the Bronx and Se Hace al Camino al Andar/Make the Road by Walking of Brooklyn that later became the Urban Youth Collaborative; the Leadership Institute, a proposal for a new small public high school focusing on social justice curricula; and Small Schools Strike Back, later renamed Bronx Schools Strike Back in order to be inclusive of students from the regular comprehensive high schools also suffering from overcrowding. (As described in chapter 2, New York City allows educators to submit proposals for "small schools," often beginning with just a few dozen students each. These small schools shape their curricula around a specific theme or pedagogy and attempt to give students more individualized attention, but they are often placed in just a few classrooms, in large buildings with regular high schools. Educators of these small schools have stated that they are given inadequate space to successfully carry out their school activities, and as a result there is often friction between small school and regular high school students.)

Most of the regular meetings for these campaigns were each attended by around a dozen members; some included many more, but most were consistently attended by at least seven or eight leaders. Unlike ACORN Bronx, SBU always scheduled preparation meetings, with set agendas, before meetings with school officials. These tended to be rather informal, asking for students' suggestions for other agenda items, accompanied by the organizer's questions about how school, family life, and the like were going in general. In this way meetings explicitly addressed campaign issues, but they were also more open to member-suggested changes and general conversations about concerns and aspirations than those described in chapter 3.

They also prepared leaders for a greater role in campaigns, in a way that allowed organizers to take a backseat during prominent meetings.

SBU's campaigns did not ignore the impact of power in numbers, calling on large rallies and events to make an impression on public officials. For example, after repeated refusals to meet and discuss school budgets by then governor George Pataki, SBU won meetings with him by protesting at his office. As Lisa, a leader at SBU, explained, they believed in the value of collective efforts. She noted, "Before...I never knew where to start, or where to go from here. I would think, 'This vacant lot is filthy,' but nobody would agree with me, and say, 'Oh yeah, but whatever.' I thought, 'What could I do, here, by myself?'... When I came here to SBU, people said, 'Hey, you think school sucks? So do I! That's great; let's work on it!'"

Regardless of the size, SBU's turnout was qualitatively different from that at Alinskyite SCOs. Here, participants spent a lot of time with the organization. Every day from 2 to 8 p.m., dozens of students—sometimes several dozen—showed up to volunteer on outreach and political strategies for these campaigns. Often, pragmatic strategies were not foremost on their mind. Instead, they began just by learning about one another, what their motivations and interests were, and where they would like to go before they began discussions about how to get there.

SBU also emphasized the importance of close relationships and included services like tutoring and poetry workshops in its activities. Tutoring often became a personal rather than organizational activity; Jeremy spoke of how, "Like with tutoring, I made brainteasers for the members to work before meetings, so that they wouldn't just be sitting around. I think we just come up with these things on our own because we're constantly helping each other, and because we want to be developing leadership skills." Other leaders like Rosalinda, who first became involved in SBU as a tutor, became politically active in campaign activities but concurrently emphasized the importance of activities like "hanging out."

SBU's wide-ranging activities led to strikingly different social networks from those apparent at ACORN Bronx and the NWBCCC. In the context of social networks, Granovetter emphasizes the importance of weak ties—people you barely know but who lead you to entirely new social circles so that your social network can quickly become that much bigger (1973). While the Alinskyite category's tool kit in some ways utilized the "strength of weak ties" (and strong ones) by tapping into social networks and emphasizing recruitment, it can be argued that SBU was concurrently trying to *build* strong ties. That is, SBU managed to create tight, lasting relationships with constituents who seemed hardest to reach, and who might not have been embedded in overlapping social networks before. Rather than building on existing groups of friends, it compelled leaders to rethink what their social spheres might look like. It did this with activities that emphasized dialogue among members and emotional exchange but were just as likely to *not* be directly related to campaigns or to involve organizers.

Partly because they focused on more than just campaigns, the SBU youth frequently spoke of the importance of cultural exchange and a welcoming community. As stated earlier, the Alinskyite tool kits at the NWBCCC and ACORN Bronx emphasized the substance of campaigns and winnable issues. By contrast, SBU members like Nathaniel also emphasized activities that might appear irrelevant at first: "We have fun things. We do trips. And, on a personal level, we chill with each other." At the SBU offices, the youth could constantly be heard yelling greetings of affection across the room. Nathaniel elaborated, "We definitely relate differently, because we spend a whole lot more time together....It's just more of a sense of community. More of a love thing in our SBU thing. Sometimes, people can get a little too involved...but it's all good."

Admittedly, these socializing activities might seem apolitical at first glance. However, to these leaders, hanging out and talking about what it was like to be living in a shelter, even if it had nothing to do with the latest school reform campaign, was a deliberate way of *not* doing business as usual. At the very least, these conversations helped the leaders better understand each other (and their performance in schools). Sometimes, in an iteration of "the personal is political," these discussions also helped leaders realize the sorts of power-sharing relationships they wished to reproduce with teachers, collaborators, and—with some adjustments—policy makers. Like specific decision-making processes practiced by participatory democratic groups in Polletta's study, SBU's tool kit constituted "a kind of politics—just not the politics of parliamentary maneuver and bureaucratic manipulation...to effect political change without reproducing the structures that they opposed. To be 'strategic' was to privilege organization over personhood and political reform over radical change, and this they would not do" (2002, 6). One leader, for instance, reflected that it was because of her friendships at SBU that she was "able to understand people better, not only personally, but what they're trying to say when they speak at [campaign] meetings."

Further, seemingly apolitical social activities often became opportunities for personal reflection and critical pedagogy. They enabled individual leaders to compare experiences and situate their own lives in the context of larger social structures, critically analyze their surroundings, and pinpoint social inequalities as key elements of injustice. In the context of SBU campaigns, a seemingly innocuous activity like tutoring can act as a trigger for political action: "With my little cousin," noted one leader, "I am helping him with his homework and picking up his book, I see that I can't help him with his homework because there's a hundred pages missing. Before, I would just feel like it is all right, that's the way it usually goes, and just leave it alone. This time, I thought of the history of resources going into the different schools, and about school budgets, how they are determined. Me, myself, and I need to learn about the larger picture. I got mad."

While such personal experiences may have triggered leader participation in other SCOs, social activities provided *consistent* opportunities for such critical reflection among SBU members. Further, so many leaders experienced personal transformation at SBU because these opportunities were accompanied by substantive workshops on education policy, politics, and organizing.

Likewise, exchanging CDs and downloading music off the Internet can be a social activity or a political one. A former SBU leader decided to formalize music as a tool for critical pedagogy when he hosted a hip-hop workshop where members both wrote their own rhymes and analyzed existing ones in popular songs, spoken word poems, and written poetry. To him, "hip-hop can be used as a medium to send a message...it's a social force." Thus, the workshop emphasized cultural and political literacy as well as socializing and more traditional reading and writing skills. After taking the class, some SBU leaders regularly analyzed the lyrics of new songs they heard via a similar political lens.

Finally, by engaging in a wide range of activities, leaders had more opportunities to build more holistic views of school reform issues. It was via discussions about housing conditions, for example, that one leader first concluded that school and housing segregation were fundamentally intertwined, and that in some ways the key question for policy makers was not how much money they had but how (and where) that money was distributed. From then on he chose to focus on inequality, rather than underfunding, as the main culprit in New York City schools.

The closeness and "love thing" forced the SBU youth to reshape their political visions, and to confront each other in a way not expressed in the other three case study organizations. The youth relished teamwork and mobilized each other in a way that fed upon their personal experiences, activities, overall interaction, and other cultural practices at SBU, rather than winnable issues, allegiance to the SCO itself, or ownership and investment.

Individual Development

Peer tutoring, hanging out, spoken word workshops, and other "non-campaign" activities not only strengthened relationships between leaders and organizers but contributed to development of individual leaders at SBU. As Ernest, an organizer, stated, "I spend quality time hanging out with leaders, and this is part of our education strategy. We talk about how they're doing in schools. We get into family business, get them to the right resources, and get them to advocate for themselves. Building them as individuals is as important as campaign work. At other groups, social services and organizing are in separate worlds. Not here. This approach has a connection to the mission and our organization. We need to build the skills and inner confidence so that they can maintain a certain level of conversation amongst themselves."

Again and again, the SBU participants spoke not so much of developing the organization as a whole but of how the individuals *within* the organization had developed and were now contributing to it. A recurrent theme was how their SBU experiences "opened their eyes." According to Nathaniel,

> SBU made me...more of a person that is open to things and realizes that everybody is not the enemy. At SBU, when people first come here, you have to introduce yourself to them. Me, I was always closed, "I don't know you," so I kept my mouth closed, "I don't need to meet you." But after a while, you got go up and introduce yourself, you gotta be a leader, and say, "Hi, my name is Nathaniel, and I do this; may I help you?"...And when I see people on the street, I go and help them, and say, "Hello" and "You have a good day." I just got more, like, "No one's against you, don't worry, nobody's trying to kill you."

Just as he drew lessons from the tool kit at SBU and applied them to his own life, Nathaniel also listed personal reasons for his "closed" persona and their implications for SBU's campaign work. For example, his analyses of racial inequalities in the school system, as well as how New York City bureaucracies work, were specifically drawn from his brother's run-ins with jail; his year in ninth grade in a rural Pennsylvania town while living with his father, where he was one of five black students in a school where many students carried Confederate flags; and his subsequent years living with his mother in a poorly run homeless shelter, where drug deals and violence pervaded.

Other leaders also spoke eloquently about personal transformation via SBU. Michael, the son of a gang leader, flirted with gangs himself at an early age, and was briefly placed in a mental health institution by age twelve. He originally joined SBU because his mother had forced him to, not because he was interested in school reform. Yet he echoed Nathaniel's remarks about learning to trust people, and learning about positive collective activity and a sense of agency, via political participation in SBU.

Lisa phrased the evolution of her outlook by asserting, "I've become more tolerant; I'm trying to see things from other people's point of views a little more. Just because, before, I really, really want to say something, I'd usually flip out and get angry. And now, I say, 'Okay, go ahead, speak,' and I can handle things in the room and make sure one person speaks at a time. [Before] I was not a friendly person."

On the other end of the spectrum of high school stereotypes, Rosalinda first got involved in SBU because it seemed like a noble thing to do; at school, she was an honors student and previously went out of her way to avoid people like Michael. She stated that SBU made her a less judgmental person, helped her "to get to know them and know what they've gone through, and why they made the choices they made."

While SBU leaders appeared to be incredibly committed to the organization, it might be more accurate to state that they were incredibly committed to one another, as a collective of individuals. Lisa stated, "Yeah, the campaigns are cool…I liked SBU as soon as I got here, but mostly, it was because of the people…I couldn't leave if I wanted to…Even if for some reason, SBU were to end tomorrow, I know we'd still all be close, and we'd probably start another organization that we could work on."

It was not just school outcomes or the organization's success that drove the leaders but their social bonds. This rendered the leaders' commitment that much more sustainable. Most of the youth began working at SBU around age fourteen; at seventeen they continued to work on long-term campaigns, despite the fact that they themselves would not reap the fruits of their labor. This is especially poignant in their efforts to construct a new, social-justice-themed small high school in the Bronx, which opened in September 2005, several years after efforts began, and after some leaders had graduated. The leaders said that experiencing their own social consciousness blossoming was reward enough.

Their commitment was remarkable not only because it transgressed typical notions of self-interest but because their campaigns were not obviously winnable. Many of the youth expressed anger at the systemic inequalities in New York education, which they condemned as "a trap."

Ironically, a combination of vision and social cohesion sometimes compelled a leader to recognize her self-interests in the work, which were not fully articulated when she first arrived. SBU's peer tutoring program greatly affected Lisa: "My grades were horrible when I first came to SBU. I had a sixty-something average." After working at SBU, she brought it up "to an eighty-something average." The opportunity to engage in political campaigns served as the motivation for her achievements in school rather than the other way around.

As Lisa's last statement exemplifies, SBU organizers and leaders did not dangle school reform as *the* incentive for membership and leadership. The youth considered whether an issue was winnable when pursuing campaigns, what the politicians' and teachers' self-interests were, and what their schools did and should look like in their campaign work. In this way, the SBU "love thing" was not just a social glue but a kind of moral vision and cultural tool.

Clearly, the tool kit at SBU made a difference to leaders. The interviews attested to the fact that an organizer was rarely seen as a neutral recruiter; rather, participants considered the power they possessed vis-à-vis organizers.

Leadership Development with Organizer as Partner

The youth organizers insisted that they operated differently from other NWBCCC staff; they felt compelled to prove to other youth that they cared and were friends, not just organizers. In fact, most outreach was not done by organizers, as in most organizations, but by leaders themselves. Nathaniel, for example, got involved in SBU through another leader, Michael. This only worked because "We were friends already; it was a connection we already had. It was partly because it was *him* asking...I thought I could relate....If it had been a regular...organizer, it would have been, 'Oh, another routine thing, you got to listen to older people do this, and say that.'" Thus, the leadership development model at SBU reflected key Freirean ideals: it was one in which the organizer and a burgeoning leader critically engaged each other rather than one in which the organizer transferred or "banked" skills and information into the leader.

Even when an organizer did the recruiting, it was done in the context of a friendship. Lisa got involved in SBU through organizer Ernest; "We were in this group together called NYC, New York Conservationists....We got really close, and talked about our lives....I loved him, and he told me to check it out....I could relate to all the people here." Eventually, Lisa left New

York Conservationists and spent all her time at SBU. Her reasons partly concerned the content of the work, because she felt that SBU was more active and constructive, and partly because she felt the SBU youth understood her better. Nathaniel's and Lisa's comments also revealed the implicit power relations between recruiter and potential participant, and the fact that they were only willing to join an organizations after being invited by people they perceived as peers or partners.

Of the organizations in the study, SBU was the only one that regularly held meetings and orientations without organizers present, giving leaders that much more importance. The interviewees also expressed that they were inspired to become leaders because they had seen others *just like them* in powerful positions. Nathaniel's story resonated with those of other SBU youth: "When I first came here for my orientation, I heard a whole bunch of youth speak, and actually, Michael was in charge of my orientation, so I really felt like, 'Whoa, my homey's really doing it!' It challenged me! 'Wow, they know so much! I want to get to that level!' And I worked until I got to know that much stuff, too....Maybe I can be just like them. I want to be a leader, to be called a leader."

In reflecting Freirean ideals, leadership development was seen as an end unto itself and not just as a means toward organization building and campaign wins. While Nathaniel certainly cared about high schools in the Bronx, he primarily cited social aspirations, not better grades or better schools, as the primary motivating factors for his active participation in SBU. Affirmation and respect by peers made the campaigns truly special to the youth, so that there was no distinction between the collective and the individual aspects of work.

Lest all of their previous intolerance be attributed to age, the SBU youth also contrasted their tool kit to that of the NWBCCC as a whole. According to Lisa, "The coalition is way more immature. They say hurtful things! I've actually had to tell them to be sensitive to each other, 'Get your act together, and work this out.' They'll say really vicious things; it's horrible! Which is funny, because we don't do that." Such opinions of the adults were echoed, unprompted, by other SBU interviewees. The adults themselves have also noted that they have begun to emulate SBU practices and styles of interaction and recruiting. Thus, just as the practices at SBU were influenced and reinterpreted by the youth they should not be construed as essentialist or limited to them. Rather, individuals in an organization can play with and incorporate cultural practices over time.

SBU's wide-ranging activities, focus on individual development, and partner relationships between organizers and leaders helped to build a powerful tool kit, one with substantive, sustainable leadership development and deep-seated commitment among members. These cultural tools were obviously time-intensive, however; few SCOs could handle as many as sixty members for many hours each day. While SBU's Freirean cultural practices may have taken longer to implement and take hold, they may also be longer lasting. In addition, the fact that SBU was able to achieve this with the same number of staff as the other case study SCOs suggests that time- and labor-intensive social change work did not have to be organizer- or staff-driven. Freirean cultural practices did not appear to produce the same scale as Alinskyite ones, but this weakness might be overcome with further use of peer recruitment and training.

Mothers on the Move: Building Well-Rounded Leaders

At first glance, the cultural practices at Mothers on the Move might bear a striking resemblance to those at the NWBCCC. There was intensive leadership development, including research groups and workshops, and the organizers and members spoke explicitly about how to build the organization. Also, the organization had a similar nominal dues system of ten dollars per year per person. Yet, MOM leaders engaged in cultural practices that placed it squarely at the Freirean end of an Alinskyite-Freirean spectrum. Specifically, activities at MOM were shaped so as to emphasize the individual at least as much as the organization, and personal growth became a focus of many activities and protocols. Furthermore, other practices, such as intense scrutiny of organizers and all organizational documents, worked to mold organizers as partners rather than teacher-guides.

MOM worked with neighborhoods with distinct borders, namely Hunt's Point, Longwood, and Intervale Valley. This area formed the southernmost area west of the Bronx River and north of the East River. Its services were decidedly poorer than those in the northern and western parts of District 8.[4] There were many noticeable vacant lots in the area, filled with decades' worth of trash. The neighborhood's most defining characteristic, unfortunately, was the local sewage treatment plant that processed half of the city's waste. Ironically, Hunt's Point was also home to the city's docking point for all organic produce arriving in New York City; none of this produce remained in the neighborhood.

Approximately one-third of residents received public assistance, and children's asthma rates were the city's highest.[5] Like the populations served by the other case study SCOs, that of Hunt's Point was overwhelmingly black and Latino. However, most older residents, including many MOM leaders, remembered when Hunt's Point was more diverse, with large Irish, Eastern European Jewish, and Cuban populations, as well as the Dominican, African American, and Puerto Rican communities that are still there today. Recently, as with the Northwest Bronx, there has also been an increase of immigrants from Africa.

Unlike ACORN Bronx and the NWBCCC, which began organizing around housing issues and later branched into school reform campaigns, MOM began and continued its struggles because of the poor state of public education in the South Bronx. In another similarity to SBU, MOM straddled services and organizing since its inception.

In fact, MOM began as an adult literacy class, the kind that first inspired Freire himself. In October 1991, adult literacy students at Bronx Educational Services (BES) were shocked when they investigated their neighborhood schools' math and reading scores as compared to others in the city. Mediratta and Karp (2003) write about how the mothers' outrage grew when they realized that even other schools in their own district, located in the adjacent, wealthier Throggs Neck neighborhood, performed better than those in Hunt's Point. If the Latina mothers who first formed MOM had learned English with *Dick and Jane* books rather than newspaper articles and statistical reports about the state of South Bronx schools, they might not have moved onto critical analysis or mobilized education reform campaigns quite as quickly.

Mothers on the Move was formed in 1992, after BES parents visited PS 62, a local low-performing school, and realized that their children's academic problems were not simply reflective of their own limitations. During their trip they saw students being neglected in poor facilities and some teachers mistreating the children, even in the presence of visitors.

As the parents ramped up their protests of school inequalities, BES became uncomfortable with their organizing activities, and the mothers broke off from BES to form MOM. With funding from the Edna McDonnell Clark and Aaron Diamond Foundations, the group drew from BES teacher Barbara Gross's previous experience with ACORN and hired a full-time organizer, Millie Bonilla, who had previously worked for South Bronx People for Change, focusing on housing. A participatory model of organizing was set from the beginning. The parents took the lead in making decisions, and they made conclusions based on local and personal circumstances. Through research help from the Data Consortium at New York University (NYU), they quickly moved from organizing at PS 62 to protesting disparities at the district level.

MOM organizers discussed specific finances more openly than staff in the other case study SCOs. Because the overwhelming majority of its funding came from foundations, MOM was sensitive to the traditional funding cycle, marked by renewal limits, specific outcomes measures, and trends in education policy, community organizing, and social movements. Its annual budget nearly doubled, from $200,000 to $450,000, in the years immediately preceding the fieldwork period of this study.

MOM has also received the attention of some academics at the Institute for Education and Social Policy at NYU, as well as the City University of New York Graduate Center.[6] The publications describing MOM's work thus far focus on the organization's early victories, documenting the work via participatory action projects and monographs rather than evaluating them regarding their tool kits.

During the present study's fieldwork period, MOM sustained collaborations with other SCOs and planned new ones. The main education organizer continued to develop after-school social justice curricula for students in other high schools, such as the Satellite Academy, as well as morning workshops on organizing for parents in several local schools. MOM also maintained formal affiliations with a citywide organization called the Parent and Youth Transformation Collaborative that had similar organizations in other boroughs, and the Training Institute for Careers in Organizing, which MOM founded with ACORN New York and the NWBCCC. Finally, MOM also began education organizing among youth, with a group called Youth on the Move.

Research, Retreats, and Other Activities

More so than other organizations, MOM boasted of a wide array of activities in addition to typical education committee meetings. Agenda-setting meetings for special events, for instance, were open to all members and always preceded regular education committee meetings by exactly one week. Core leaders were most likely to show up at these preliminary meetings, but generally, different leaders attended each time. These meetings usually included a good deal of brainstorming, presentations about potential campaigns ideas, and decision making about which issues to prioritize for meetings with larger audiences. The fact that these meetings followed specific patterns in their scheduling and overall agenda did not feel restrictive; rather, the meetings allowed relatively new members to quickly become comfortable in voicing their opinions and assuming new organizing responsibilities. Leaders did not have to attend too many of these meetings before feeling like they could chair a subsequent one.

One such preliminary meeting included a video about parent-teacher home visits created by Sacramento, California's IAF affiliate. This video had been previously viewed by one of the members at a conference she attended with MOM, so she presented it. The reception was mixed. While some members were clearly enthusiastic and immediately began throwing out questions about implementation, others doubted that it could work in New York's new centralized system, and still others did not believe at first that the parents portrayed in the video were actually low-income, since they all lived in free-standing houses rather than in housing projects. Once caveats were articulated, a consensus emerged to present the idea to the general membership, as long as members made sure to develop a new, MOM-centered home-visit plan along the way.

For members who wished to assume leadership responsibilities, other opportunities abounded. For the month or so before any of MOM's two or three large rallies and events each year, general education meetings were held once a week instead of once a month; calendars detailing the specific issues to be discussed were prepared long in advance and distributed widely. During some months, breakfasts were arranged to encourage the interested, or just the curious, to drop by the organization's storefront office and learn more about MOM.

In addition, there were opportunities for further dialogues on Bronx schools, MOM's efforts, and social change overall. For instance, an informal book discussion group met monthly; this group met at a local bar on certain Fridays to discuss books that addressed the Bronx, community organizing, or, more commonly, both. Books discussed included *Organizing the South Bronx* by Jim Rooney, *South Bronx Rising: The Rise, Fall, and Resurrection of an American City* by Jill Jonnes, and *Tilting at Mills: Green Dreams, Dirty Dealings, and the Corporate Squeeze* by Lis Harris.[7] Leaders also attended conferences, usually hosted by foundations, community organizing alliances, or social justice groups, around the country. One leader, George, commented that after he asked a Department of Education official a pointed question at a MOM meeting, one of the organizers "asked me if I wanted to go to Chicago for the Cross-City Campaign. I didn't know at the time what that was. But in meeting people from around the country, it opened me up to looking at education from a different standpoint. A national one, as opposed to my little school." Such trips helped George to see his work as part of a social movement, transcendent of his school or even the Mothers on the Move organization.

Like so many SBU leaders, Michele, a leader at MOM for over a decade, also cherished activities that did not pointedly relate to the organization's campaigns. Instead she suggested that MOM host even more events with soul food or wine and cheese, "rap sessions," and "sister-bonding" events. Like SBU, Mothers on the Move attempted to create cultural practices that encouraged members to express their personal interests, even if the political ramifications were not readily apparent. To this end, the organization also hosted a variety show and incorporated leisurely visits to the park across the street into its meetings. Organizers, leaders, and members also traded other books, like those in the *Harry Potter* series or beginner's guides to yoga. Together, these shared practices emphasized personal transformation and development.

MOM also invested in day-, weekend-, and weeklong retreats facilitated by consultants and community organizers from across the country. Although such retreats took place in both the Alinskyite and Freirean case study organizations, the Freirean SCO retreats were more likely to be centered on the individual and on discussions about philosophy, vision, and values in general rather than campaigns, skills, or self-interest per se. NWBCCC organizers and members tended to focus on workshops and learn new skills; SBU members had the opportunity to write their own bylaws and have uncensored, no-holds-barred conversations about race without the supervision of organizers; and MOM members had the opportunity to write up vision and mission statements, as well as a long-term plan, for the entire organization. MOM leaders thus created the rules and policies they would live by in the SCO.

As at SBU, socializing activities often acquired a political tenor because they were accompanied by critical reflection. At MOM, this critical reflection was most clearly manifest in the leaders' overt practice of reflection-action, whereby leaders (1) see the problem, (2) analyze it, and (3) act on it. To Katerina, an organizer trained in both Freirean and Alinskyite organizing, reflection-action was distinctly Freirean because Alinskyite preoccupations with winnable campaigns did not enter the picture until the third stage, that of action. It was only then that organizers and leaders drew from their knowledge of practices usually associated with Alinsky—that is, "cutting" issues into "actionable" slices and finding a winnable campaign idea.

Clearly, Mothers on the Move was also preoccupied with typical SCO concerns like recruitment and fundraising. MOM organizers spent a substantial percentage of their time on one-on-one conferences and door-knocking, just as Melissa did at ACORN Bronx (as described in chapter 3). However, as Katerina noted, "In our weekly staff meetings, our group evaluations of membership and public meetings and events did not focus merely on measuring the success according to Alinsky evaluation priorities like turnout and our checklist of demands. Rather, we also evaluated whether the meeting [or] event and the preparation for it was grounded in MOM's values and mission—our race/class analysis and our emphasis on members' leadership development. These practices were organically part of MOM culture, so only now do I realize that they align more closely with Freire's processes of reflection-action than with Alinsky's model." Although MOM meetings often turned to the issue of rebuilding a membership base, it was always accompanied by inclusive discussions of personal goals.

Thus, it was not just what was done but how and to what ends that mattered. At one meeting, when a leader asked the organizer for an overview for the types of foundation money most available right now, the organizers aggressively refused to answer the question; they insisted that they would find money for whatever the members wanted, no matter how outlandish the wishes were, that "we're not chasing the money."

Many of the cultural practices at MOM—the constant discussion, the book exchanges—may have added to a sense of learning, but they originally struck some members as, frankly, a waste of time. As George described it, when he first interacted with Mothers on the Move, there would be "a lot of stuff at the meetings, I would have people complaining and making statements about how a school worked, and I'm saying, 'Well, that's not what's going on at my school,' so there used to be a whole lot of back-and-forth debate, and I used to be short-patienced [*sic*], because I have a short temper. And I thought they were moving too slowly." However, he eventually changed his mind. At first, "I didn't understand…really wasn't interested in organizing, I was really looking at it as a means to an end, and I realized that they [MOM] were worth it when the city was reorganizing, and they got to sit down with them." In changing his mind, he also suggested that organizing is an end unto itself, in a way that contrasted ends-oriented cultural practices in the Alinskyite organizations.

Individual Development

A good example of MOM's focus on individual development was the Social Justice Organizing Training Matrix, which was still being developed with leaders during the present study's fieldwork period. This training matrix was a means to encourage the development of whole, well-rounded, capable, and healthy individuals, not just dues-paying leaders and organizers. (Not that any of the case study SCOs would be unhappy with lots of dues-paying members! Still, outside of dues payments, the SCOs had different expectations of their leaders.) At that time, the matrix included ten categories with a list of skills for each, including predictable ones like relational organizing (clarifying self-interest, membership recruitment and relationship-building, mentoring new leaders); public action leadership (issue identification, negotiation, celebration); public relations (generating press coverage, public speaking); and fundraising (grant writing for foundations, benefits for grassroots activities). More unusual were categories such as culture and art practice; body practice (the integration of healthy living practices in personal life through diet, exercise, and recreation); inner life practice (development of a coherent values statement, reflection); and leadership for family, work, and life. The training matrix therefore emphasized quite a few areas of individual development and learning that bore no direct consequences upon MOM's organizational development.

Such emphases on individual development were illustrated the day before the Still We Rise march (originally coordinated with dozens of other grassroots groups and the Hip-Hop Action Summit, headed by record industry mogul Russell Simmons) during the Republican National Convention in August 2004. Sara, the teenager who was supposed to speak on behalf of Mothers on the Move, became sick and had to visit the hospital. MOM organizers scrambled to find another youth willing to represent the organization. They found someone, and her speech was well received. However, MOM staff did not declare the event a success because this speech was not as organically developed, and it therefore did not reflect the experience of the substitute as well as the original speech had reflected Sara's passion and personality. This incident indicated that organizational success is not the only goal; even in cases of emergency, leaders were to be developed in specific ways.

Leaders took great pride in their intensive participation; Isabela, for example, boasted at the MOM's quarterly membership meeting that out of everyone who gathered at NYU for a conference the night before, she had been the only nonstaff member who spoke.

Another important component of MOM's individual development was an emphasis on transparency. More than other organizations examined in this study, MOM placed access to information at the forefront—both literally (displaying archival portfolios and binders with all of the meeting agendas, attendance lists, reports, foundation documents, etc., at the front of the storefront office), and figuratively (highlighting the importance of transparency as an explicit value). The office also served as a library, with archives, books, and periodicals such as *City Limits,* a magazine that covered New York City politics. Because of this a leader did not have to ask an organizer for important documents; they were already accessible. Organizers and leaders also suggested initiatives such as recording oral histories of all of the leaders. Some members emphasized these practices as integral elements of organizational learning, since they had seen too many lessons forgotten with staff turnover.

MOM's multifaceted training, transparency, abundant use of resources, and active solicitation of individual leaders' ideas added up to a well-developed set of cultural practices that lent depth to their participation in MOM's activities, in a way that rendered them that much more committed. Ultimately, MOM staff hoped that these members would, in turn, help the organization pursue more impressive campaigns.

These cultural practices also helped MOM's leaders to develop and build capacity as whole individuals, not just organizational members. As Katerina described it, "The foregrounding of leadership development processes [was] not just as a necessity for achieving winnable campaigns...but as the end in itself—the basis upon which a socially just society is built." Her hope was that members could eventually create social change in their everyday lives, at their workplaces and in their own homes, even when they were not working on MOM campaigns.

Finally, MOM's focus on individual development also had practical implications for its leadership development model. Specifically, MOM's tool kit specified that no one-size-fits-all approach to leadership development exists. Katerina observed that for her, "One-to-ones, Alinsky's tool for leadership development, were generally taught in one two-hour training in the organizer and membership trainings I've witnessed, participated in, [or] developed. In fact, I was taught the organizing mantra, 'Do one hundred one-to-ones, and then you'll know how to do them.' Well, I've done those hundred one-to-ones, and I'm still learning, reading about, reflecting on, and practicing Freire's...techniques—and I *still* feel like I can learn about these processes for the rest of my life! And, in fact, that feels *good*."

The practice of focusing on the individual, and engaging in dialogue with others, helped leaders to step outside of narrowly confined roles of what it meant to be a "leader" instead of an "organizer." Katerina concludes that she is "glad" that the Freirean tool kit forces her to learn as well as teach, and to pay attention to "the needs of each particular group of people you're working with, and...propose a process and tools for exploring the uniqueness of each context."

Leadership Development with Organizer as Partner

Leadership development at MOM occurred most overtly via a series of ten two-hour workshops held twice a year, usually during the daytime hours, and another seminar series of workshops held two nights per month. These workshops covered topics like political analysis, disentangling the political system in New York City, using the media, and translating big issues into policy proposals. For example, members at one workshop session worked on a specific issue each of them wished to tackle and performed a sequence of exercises, like paring treatises down to sound bites, brainstorming on the visual and auditory imagery that would support their case, and engaging in videotaped and critiqued mock interviews with either policy makers or news reporters.

One critical reflection element of MOM's tool kit is apparent in another Freirean practice, "Naming the Root Causes," that also appeared regularly in MOM's leadership development workshops. For this activity, leaders created a "problem tree" where the leaves were the "problems" they saw in the community, the trunk was labeled with the "immediate causes" of their problems, and the roots were the "root causes." In this way, as one organizer noted, leaders identified "racism, classism—all the *isms,* as we used to say— and … oppression … at the root of the local problems that we see around us, [like] housing, education."

MOM leaders were quite committed to "Naming the Root Causes." Even as everyone wanted campaign wins, noted Katerina, "the board and the membership held [Alinsky-trained organizers] accountable for guiding the organization toward concrete, Alinsky-style organizing victories while also insisting on Freire-style … root cause analyses … that do not factor into the winnability of issues but that they felt are critical to MOM's visibility [and] resonance within the community." By insisting on continuing certain cultural practices, MOM leaders also maintained relationships with organizers as partners in social change.

MOM's tool kit also included consistent cultural practices that crafted all campaign activities as learning opportunities for new leaders. For instance, at a typical education committee meeting, attendees introduced themselves by name and cited the issues that most interested them. Agendas were usually developed and available beforehand, but most people picked up a summary as they sat down. A projected number of minutes allotted to a topic was listed next to each agenda item. At most of the meetings, there were also informational handouts to pick up. Sometimes this was an academic article about organizing or a case study of a particularly illustrative success or failure; at other times there were recent newspaper articles about Bronx policies. After introductions, members and organizers broke into pairs, spending approximately five minutes in quick one-on-one conversations about a specific topic, such as the pressures most affecting them at that moment in life or their personal goals for the next two years. Even a typical meeting introduction, then, forced members to articulate their current concerns and potentially relate them to discussion topics based on readings.

Different leaders then presented updates on different campaigns or events, such as reports on recent conferences or meetings with politicians. Other recurring items for discussion included surveys of people's experiences with new Department of Education policies, persistent problems at specific local schools, the building of a new school, New York City's capital plan and city budget allocations for school construction in the Bronx, and different ways to tackle overcrowding. Before each item on the agenda was resolved, each attendee spoke and either approved the protocol or raised an issue. Meeting discussions at MOM were dramatically more varied and spanned more topics than those at ACORN Bronx, and overall, they were less structured than those at SBU and the NWBCCC, where each meeting tended to focus on a specific campaign issue.

The extensive and intensive preparation that occurred before all MOM meetings, even internal ones, was obvious. Members rather than organizers usually presented all updates, not just overall campaign platforms, and they often included personal commentary in speeches. At meetings, MOM members were more likely than those from other organizations to cite bylaws from the Department of Education, and to easily recall the names of schools officials responsible for specific grievances, dozens of acronyms for legislative acts and administrative agencies, the names of a dizzying array of governance structures at different governmental levels, rules concerning checks and balances between different administrative and instructional roles, and the names of documents listing all these rules, such as the Blue and White Books. While members of other organizations also alluded to such information, it most permeated MOM conversations. This is partly because some members had recently become parent coordinators or begun to collaborate with schools and thus had easier access to some information; this should not be construed as the decisive factor, however, since MOM members who prided themselves for their "outsider" status were just as knowledgeable, while some "insider" members of organizations were not. Rather, the common denominator was that education committee meetings at MOM emphasized nitty-gritty policy making and critical reflection, in ways similar to the NWBCCC's focus on policy implications found in research.

MOM's combination of formal leadership development workshops and hands-on training allowed its leaders to take on impressive amounts of responsibility. While the leaders at MOM were not necessarily as close to each other as were SBU leaders, they collaborated closely with organizers, partnering up with them on a variety of campaigns, and became quite committed to the organization.

MOM's extensive tool kit showed leaders and outsiders alike that its members valued learning for learning's sake, not just for campaign wins. Indeed, the organization acquired a reputation as a hub or connector in the local organizing foundation world. As such, many of its more recent foundation grants were not for social justice or organizing work per se but for the administration of informal research groups or institutes connecting policy think tanks and community organizing groups in the city and around the country.

Overall, the two Freirean SCOs exhibited a greater range of organizationwide activities than the Alinskyite SCOs presented in chapter 3. Education-specific activities and meetings had set meeting protocols, but these protocols tended to more overtly accommodate differing individual needs and preferences. For example, leaders and organizers made sure that there were numerous official feedback opportunities before an agenda was set, that there was rotation among leaders presiding over meetings, and that child care was always provided.

Learning and exploration, even if performed by leaders as individuals rather than MOM or SBU members per se, were seen as social processes; each person's learned lessons contributed to the organizational whole. The challenge was to ensure that the organization's lessons were simultaneously and effectively shared with and applied by individual leaders.

Partnerships as Individual Development

As illustrated by MOM and SBU, a Freirean tool kit excelled in helping members develop into substantive leaders. The activities were varied and multifaceted enough so that leaders identified with more than specific campaigns, and they acquired enough transferable skills so that they quickly assumed more responsibilities than was common at the two Alinskyite SCOs. They helped to set agendas and conduct campaigns, and built fairly close working relationships not just with organizers but with each other. In short, members at Freirean SCOs experienced personal transformations. They were not just members of MOM or SBU; they became activists working toward social change.

Most of the members I interviewed did not join these organizations when prompted by factors of sheer self-interest or policy support. They were not prompted to ratchet up their participation by the appearance of a new drug-ridden house down the street, the election of an unwanted politician, or even a personal crisis at school or combative run-in with a school administrator or safety agent. The leaders spoke of personal circumstances, whereby the organization filled a gap at that moment in their lives. The SBU youth, for example, joined specifically because someone they admired and trusted spoke of it passionately. Along these lines, all of the members spoke of a lifetime commitment to their organizations, regardless of expected victories or the lack thereof.

These findings about culture and emotions make some intuitive sense, but they are nevertheless neglected in most academic work.[8] Katerina explicitly contrasted "Alinsky pragmatism versus Freirean values" this way: "We have a moral imperative—that we as organizers of color also deeply feel—to take on…nonwinnable issues *if that is where the people are at and what they are feeling!*"

To the extent that key practices are examined in organizations, they are often portrayed as static or taken for granted, as outlined by the elites in the organization. Here, members and leaders as well as organizers constantly enacted cultural practices. The SBU youth formed intensely personal relationships that, in turn, shaped their campaigns and helped them to build long-term commitment and sustainability. At MOM, meeting protocols and preparation, conferences and reading groups, retreats and other activities, and the strong conventions of transparency collectively formed cultural practices that emphasized popular pedagogy, learning, and personal development.

The work at each organization reflected a set of shifting practices rather than values set in stone. Social activities usually deemed out of bounds or superfluous in other organizing groups were considered integral aspects of political work at SBU and MOM. These activities gave leaders time to reflect upon the ways in which personal experiences connected to larger sociopolitical struggles. Emotional commitment then helped organizational work to remain sustainable in the face of greater obstacles because leaders and constituents had something to gain besides concrete victories and policy reforms.

An SCO's original practices, those existent when the SCO was first created, did help to set a path. MOM was first developed as a popular education reading course, one that incorporated critical analysis of educational disparities in its curricula. Such classes were integral to MOM's tool kit and helped it to become a Freirean organization. Several MOM leaders also explicitly mentioned being inspired by Freire in their discussions. During a meeting on uses of the media, for instance, several recalled their experiences with popular education and liberation theology in El Salvador and the United States during the 1980s. While other leaders took to Freirean practices just as well, Latino constituents were more likely to have had previous grassroots exposure to elements of the Freirean tool kit. As chapters 7 and 8 discuss in more detail, it is difficult to abandon the cultural tools through which members and organizers have developed strengths and preferences.

SBU emerged from the NWBCCC, an Alinskyite organization, yet it developed an entirely distinct tool kit. From the beginning, however, there were informal practices of peer tutoring and support. Further, because all of the leaders participate in the SCO during after-school hours, "hanging out" quickly became an integral part of SBU culture. Such practices were later institutionalized through official activities and workshops, such as the one on hip-hop.

Despite these practices, SBU and MOM do not closely resemble some of the most prominent case studies of Freirean education organizing already in the literature. Oakes and Rogers (2006), for example, describe work with students and parents aimed at community empowerment via critical social inquiry. Their work with poor communities in Los Angeles is founded upon principles outlined by educators John Dewey and Paulo Freire, but the practices that they emphasize are different from those of the SCOs I got to know in the Bronx. Namely, the practice of social science research and overt theoretical or academic sociological language play a much smaller role, and actual collective action campaigns play a much larger one, in the Bronx case studies.

Accordingly, the role of pedagogy and education policy experts was much more limited at MOM and SBU. The hip-hop workshop at SBU was just one of many activities there, and "Naming the Root Causes" one of dozens of activities in a long organizing curriculum that also included classes on the merits of petitions vis-à-vis rallies. SBU and MOM leaders engaged in critical reflection, but unlike leaders in the Los Angeles case studies, almost all of them did so without reading books by Freire himself or critical theory texts. They learned about the New York City educational bureaucracy and basic statistical analysis, and they sought additional research help from university collaborators, but the university collaborators had no formal role within the SCOs themselves.

Thus, some of the critiques lobbed at Oakes and Rogers's work, regardless of their validity, do not quite apply here. The contentions that social inquiry focuses too much on alternative institution building and not enough on concrete policy proposals or gathering power, and that discursive practices do not mesh well with working-class constituents, for instance, are belied by MOM and SBU.[9] Further, SBU and MOM were able to succeed in facilitating personal transformation in leaders without hiring more education organizers than ACORN Bronx or the NWBCCC. This may be because these two organizations have, to some extent, successfully melded cultural practices from both Alinskyite and Freirean tool kits. For instance, MOM was the case study that most seriously considered PICO Sacramento's home visit system, and both MOM and SBU meetings included discussions on "cutting" issues into "actionable" slices. They combined discursive practices with the sort of "democratic solidarity" that Schutz (2008) argues is more pertinent to working-class life.

Polletta has examined the ways in which other organizations that encourage friendship have faced similar challenges: "For instance, friendship's tendency to exclusivity and its aversion to difference made it difficult for 1960s activists to expand their groups beyond their original core," partly because these groups often resisted formalization of rules (2002, 4). For the most part, MOM and SBU appeared to avoid this problem by melding formal and informal practices in agenda-setting and meeting protocols. There was nothing quite so artificial as a "disc" system in which each person spoke a predetermined number of times per meeting but meetings had rotating chairs. Making friends was not a "private, personal activity," and recruitment and hanging out were largely performed as official organizing activities rather than something that occurred during meals before or after campaign meetings, as in the feminist groups analyzed by Polletta (2002, 167). These procedures were all formalized so that newcomers could quickly learn the rules and not have to become buddies with the organization's most charismatic or powerful leaders before assuming responsibilities, but there was a wide enough range of responsibilities so that leaders could assume the tasks most to their liking. In a way, the Bronx SCOs' Freirean tool kits contained elements from Polletta's tutelage model (where organizers act as tutors, and under which Polletta categorizes faith-based organizing groups like the IAF) as well as her friendship model.

These case studies demonstrate that Alinskyite and Freirean tool kits may have different foci, but that they are not antithetical. While the Alinskyite tool kit encourages SCOs to become hierarchical, the Freirian case study SCOs I examined were more than tiny, egalitarian circles (or worse, tiny circles filled with subtle domination and false rhetoric on equality). Instead, they were fairly large, tightly knit webs of activists. These activists were not all equally involved. Far from being interchangeable, these leaders generally had more varied and substantive roles in their SCOs' campaigns than those in the Alinskyite SCOs did. Just as Freirean groups have something to learn from the Alinskyite tool kit, Alinskyite SCOs have something to learn from the Freirean one.

Nevertheless, some of the critiques lobbed at Oakes and Rogers's work may in fact apply to the Freirean tool kits examined herein, and they merit significant consideration in subsequent chapters. Schutz (2007), for instance, has been quite forceful in arguing that approaches like the Freirean one do not necessarily help groups to build concrete political power, especially in terms of scale.

Indeed, while the Bronx Freirean SCOs were especially adept at in-depth leadership development and eliciting substantive personal transformations among members, all of this work took time, and MOM and SBU did not always garner policy wins on the same scale that those at the NWBCCC and ACORN Bronx did. Since these SCOs could not afford to hire more organizers, the question lay in whether their leaders could also do the work of organizers, especially in terms of recruitment and leadership development. I argue that this can be done—not by further copying other organizations and appealing to organizational development, however, as the Alinskyite SCOs did, but by connecting short-term activities to larger, long-term visions of social justice.

CHAPTER FIVE

OFF THE CHARTS

Tackling Issues of Race in SCOs

In this chapter I examine social change organizations' untold stories, contradictions, and other factors not easily labeled as activities, organizer-leader relationships, or other key practices. In other words, I analyze patterns in the conspicuous, awkward silences that unfolded in my fieldwork. It so happens that, more often than not, what was not being openly talked about (even though participants later admitted that they all were all thinking about it) dealt with issues of race. Whether and how the social change organizations (SCOs) discussed these issues helped to shape the campaign issues they ultimately chose to tackle.

SCOs adopting the Freirean tool kit were more likely to face issues of race head on. Their socializing activities, combined with critical reflection, sometimes became vital, safe spaces for relatively judgment-free discussions on race. Because of their emphasis on individual development, leaders and organizers at Mothers on the Move (MOM) and Sistas and Brothas United (SBU) created a culture in which leaders did not have to be exactly the same in order to form a collective. They were able to broach race as one of the many important forces shaping any individual's life. (Gender, neighborhood of residence, age, class, sexual orientation, political affiliation, and even taste in music were other obvious forces.) In these SCOs, even when two leaders did not share the same racial background, they were likely to nevertheless recognize that they had overlapping interests. Partly because the Freirean tool kit involved a much wider array of activities, MOM and SBU leaders had the safe space to have a lot more informal conversations in which they could be race conscious without seeming racist.

By contrast, a focus on organizational development at the Bronx chapter of the Association of Community Organizations for Reform Now (ACORN) and the Northwest Bronx Clergy and Community Coalition (NWBCCC) helped leaders and organizers to quickly unite on broad-based, usually class-centered, campaign issues, but they did not always possess the cultural tools with which to talk about issues of race without seeming divisive. As a result, ACORN Bronx adopted "color-blind" terms in their conversations, even when the leaders and organizers were talking about issues that affected different racial or ethnic communities in different ways. Unfortunately, these color-blind practices perpetuate existing racial inequalities in mainstream American society.[1] For example, none of the SCOs would argue against public safety officers in schools, but adding more officers will not change the unfair treatment experienced by some students unless patrolling protocols are changed as well. Likewise, calling for more funding for public schools is a laudable goal, but unless funding is centralized so that criteria are based more on need or academics rather than dependent on local tax bases and private property values, most of this money will continue to go to wealthier schools in predominantly white districts.

We can see how the two tool kits end up treating issues of race so differently by examining the respective case study SCOs' practices in three key areas.[2] First, demographic breakdowns of the SCOs' staff and base constituencies show that paid staff and organizers at all four SCOs represented constituent "racialized minorities [and majorities]" (Agocs 2004, 2) fairly well, but nevertheless, some leaders questioned the predominance of white directors in the top ranks of three of the SCOs. What differentiates the different groups here was how staff members then responded to touchy questions of race and rank.

Second, patterns in "communication [and] informal social relations" (Agocs 2004, 2) salient to race varied greatly at the four SCOs. These included unwritten dress codes at the organizations, patterns of segregation among leaders and organizers, and the extent to which conversations about race took place. At the Alinskyite SCOs, campaign issues had to automatically gather the support of most members in order to be broad-based. Other issues were often sidelined as divisive.

Finally, the two tool kits were associated with different decision-making rules and practices so that the SCOs could either affirm or contest color blindness in their campaigns. The SCOs had dramatically different "policy and decision making process[es]" that affect everyone in the organization. Social change organizations in multiracial contexts need to create "organizational space" that allows members to discuss issues in their own language, or in ways they feel comfortable (Delgado 2003, 104), but there must also be organizational space for substantive conversations between different member groups (Sen 2003, 34–38). A recurrent motif, then, was that silence or perfunctory consensus processes routinely led to a smothering of race- or ethnicity-delineated issues.[3] The Freirean SCOs were more successful in giving leaders the organizational space in which to voice their opinions and help to make important decisions. Recall that, like the participatory democratic organizations examined by Polletta (2002), leaders at SBU and MOM felt that "[e]xperiments with egalitarian and cooperative decision-making are a kind of politics" (Polletta 2002, 6). Thus, engaging in critical analysis and resisting hierarchies was just as important inside the SCOs as in society as a whole.

In the Alinskyite SCOs, leaders sometimes felt that they did not have the opportunity to honestly express their views, and so they ended up leaving the organization. While Freirean SCOs desire broad-based alliances as much as Alinskyite ones do, they may be more likely to pursue racially delineated strategies or campaigns because their focus on the individual allows members to discuss race as one of many factors and characteristics associated with an individual. A leader in ACORN Bronx might be described as "an ACORN member for two years, fighting for benefits for the working class, including better schools" while a leader in SBU might be described as "a black tenth-grader at Walton High School who's into hip-hop, used to live in a shelter in Hunt's Point, and identifies as lesbian, and she's fighting against overcrowding in the schools." When many characteristics are emphasized, race becomes an additive rather than substitutive identifier.

Numerical Indicators: The Subtext of Race and Rank

Because the constituency demographics for the case study SCOs were quite similar and were presented in chapter 2, this section focuses on racial representation among paid staff. Such a small number of cases does not provide statistically significant patterns of inequality. Still, as the following table indicates, the two Freirean category organizations employed women of color in higher ranks, when the overwhelming majority of membership

Table 7. Basic Demographic Characteristics of Staff in Case Study SCOs

	Alinskyite Category		Freirean Category	
	ACORN Bronx	NWBCCC	SBU	MOM
Staff	8 organizers	15 organizers	3 organizers/ coordinators	5 organizers
Education staff	2–3 organizers	2–4 organizers	3–4 organizers/ coordinators	2–4 organizers
Staff retention (number of education organizers remaining in 2004, out of those employed sometime during the previous year)	2 out of 6 (some periods without education organizer, 2 at any one time)	2 out of 4	3 out of 4	3 out of 3
Staff racial and gender make-up				
Higher rank	1 white female	1 white female, 1 white male	1 black male, 1 Latina female	1 white male, 1 black Latina female
Lower rank	Latino and black females	Latina female	1 mixed-race female, 1 black male	1 mixed-race female, 1 Latina female, 1 black male

in all four organizations (except SBU, which was evenly split among young men and women) consisted of women of color.

Subtexts of race and rank become clearer once we look beyond the numbers. At ACORN Bronx, questions about racial diversity among staff were largely dismissed. It was assumed that the higher-ups had the constituents' best interests in mind. As a result, a good deal of resentment and dissent simmered in the background. At the NWBCCC, such questions were addressed and discussed. Because SBU's staff consisted solely of African Americans and Latinos, its tensions were mostly related to its relations to the NWBCCC. MOM, a Freirean SCO, was quite successful at tackling questions about race among staff.

On the one hand, ACORN Bronx organizer Edgar stated, "It is no secret that the hierarchy of ACORN is mostly white." This echoed some of the existing literature about the organization, though none of the organizers interviewed at ACORN Bronx claimed to have read these books.[4]

On the other hand, Edgar noted, "But in New York, you have Elaine [an African American woman]…, you have Edgar [a Latino man]…who just happens to be working under Tara, a Jewish-Italian girl.…And we're running a staff that's made up of minority people." In turn, leaders contended that almost all ACORN chapters have primarily female, African American and Latina organizers, but few people of color in high-ranking positions. While several interviewees agreed that Elaine's leadership made the local staffing an important exception to national ACORN patterns, they were not so readily convinced that even ACORN Bronx was free of issues surrounding race.

Perceptions of racial inequalities along lines of rank simmered among most of the organizers. Melissa, who graduated from an elite college and identifies as Middle Eastern but is phenotypically white, commented, "Tara does sometimes have a different demeanor with minorities or poor people, even though she would never admit it. I don't know, some of the comments she makes.... She's clearly an outsider. I think that that's another reason she was sad to see me leave; I wonder if she thought we would share a bond because we're from a similar demographic," both being white, middle-class college graduates from prestigious liberal arts institutions. Other staff, all African American or Latino, also occasionally expressed resentment toward Tara because she was younger and yet seemed to be promoted more quickly than other organizers, including some who had been there longer.

Some organizers stated that even if racial inequalities did exist within the organization, they were inconsequential. As Edgar explained, "Chris [a high-ranking organizer] is a nice guy. He's not a racist. I mean, he's a Jew. Jewish people have been persecuted throughout history. Hitler was not a nice guy, right? I have a lot of white friends, a lot of Dominican friends, a lot of Asian friends.... People who blame it on racism...are just lazy." Carried through, this line of argument has significant implications. First, it suggests that minority representation in itself is not necessarily a goal in the high ranks. As long as one gets along with members of different racial and ethnic groups, then it is also assumed that he has everyone's best interest in mind. Second, by equating concerns about racism with laziness, Edgar left little room for constructive, frank discussions about possible racism. Any reference to issues of race would have run the risk of sounding like an accusation, rather than a reflection of concern.

Still, Chris himself had his share of detractors: "[He]...has strong issues with racism," noted one member. "He makes racial and cultural assumptions. He's also paternalistic with women on staff. He clearly views himself as a white father." In this instance it was difficult to glean whether the crux of the question was a lack of minority representation in high-level decision making, top leadership, or both. Because no frank discussions about Chris took place, such dissent festered among other organizers and leaders. Ideally, either conversations about Chris's leadership would have shown that complaints were unfounded, or if these complaints were legitimate, they would have been addressed. Either way, race clearly played some role in ACORN's internal dynamics among staff and membership.

At the NWBCCC, too, the people holding the top two positions were white, even though most of the membership was African American and Latino. While few members and leaders openly questioned their leadership, the subtext of race and rank flared into the open in times of crisis. At one meeting, two organizers, Sam, who is white, and Ernest, who is African American, disagreed about the next strategic move in a small schools campaign. Their deliberation quickly turned into a shouting match. Ernest felt Sam was interrupting him, and he began to raise his voice. Sam wanted them to talk then and resolve the situation immediately, but Ernest wanted to be left alone, saying, "Don't talk to me right now; it's just making me angrier." Sam and Ernest then went into the hallway and closed the door behind them to discuss this, but everyone who remained in the meeting room could easily hear the loud argument. "You're just like Linda [another supervising organizer]," Ernest said, "except you don't yell." When Sam and Ernest came back into the room, Ernest angrily announced that he had been suspended by Sam. Because there was so much palpable tension in the air, the meeting was adjourned. Neither Ernest nor Sam had mentioned issues of race. Still, when members circulated stories about what happened among themselves, they described the incident as just one in a series that pitted a high-ranking white organizer against a lower-ranking black or Latino one. For weeks afterward, the incident served as fodder for both gossip and substantive discussion in the organization. In such conversations, member leaders questioned not just whether Sam was right to suspend Ernest, but whether Sam appropriately represented the NWBCCC's black and Latino constituency.

Ernest's statement about Sam and another organizer was interesting not only because it named the high-level staff members in the organization but because it pinpointed them as different and accused them of sharing similarities in faulty leadership. Regardless of whether Ernest's judgment was well-founded, its sentiments were nonetheless shared by other organizers and leaders. In spending time with members of the NWBCCC, and especially SBU, one noticed that Linda's voice in the hallways was accompanied by seemingly automatic, low groans from members. "So annoying," someone usually muttered. Even if the rift between leadership and this organizer was not always substantive, it remained significant in the organization's everyday activities and cultural practices.

Months later, when I asked one member if race was ever an issue at the organization, Rosalinda immediately answered, "It plays out on campaign issues, like the decision to take Ernest out of the campaign." She continued,

> I don't want to bring this topic up, but since I'm really angry about it....Ernest was the staff leader for the Leadership Institute [campaign]....He's always on top of everything; he's doing his job. But some personal things happened with Sam, who recently joined the [campaign] thing, and was kind of costaffing it with Ernest. He doesn't have so much time to dedicate to the campaign, to a brainy, flexible campaign that needs a lot of time, and some personal thing [happened], and him and other staff people decided that Ernest was not going to lead the campaign anymore. So Sam stayed on the campaign, and they chose a person that is really active. She's really prepared for the campaign, our tutor coordinator. I agree with it, but she doesn't have organizing experience, just the educator side of [the proposal for a small school]. She had been helping Ernest, but she wasn't the leader of it; she has other things to do, especially the tutoring program.... Right now, we don't know why he was taken out of it. They did explain the reason why, but we felt that that wasn't a good enough reason.

To Rosalinda, Ernest's dismissal was illegitimate, the campaign had been put in jeopardy, and the entire incident revolved around issues of race. Because she felt that the reasons cited by the supervisors were insufficient, this leader attributed Ernest's removal from the Leadership Institute campaign to an abuse of power by the staff, without sufficient consultation with the membership. Because both the supervisor organizers in this case were white, she also then pointed to the incident as a reflection of racial inequalities in the organization.

Rosalinda's dissatisfaction with the situation stemmed not only from the events that transpired but from, as she perceived it, the inadequate staff response. The subtext of race and rank was borne at least as much by each staff person's activities or inactivity as it was by the demographic breakdowns of organization's overall staff. She continued, "[Another leader] and I, as board members, met with them separately, with Sam and [another staff member], but there hasn't really been a response. [They] told us the situation three times, [the] explanation, that Ernest had mixed data, mixed facts, that he wasn't as experienced or as adequate as the campaign required, those sorts of things.... To be honest, Sam doesn't have enough time to be dedicating so much time to the campaign. We felt it was personal reasons.

And Ernest is not the lead staff person, and he's still doing a lot of the work on the campaign."

Nicole, another staff member whose role in the campaign expanded after Ernest left, felt that it was not a "big deal" in the long run, but that the incident nevertheless marred her perception of staff relations: "They didn't ask me—they told me to lead it—which is fine, but I felt pulled in different directions, without enough support....I was supposed to be the lead educator, with Sam being the lead organizer, but because of schedules and emergencies, different roles were transgressed," and she felt caught unprepared in some instances. At the same time, she also felt that there may have been substantive, strategic decisions for Ernest's removal from the campaign, such as the lower credibility he might have had on a school proposal because he did not hold a college degree. Notably, such reasoning was not mentioned, let alone cited, by the SBU leaders who were angry about the incident.

These simmering comments suggested that bringing up potentially touchy conversations and tackling them head on might have seemed uncomfortable or potentially divisive in the short term, but doing so would have ultimately brought more long-term unity. There may have been several reasons for Ernest's removal from the campaign, but the fairly widespread perception of power inequalities along lines of rank and race exacerbated tensions among the membership.

To the NWBCCC's credit, while the quarrel between Ernest and Sam sparked quite a lot of commentary about race and power in the organization, Sam and the organizers themselves subsequently initiated discussions about race. Substantively, they encouraged meetings among leaders and members on the topic. These meetings were organizer-free so that members did not feel like they needed to censor their comments. According to Rosalinda, "At the leadership retreat, we talked about race. It's just so complicated. I think it's a power issue, because too much power relies on the staffing."

The issue of minority leadership was by no means limited to ACORN Bronx and the NWBCCC. Michele, a leader at MOM, noted, "When Stephen [an organizer] first came, I think that people had questions because he was a white male. Now, I know that when we went to other states with MOM, people said, 'Who's that white guy?' and I just tell them, 'Stephen is a great person,' there's nothing to it. I'm glad he's on board. He brings new ideas and perspectives. We're very accepting of people from different nationalities. I think people might not know that at first, because people might seem withdrawn, but you can't blame them, because you can't trust everybody."

It is notable that Stephen himself had brought up issues of race, stating that it was important to be conscious of its effects on dynamics within the organization, and that it was important to encourage organic, indigenous leadership. This helped the members to feel confident in him when they met with other SCOs. Stephen's actions implied that color blindness was impossible; it was not as if people did not register a new acquaintance as black or white. One could meaningfully work on issues of race only by acknowledging whatever issues existed. Further, since people of different racial backgrounds tend to have different experiences in American society, their perspectives might also be different. This was a delicate point, since no one forwarded the notion that there was one white view, or one African American view; still, racial diversity was one step toward a diversity of ideas, even if incomplete.

(One of the reasons I received entry into Mothers on the Move was that, according to MOM organizers and members, most of the literature on community organizing and cultural analysis had been written by white male academics. In making such a statement, they presumed and/or hoped that I would bring a new perspective. This did not imply that there is a definitive set of specific "white" or "immigrant" or "person of color" perspectives. Still, some SCO leaders brought up issues of race when they opened up to some researchers more than others. Their comments suggested that, at the very least, *perceived* race shaped their experiences, and these experiences, in turn, shaped their opinions and perspectives. They hoped that my background as an Asian American woman from Brazil would render me more sensitive to different cultural practices than previous researchers.)

While basic demographic characteristics of the staff of all four case studies were generally similar, stories from different organizations suggested that the subtext of race and rank was far from straightforward and, to a certain extent, remained covert. The groups that allowed leaders to air their concerns were ultimately more successful in tackling issues of race both inside their organizations and, via their campaigns, in the school system itself.

Informal Cultural Practices: Contesting Color Blindness

At meetings and interviews in each of the organizations, there was at least one instance where a member muttered, "I'm not racist, but…" and followed this with a statement pinpointing a specific ethnic group as more conducive to engage in some undesired behavior. None of these instances led to immediate discussions about stereotyping or race. In some instances, organizers felt that racism should be countered by color blindness, and that comments that explicitly addressed the issue of race could be interpreted as divisive, if not racist. Some critics of this viewpoint, however, argue that to contest color blindness and be "color conscious" is not equivalent to being racist.[5]

In interviews, most leaders and organizers asserted that race was not an issue. At first glance, this may have been surprising, since the SCOs' constituencies are overwhelmingly African American and Latino, and many believe that the South Bronx is the poorest area in the city partly because of institutional racism. Plenty of leaders and organizers, for instance, mentioned 96th Street in Manhattan as the dividing line between the primarily white, wealthier neighborhoods and the primarily African American and Latino poorer ones. Still, in several instances, interviewees stated that a person's ethnicity did not matter, since everyone is in the same economic boat. Yet, their later comments revealed that race clearly *did* matter. One ACORN leader noted that to the extent that race did appear to be an issue she was not sure it was justified. This leader, a visiting public school teacher from Jamaica of African descent, explained,

> I'm probably too educated to say there is racism. I would say that yes, there are racist people. But I don't think we must cry wolf too early…that is the basic nature of the African man [*sic*]. The African man attempts to give each person a chance, and does not stereotype, but other people stereotype very quickly.…I am very much a personality of education; I'm also a religious person, a strong spiritual person. I tend to see Christ in every person first. So the chance is very low that someone will be discriminated against.…I have grown up in a society where we have two major races, Indians and the Africans. And the Indians, very, very much and very, very often, talk about discrimination in our [Jamaican] society. When I do not even see it.…I think some people, tend to shelter and use it [allegations of racism] very quickly.…But I think we tend to play on that sympathy, cry it too easily.

While others did not go so far in their assertions, organizers and leaders at some SCOs clearly believed that color blindness supercedes any isolated incidents of racism. The dominant perception here was that racism is always intentional and committed by individuals. Such a perception left little room for structural analyses of institutional racism, or for policy responses in situations where no specific "evildoers" could be pinpointed.

Sometimes, frank discussions about race were also submerged because a focus on sustaining majority support prevented organizers from addressing issues of race head on. Even though most of the organizers and leaders at all four case study organizations sometimes spoke of issues of race in American society at large, they nevertheless largely exempted their organizations from this critique. This was partly because they clearly had good intentions, and they were working on progressive campaigns to strengthen the public school system in the Bronx and, by extension, to fight racial inequalities in American society.

A consistent theme that arose, in both the literature on community organizing and in the fieldwork data for the present study, was whether an issue that disproportionately affected a specific racial or ethnic population, but which could be addressed by all members in the name of social justice, was automatically labeled as a divisive issue, one that was in danger of pitting some members against others.[6] As Check writes, there is "no blueprint for how culture is supposed to be reformed to address race and not perpetuate 'whiteness,' to address belonging to different communities" (2002, 202–3). This tension partly exists because such strategies or campaigns are unlikely to be deemed "winnable" unless they automatically garner the support of *most* members. Since members belong to different racial groups, it appears too risky to confront a racially delineated issue—that is, something that seems to primarily affect African Americans or Latinos but not both groups. In contrast, an issue that involves the entire neighborhood or all working-class people is likely to affect, and therefore win the support of, all members.[7]

This latter statement, however, makes assumptions about whether a member would support a strategy that disproportionately affects members of another racial group, and it is itself vigorously debated.[8] It is possible, for example, for an African American family to support a Spanish-English bilingual program that primarily affects Latino children, or for a Latino teenager to support a campaign to address local racial profiling that primarily targets Muslim men of African descent.

For the most part, when some organizers and leaders explicitly talked about the notion of divisive issues, it was clear that they were talking about issues that appeared to affect one racial subgroup more than another. Divisive issues were always discussed pejoratively, and so it was important to investigate how different organizations classified which issues fall into the category of social injustice and which are instead labeled divisive.

Tara, an ACORN Bronx organizer, remarked, "We have to be a democratic organization, but we also have be thoughtful and do our homework…

any meeting can deteriorate into people blaming the parents or the teachers, or wanting to organize around issues that are divisive." When asked to give an example, she added, "Last week, I got phone calls from parents at [Public School] 88 about a teacher brought up on charges. It was a popular teacher, some kids were crying. But was it something that our members were ready to jump into?"

In this case, it is worth noting that the task of avoiding divisive issues was portrayed as a trade-off for being "democratic." In order to accomplish the tricky work of encouraging overworked, weary parents to pursue education organizing campaigns, Tara chose to focus on facially neutral issues, those that needed little further investigation. More specifically, Tara also noted that the SCO worked by "avoiding divisive issues. Like, I can imagine Latino parents organizing because there aren't enough Latino teachers in the schools, but African American parents would be offended, or would be upset." On one hand, this ensured that a subgroup was not ostracized; on the other hand, it also ran the risk of avoiding campaigns that disproportionately affected a minority group, such as police brutality against black or Latino men. While one can imagine obviously divisive issues in which one subgroup attempted to exclude another, the situation hypothesized by Tara lay in slightly murkier territory. After all, in a context of ever-quickening globalization in business, migration, and other sectors, a diverse teaching staff that includes Latinos as well as African Americans could raise the quality of education afforded to all students. In attempts to be race-neutral and form broad-based coalitions, race-delineated issues were sometimes avoided rather than tackled, even when it could have been cast in positive terms and did not necessarily exclude the participation of others.

Unfortunately, since significant segments of society currently benefit from existing power inequalities, appealing to the articulated self-interests of a majority of constituents can sideline deep-seated issues of race. Others have argued that such a stance uses class as a "lowest common denominator."[9] Still, even when everyone is gathered to denounce overt racism, colorblind strategies make it difficult to work toward substantive social change. As long as no overtly racist acts are committed, issues of race remain unexamined, and institutional racism goes largely overlooked. According to this logic, school reform is best achieved by rallying everyone together, downplaying patterns of inequality that might exist among the supporters.

For example, one way in which the Alinskyite SCOs may have downplayed differences among leaders was by implementing dress codes. This might seem superficial at first, but it was a concrete manifestation of different attitudes toward sameness or difference among members. Such dress codes helped to forge organizational identity, but because clothing styles are often seen as social signifiers and reflections of identity, some leaders argued that they also help to deflect issues of race, gender, and sexual orientation. Daniel, a former SBU leader and part-time organizer, complained about dress code policies in the larger NWBCCC organization: "The other thing I don't like is [the] dress code. Have you noticed that all the women at the office, they dress a certain way? [They usually wear large T-shirts associated with the NWBCCC, or in plain colors.] That's because of [other staff members' opinions]. Me, I think that sexuality is an important part of being a person and something that gives you power. Like Natasha, she had big breasts, and you'd notice them. She got reprimanded. But not dressing like you want, first of all, you stand out from everyone else on the street. You're not part of the community."

While other organizers may have bristled at the overt references to sexuality in such comments, Daniel felt that formal dress codes sometimes alienated organizers from the membership, and instead of fostering solidarity and recruitment, they undermined it. As with a focus on winnable campaigns, dress codes were meant to unite all leaders in an SCO; but they caused some to feel inadvertently sidelined.

Daniel's opinions fit well with SBU's Freirean tool kit, in which the focus was on individual development, rather than the Alinskyite tool kit at the NWBCCC, which focused on the organization as a whole. He saw dress as a political statement integral to expressing oneself as an individual: "Dressing sexy is not improper—it's empowering, intimidating. You can use it. How do you teach empowerment if you're not empowered?" Along these lines, it was notable that some organizers and leaders sported clothes that emphasize African American or Latino identity, or wore rainbow nose rings and other signifiers of lesbian, gay, bisexual, and/or transgendered identity. Since hair and clothing styles were rarely race neutral, SBU leaders sometimes feared that strict dress codes imposed discriminatory definitions as to whose style was considered proper and whose was not; often, the approved styles were reflections of whatever group held dominant status. Like some direct action activists, these leaders believe that racial and sexual identities can be "as much the bases of political commitments as are more traditional political creeds" (Polletta 2002, 192). SBU's cultural practices conformed to a Freirean approach and flouted an Alinskyite one, which would have emphasized organizational identity through uniform dress.

Finally, the potential pitfalls of color-blind strategies could sometimes only be gleaned with direct observation of the everyday struggles of campaigning for education reform. Every once in a while, racial divides were overt. This was indeed the case when I accompanied ACORN Bronx on a bus trip to Washington, D.C. The day's agenda included meeting with ACORN members from all over the country, union leaders, and William Gates Sr. on the lawn in front of the U.S. Capitol; delivering a letter to then secretary of education Rod Paige; and protesting predatory lending at Jackson-Hewitt Income Tax Preparation Services.

I arrived at the ACORN Bronx office at 6 a.m. Two chartered buses were leaving from the Bronx. On the bus I boarded, the riders were split by race. In the first three rows sat an African American organizer, her mother and brother, and a friend. None spoke Spanish. The rest of the bus was composed of Latinos, most monolingual Spanish-speakers. Several had brought their children with them. The group was fairly evenly split between men and women.

Before we took off, Tara, a head staffperson, came onto the bus and instructed Carol and the other organizers (Carma and Susana, both Latina) to give all members the agenda and go over it, with discussion, thirty minutes before our arrival in Washington. Tara then left and joined the other bus for the actual ride. We took off between 6:30 and 7 a.m. As soon as we took off, the agenda was passed out and read aloud. There was no discussion or question-and-answer period. Carol also repeatedly spoke to monolingual Spanish-speaking people in English, and sometimes went on in her instructions without allowing for them to be translated into Spanish first. For most of the remainder of the bus ride, people slept.

We arrived in Washington around noon. There was a scramble for the box lunches and ACORN hats; organizers from different buses were arguing with one another for them. The box lunches were distributed by a specific catering company; Carol's friend said that she was frustrated they were not getting food, and, based on the her conjectures about the caterers' racial and ethnic background, she made derisive remarks about "Jewish people" that were neither rebuked nor answered by others on the bus. After receiving our lunches and eating on the bus, we attended an assembly of national ACORN representatives and union leaders at a large church.

For the remainder of the day, the group marched in several actions, primarily asking for more school funding for the government's No Child Left Behind policies. During some short, ten-minute stretches of the day, marchers plodded against windy, wet snow. Nevertheless, people appeared to be very enthusiastic. Along the way I spoke to many marchers, and they were all excited by ACORN. They spoke eloquently in terms of "social justice," earning a decent wage that they deserved, and distributing this country's wealth in a more equitable way. However, none had been involved with

ACORN for more than a year. One person, from the Responsible Wealth Foundation (associated with William Gates Sr. against the repeal of the estate tax), asked me what the acronym ACORN stood for. I told her it stood for the Association of Community Organizations for Reform Now, and she said that she had asked many leaders and organizers that day, and I was the first who had an answer.

As the day wore on, however, ACORN leaders began to look tired. When we met in front of the Capitol and then the Department of Education in the late afternoon, most of the people there were not listening, as it was often difficult to hear. Other than the first few speeches at the church, there were no translations into Spanish provided, so many Spanish-speaking members had stopped trying to follow the conversations. As we were getting ready to leave the Department of Education, there were organizers from other cities telling us to go to the Jackson-Hewitt protest. Carol kept repeating that she wanted to go back to the Bronx. One (from Pennsylvania) said, "As far as I know, we're all going to an action at Jackson-Hewitt." Carol kept repeating, "Well, I was never told of this, so we can go home." I handed my copy of the agenda to her, but she bristled at this. We got on the highway to head back to the Bronx.

Approximately half an hour later, Tara called from the other bus. Carol said that the bus driver did not have the directions and was going home, that we were stuck on the highway, we had passed the exit, and it was too late to turn back. The bus driver told her to not blame it on him. Tara told Carol to take a vote on the bus. Carol proposed it to everyone on the bus, and eleven (of approximately forty) people voted to go home. Before she counted the number of people who might have raised their hands to go to Jackson-Hewitt, however, she turned around and said, "That's it! Call Tara back and tell her they voted, and we're going home."

On the ride home, we watched videotapes Carol had brought with her: *Rush Hour 2, Barbershop,* a Marvin Gaye concert, and the filming of an African American play about adult sexual relationships, *Madea's Class Reunion* by Tyler Perry, on the bus. There were repeated requests from the rest of the bus for something appropriate for children, but these were the only tapes brought on the trip. While the first two videotapes were watched by a good number of people on the bus, the latter two were not.

Some of the Spanish-speaking people behind me told one of the organizers that Carol was enthusiastic, but that she was too new and lacked experience. They were disappointed that we were not following the agenda. Meanwhile, Carol spoke to her mother and her friend about her dissatisfaction with ACORN's protest strategies. She felt that confrontational events like embarrassing politicians by going to City Hall were rude and wrong; both she and her friend declared that they did not believe in such tactics or strategies; they were "not right." We arrived back in the Bronx around 8 p.m. A few days later, when I spoke with Tara, she said, "It's too bad that your bus couldn't go to the Jackson-Hewitt action because the bus driver got lost, huh?" As far as I could tell, Tara sincerely believed Carol's story.

This story highlights some of ways in which tackling issues of race remained difficult in education organizing groups. First, organizers and leaders had to overcome language barriers. If building a large leader base is a group's only goal, then monolingual organizers suffice. However, building a large, deep, and *cohesive* base, one that forwards an integrated vision of policy change, is much more difficult. More generally, the episode suggests that organizers and leaders would benefit from greater work and training on moving across difference overall. Second, organizers feared that any critique of racial divides would be construed as racist or as detracting from the larger mission of the organization. They were, after all, in the same boat, trying to fight formidable forces of disenfranchisement from outside the organization.

Again, the day's events did not reveal many moments of overt racism by individuals as much as institutional segregation and disparate treatment by race. Carol probably decided to go home because she was exhausted, not because the Latino leaders would have wanted to stay. Further, focusing on winnable campaigns worked in ACORN Bronx's favor in some ways. The organization succeeded in joining thousands of supporters from around the country, and it successfully pressured the Department of Education to award grants to some poor schools.

A final, very brief anecdote about local graffiti also illustrates the dynamics of some racial divides in the organizations. One protester had filled the sidewalks on several blocks around the ACORN Bronx with the words "ACORN: Bloodsuckers of the Poor." The graffiti refers to a phrase used by a social and religious group called the Nation of Gods and Earths, also called the Five Percent Nation of Black Islam. According to the Five Percent Nation, any large community, especially the African American community, can be divided into three categories: 85% of the population remains the "ignorant masses," and 5% of the population is enlightened and must lead the rest out of ignorance; 10% of the population is partly educated, but uses this partial knowledge to exploit the 85%, acting as the "bloodsuckers of the poor." The graffiti lobbed specific critiques at the organization, including the notion that African Americans might sometimes work against the interests of their larger community, but this remained unbeknownst to the office head staffperson, who dismissed the graffiti as the work of a "crazy guy [who] obviously should be institutionalized." Still, considering the fact that the graffiti gathered media attention, it presented ACORN Bronx organizers and leaders with an opportunity to submit their side of the story, and to highlight campaigns in which they obviously served the interests of the poor. Ignoring the graffiti did not make it go away, and it may have fueled rumors about ACORN Bronx.

Coincidentally, a contrasting conversation about the Five Percent Nation took place between Nicole, a coordinator at SBU, and Jeremy, a leader. Jeremy talked about a friend who had taught him special code handshakes; these gestures were fairly witty, and Jeremy was impressed. A few people in the office knew members of the Five Percent Nation, especially since the group is promoted by some hip-hop groups. Nicole stated that she found them interesting, but that they denigrated women. She also wondered if they were anti-Semitic. Jeremy, who did not know what "anti-Semitic" meant, was told to look it up on the Internet. They then discussed the politics surrounding the Five Percent Nation's definition of community, though not quite in those words. Here, leaders asserted color-conscious difference, but in a way not construed as racist.

This suggests that it is possible to pay attention to race-specific narratives without ignoring the fact that these narratives, too, are historically and socially constructed. While a lack of dialogue about race, then, can prevent education organizing groups from engaging in more general conversations about urban and racial politics, uncomfortable moments touching upon issues of race can be transformed into opportunities for nuanced contestations of color blindness.

Decision-Making Processes: Bonding and Bridging Difference

In order for education organizing groups to truly engage in antiracist views of school reform, they need to build community power and pursue more than broad-based, winnable campaigns. In the case study organizations, such winnable campaigns were not always sustainable.

The decision-making processes that affected everyone in the organization, including the grievance procedures meant to handle episodes such as the argument between Ernest and Sam described earlier in this chapter, helped to determine the level of communication and trust that existed between leaders and organizers. First, active consensus ensured that everyone has had some say in important decisions; the final decision was then a lot more likely to be seen as legitimate by all leaders and organizers, even if some did not love it. Other processes, such as passive consensus or majority voting, failed to build quite as much trust among leaders.

Second, according to the case studies, organizational spaces helped the SCOs to resolve issues of race. Here, organizational spaces were not just physical meeting places. Rather, they consisted of consistent opportunities for meeting, conversation, and exchange in forming a collective identity, somewhat akin to so-called free spaces.[10] Borrowing terminology from the social capital literature, "bonding" spaces facilitated meetings among members of fairly well-defined subgroups.[11] "Subgroups" refer to small, relatively well-defined cliques or clusters of members within the larger education-organizing groups or organizations. These subgroups were largely identified by racial background and immigrant status—that is, as African Americans, Latinos, and African immigrants. "Bridging" spaces facilitated meetings and exchange between members of different subgroups,[12] and these proved to be especially essential in turning "divisive" issues into unifying ones.

The Freirean SCOs were the ones that both regularly adopted active consensus decision-making procedures and provided leaders with ample bonding and bridging organizational spaces.

Predominant Decision-Making Processes and Mechanisms

The primary types of decision-making processes exhibited in the case study SCOs were active or passive consensus, voting, and exit. *Active consensus* occurred when each participant was directly asked for an answer in the affirmative before a decision was made; *passive consensus* is defined here as presumed assent by every participant unless an objection was verbally made. In *voting* processes, a simple majority usually determined the outcome of the decision. A person is described as having utilized an *exit* mechanism if she expressed dissent (whether at the meeting or in another setting, such as an interview) and then chose to leave the group, project, or SCO because of this disagreement.

At ACORN Bronx, projects did not seem to change course often; rather, differences in direction were asserted when a new project was initiated. In part, this appears to be related to the SCO's emphasis on recruitment; new projects were often accompanied by new members. Rather than bringing immigrant issues to the table during a parent meeting, organizers were more likely to encourage members to bring friends, coworkers, or fellow parents with similar grievances, and to conduct weekly meetings until this group grew large enough to launch its own campaign. If the leader had the resources and liked ACORN Bronx's overall strategies, he probably followed this advice and worked on a new campaign. It was unlikely, however, that a parent would succeed in convincing an already existing group to launch a campaign on bilingual education if a significant percentage of the group did not feel it was in its interest; this was a fairly common scenario involving groups with Spanish-speaking Latinos and English-speaking African Americans. In any campaign, the leaders who did participate were assumed to approve via passive consensus.

In the end, many members and organizers used an exit strategy to voice their dissent. Akin to its use in Hirschmann (1970), *exit* is not defined here as inherently a physical act or membership withdrawal, although there is evidence of such exits, but as withdrawal from active participation in the SCO. For example, if some members became passive, stopped attending meetings, and eventually let their membership expire, their exit was marked when they ended meaningful communication with others in the SCO before their official departure.

Organizers and members who left ACORN Bronx listed a few key reasons for their exits. These included disagreement with the organization's policy to exclude community residents who wished to participate but could not afford the $120 annual dues, a clash with the SCO's chosen political strategies, and a feeling that organizers were pressured to emphasize certain cultural practices of recruitment over others. A theme that was almost tangential in some cases and central in others was the extent to which these patterns were delineated by race. That is, some former leaders and organizers felt that ACORN Bronx's cultural practices and political strategies favored some subgroups over others, or pursued campaigns closer to the heart of one subgroup. Further, the social networks tapped for recruitment at ACORN were almost always race-delineated, even if this was not overtly mentioned in the content of campaigns. While these leader and organizer comments might very well have come from a biased sample, they nevertheless indicate that high exit rates may have been indicative of dissent about issues of race.

In cases of passive consensus, some members may have felt hesitant to actively express dissent, and so they either exited or formed their own projects when they disagreed with existing ones. Passive consensus was more likely to take place in the Alinskyite SCOs, and fit well with relatively firm organizational identity and campaign goals. Although none of the case study SCOs regularly made decisions via voting, it was most likely to occur when the decision to be made was fairly small—for example, whether a meal should be provided at the next meeting—and both organizers and leaders who chaired meetings consistently stated that they tried to avoid having to hold votes, preferring mechanisms of passive or active consensus instead.

At the other end of the spectrum, Freirean category organizations were more likely to engage in active consensus. When voting did take place at MOM, a discussion always followed, with dissenters stating why they were voting against the proposal at hand. Likewise, SBU meetings generally continued until all concerns were addressed and each person actively expressed support for the final proposal. Even when it appeared that the dissenting group primarily consisted of members of a single gender or race, the discussion that followed was institutionalized, and this practice did not appear to be out of the norm. In a conversation on school safety at SBU, for example, leaders spoke about their personal experiences so that one person's negative experience with police officers did not negate another's positive experience per se, but participants were encouraged to be considerate of everyone's feelings of safety in police-heavy schools or neighborhoods.

The primary decision-making processes used by the SCOs—dissent via exit, active consensus, passive consensus, or majority voting—led leaders and organizers to either emphasize either color blindness or mitigate color consciousness in their campaign work. These differences were most concretely manifest in the campaign issues chosen by the four case study groups. Those SCOs that most consistently practiced active consensus— namely, SBU and MOM—were more likely to pursue a wider variety of campaign issues and to launch campaigns that tackled issues of race, even issues that directly affected a minority of constituents. Because these constituents were given the opportunity to articulate their concerns before major decisions, they were able to help shape existing campaigns. By contrast, leaders at ACORN Bronx were encouraged to amass support for their concerns by launching new campaigns.

Bonding Organizational Spaces

The rights of non–English speakers and organizational space for most race- and ethnicity-delineated subgroups were fairly well established in all four case study SCOs. Such organizational space, notes Delgado (2003), is used for subgroups of "participants whose first language is not English to have discussions in their language, or to creatively modify tactics to consider the experiences or cultural practices of people with different racial, cultural, and religious backgrounds" (104).[13] For example, ACORN Bronx organizers met with new constituency networks on their own time; the NWBCCC allowed immigrants groups to gather and converse among themselves for four months before a single campaign developed; SBU leaders shaped their own orientation workshops and conducted them themselves; and El Salvadorian MOM leaders met when they were free during the day, since they were generally expected to stay home at night. Likewise, MOM workshops were held at different hours to accommodate different subgroups, and socials took place in early mornings as well as during the evenings and on summer Saturdays.

Still, it appears that SBU and MOM were the organizations that regularly sent member leaders to represent the organizations at conferences and rallies without organizers present. In some ways, the constant presence of official staff may have led to member self-censorship. Although safe organizational space existed for members of different ethnic or racial groups, such safe space did not always exist for members in Alinskyite SCOs to speak without organizers present—especially in ACORN Bronx. Further, to the extent that issues of race and rank existed, some issues of race were less likely to be addressed. This is related to the assertion in some groups that issues of race did not seem to be dire because they were not raised in one-on-one meetings; critics subsequently asserted that leaders were unlikely to raise these issues themselves, especially if organizers were white and did not ask directly.[14]

Bridging Racial Divides and Organizational Spaces

Latino and African American subgroups could not bridge racial divides if they did not even speak the same language. Therefore, removing language barriers was integral to the construction of bridging organizational spaces. The NWBCCC made greater efforts and strides than ACORN Bronx did in bridging organizational spaces. The Freirean SCOs consistently provided opportunities for the different subgroups to engage in meaningful communication, both formally and informally.

At ACORN Bronx, at least half of the staff was monolingual. From February through March 2004, Carol, who spoke only English, was the education organizer. After one month with bilingual Tara as the organizer, monolingual Spanish-speaker Paula took over the job and was the official education organizer from May 2004 until this study's fieldwork ended five months later. Her job was made more difficult by the fact that one of the two public schools with which she ostensibly closely collaborated served primarily Francophone or English-speaking African immigrants. In reality, she was not able to meet with parents of that school. Since all of the case study organizations had some access to electronic translation equipment, the variance was due to informal practices more than official protocols. During ACORN Bronx meetings, translation was sporadic because not all organizers spoke both English and Spanish. Some organizers received complaints that language issues were not sufficiently addressed, and these complaints intensified with the growing number of Francophone immigrant members.

It was also difficult for subgroups at ACORN Bronx to resolve tensions when leaders were told to launch new campaigns whenever they expressed concerns about existing ones. Thus, Latinos and African Americans in ACORN Bronx participated in largely segregated activities, without opportunities to engage one another or the means to do so.

By contrast, the other case study SCOs provided resources for organizers to ensure that all constituents could go to an organizer who spoke their language. The NWBCCC paid for Spanish classes for those organizers who did not speak the language when they were first hired, at local universities like Fordham, or via immersion programs in the Dominican Republic and other Latin American countries. Sometimes, this was controversial; one African American leader accused the organization of racism when she was not hired as an organizer because she did not speak Spanish. For the NWBCCC, the translation equipment was not regularly used at meetings, except for those sponsored by a multi-SCO coalition, but there was usually little need for them since all organizers were bilingual, all agenda were bilingual, and most comments over the course of a meeting were translated informally.

When racial and cultural rifts occurred, NWBCCC staff attempted to address them immediately. Monica, the education organizer, spoke about how the Latino, primarily Catholic parents had a lot of trouble working with the African, primarily Muslim parents, and vice versa. The cultural rift could be seen along many lines, especially via language barriers and concerning shared views on proper ways to discipline children. After some meetings—held before Monica became organizer—had disintegrated into shouting matches some perceived as racially delineated, Monica made concerted efforts to learn about the grievances articulated by all individuals involved. She then worked extensively with each group independently, hoping to gain a more nuanced grasp of each group's dynamics and assumptions before working on a newer, collaborative project with all of the groups together. This slower, more customized approach echoed that espoused by the NWBCCC's faith-based organizer, who worked with several congregations, mosques, and parishes.

On the other hand, to the extent that race was explicitly mentioned, some NWBCCC members were not satisfied about the tenor of the conversations. One leader characterized some of the organizers' treatment of race as superficial: "Race, and a lot of racist dynamics, are still alive.... There's a lot of manipulative propaganda about race and diversity.... [A supervisor] will be like, 'Oh Elena, you're Puerto Rican.' It's like Elena's the representative. And then we have one group that's mostly Korean, so she needs a Korean.... [There are] certain assumptions about people." Several leaders and organizers took pains to state that authentic counternarratives were also likely to be more nuanced. Counternarratives, posit Delgado and Stefancic (2001), are storylines that "cast doubt on the validity of accepted premises or myths, especially ones held by the majority" (144).

Bridging spaces allowed members of different subgroups to speak from experience without being seen as token representatives. According to these observations, the NWBCCC had worked to provide room for voices of color, but perhaps the uniqueness of these voices did not always shine through. Wider representation of different subgroups could eventually highlight diversity as well as consistency within subgroups and make it difficult for leaders to resort to stereotypes. While some complaints were lobbed against the NWBCCC's treatment of racial inequalities inside the organization, overall these inequalities were by no means willfully ignored; nor were they met with hostility or denial. After the NWBCCC went on to launch intraorganizational events around the theme of "strength through diversity," some leaders commented that they no longer saw different cultural or religious rituals as divisive as much as simply different, but complementary, ways of addressing similar concerns.

Still, during the present study's fieldwork period, the bridging of organizational spaces was more reliably constructed and implemented at MOM and SBU. As at the NWBCCC, bilingual organizers and use of translation equipment were consistent. Conversational or fluent Spanish was also required at MOM, and the SCO had just received a large grant especially for translation equipment to be used at large meetings. Until then, MOM had vacillated between relying upon a bilingual education organizer for translation and hiring freelance interpreters for specific meetings. All SBU members spoke English. Still, one of the organizers and many of the leaders at SBU were bilingual.

The two Freirean SCOs provided substantive, antiracist alternatives to color blindness by facilitating positive and repeated exchange among subgroups. In these organizations, leaders asked uncomfortable questions such as, "What have been the experiences of Latinos or African Americans on this issue, in these schools? Are they different for African-Americans than for African immigrants?" As they did so, they began to tackle larger issues of race, but the varied personal stories they heard in response often ended up being even more unique than anticipated. Together, these stories also suggested that race is not an essentialist construct. In real life, after all, if groups of people face similar experiences, it does not necessarily follow that this is because these people are all the same. When leaders were given the opportunities to speak from their personal experiences they often broached issues of race with ease, and the results were often far from divisive.

Over time, bridging spaces allowed leaders to address issues of race in positive ways. All leaders were bound by campaign issues and troubled schools, like those at the other case study organizations, but they also shared books like *The Autobiography of Malcolm X,* poems used at meetings, and downloaded music files. Such cultural objects were rarely race neutral, and the youth treated such racial identifiers as positive tools for exchange. Because stories were so intensely personalized and interdependence was so emphasized, members were comfortable with conversations about race without feeling as if they were defined solely in terms of race. As one put it, "Culture's a mix. Mostly Spanish and black. More Hispanic than black. We're all just helping each other, basically. That's it. You always have someone to depend on, no matter what."

At SBU, bridging organizational spaces made issues of race normal rather than deviant and divisive. According to one organizer, the issue of "race is internalized during discussions, [but] not formalized, [not] using data." Humor was an important component; when meetings were disproportionately represented by Latinos, the African Americans who *were* present usually made a joke about it, and everyone else used the comment as an excuse to prod them to recruit more aggressively.

Still, a subtle cultural divide did perhaps exist in SBU, and if so, it was unclear whether it was easily overlooked. For instance, the organization occasionally worked with a group of young Muslim women who called themselves the Young Intellects. Considering the fact that the two groups collaborated on political campaigns, it was surprising that they did not work together more closely. When leaders were asked about this, they said that the Young Intellects were "real cool," but that maybe the SBU office was too far for them to visit every day, especially since most of them lived in strict households. While the explanation seems reasonable enough, it is also possible that other teenagers did not immediately feel at ease in an organization with a distinct culture of sharing music, books, and personal secrets. As much was admitted by SBU leader Lisa, in an unrelated meeting about their new small school proposal. Lisa wondered whether Vietnamese, Korean, Francophone African, and Middle Eastern teenagers were not joining SBU because they did not find the SCO attractive, or because SBU was not making enough effort to speak their language(s), both literally and figuratively. This suggests that while SBU built strong organizational spaces for groups such as the Young Intellects, it had not completely built bridging organizational spaces for mediation and inclusion across *all* racial divides.

Overall, however, it was difficult to notice clear racial divides in SBU, even to the mitigated extent found in the NWBCCC. This was illustrated by conversations between the Young Intellects, who claimed that they were contacted by their guidance counselors for private meetings several times a year, and SBU leaders, who claimed that they could not get appointments with their guidance counselors despite repeated pleas for help. Together, they examined whether these disparities were due to some students being "good" and others "lazy." Eventually they teamed up to protest. SBU's bridging of spaces helped the leaders to acknowledge difference in order to walk down the tricky road toward more meaningful equality. Further, the subgroups were united in spite of, or maybe even because of, their disparate social conditions in the schools.

The case was similar at Mothers on the Move, where issues of race were most often raised in terms of macro-inequality. For example, Michele commented that while earlier campaigns dealt with overt racism between school districts, the newer organizer managed to address the same issues and raise racially delineated issues in a different way: "Katerina's way in directing talk, it's very cool. It's very smooth. She asks us, 'What do you think about this?' when she tells us about different districts. The way we see different types of money.... 'Why do you think it's like that?'... The way she's doing it, it's not like, 'I'm going to attack you.'... It was just done in good taste. I like the way she does it.... Looking at the patterns rather than people to attack."

Katerina, an organizer at MOM, specifically cited the "Naming the Root Causes" exercise described in chapter 4 as a crucial tool in establishing a bridging space. She remarked, "We had to confront power holders' strategies of divide and conquer, particularly in schools and tenant organizing. We needed to bring African American, Puerto Rican, Dominican, Salvadorian, Garifuna, Mexican, and African people together. By using Freire's problem tree we saw that the diverse manifestations of our problems actually had the same root causes. And if you've seen the same dynamics happen in other neighborhoods, countries where you've previously lived, then this process surfaces [in] those connections, too."

Similarly, when a woman at the MOM annual meeting stated that she might vote for George W. Bush because her Catholic upbringing informed her stance against abortion, some of the other members in the room, both Latino and African American, bristled or gasped. In response, the facilitators noted her comment as an issue of "different values" rather than anyone having "higher" or "better" values than anyone else, and a constructive discussion on the presidential candidates' education policies followed. These were instances in which a person's race was mentioned as part of the person's heritage, and so, as in SBU, there was a positive language with which to raise issues related to race.

Dashed Lines

While education organizing holds the promise of giving marginalized communities opportunities to voice counternarratives about their lives, these case studies suggest that this promise is not so easily fulfilled. Rarely was racial segregation as clearly delineated as it was on the ACORN bus trip to Washington, D.C. Although there were no official signs dividing the bus into two groups, an unspoken line, even if not solidly drawn, served as a border between them. On its own, such segregation was unremarkable. The difference lay in the organization's collective reaction to such racial divides, and whether the relevant issues were ever broached in conversation or addressed in action. Similar questions regarding the SCOs' responses applied to issues arising from patterns in race and rank, decision-making processes, organizational space, language barriers, and informal practices such as dress codes.

Within the Alinskyite category, the NWBCCC was associated with more activities, conversations, and rituals attempting to build multiracial alliances and addressing existent racial divides than was ACORN Bronx. Out of the SCOs in this study, ACORN Bronx is the one that did not boast of any training programs, rituals, activities, or official goals addressing racially delineated inequities inside the organization. MOM and SBU were more consistent in tackling issues of race than were the other SCOs. Further, their cultural practices helped to both address racial divides and, by encouraging overlapping interests and everyday racial integration, to prevent conflicts along racial lines to rupture in the first place.

Partly because of the Alinskyite emphasis on the organization as a whole, there were fewer activities where discussion about differences among members might take place. In ACORN Bronx's meetings, for example, existing campaigns and new recruitment were the main topics of discussion; likewise, organizers spent most of their time on door-knocking and building networks of new members, political campaigns, and leadership development for ACORN as a whole. In ACORN Bronx's interpretation of this rubric, there was less room for activities or conversations that addressed individuals' racial identities or complexities in the members' common struggles in social justice. The NWBCCC, however, hosted many activities and workshops that dealt with racial divides, and how racial tensions could be ameliorated. This was partly accomplished through the organization's incorporation of diversity as an integral strength of the organization. These dialogues about race, then, did not so much concentrate on each individual's understanding of others as it did how the organization as a whole could grow and improve from greater internal cooperation and collaboration.

When commonalities are not *immediately* discernible but nevertheless existent among different disenfranchised constituent subgroups, how can social change organizations ensure that these subgroups collaborate in substance as well as name? The literature on coalition building, especially among different racial groups, emphasizes the importance of "cultural work" in situations where no overlapping, ready-made, concrete interests are apparent.[15]

It can be argued that members and organizers of MOM and SBU practiced this sort of cultural work. They primarily spoke of race with reference to specific people, to individuals and their circumstances. Face-to-face dialogue was an important ritual, and humor was an important characteristic in such conversations. Far from being divisive, these practices allowed members and organizers to broach issues of race more comfortably, or in more intimate settings. Of import is the fact that SBU and MOM leaders joked about social identities and the politics of representation. When group chants reached a lull at a protest against a slumlord, one SBU leader joked, "We're here! We're queer!—Oops! Wrong campaign!" These jokes allowed individuals to raise issues of racial or sexual identities with less fear of censure.

By focusing on individuals, Freirean cultural practices also had two other implications. First, such cultural practices allowed leaders and organizers to bring up issues of intersectionality, that "individuals or classes often have shared or overlapping interests" that might not be recognized without bringing up the notion of race (Delgado and Stefancic 2001, 149).[16] For instance, leaders spoke of the dynamics specific to a black woman, and not black men or white women, to grapple with how her issues could not be understood in terms of either race or gender alone.

Even practices that may appear to be superficial or irrelevant at first glance, such as dress codes and music exchanges, turned into cultural tools. Dress, music CDs and MP3 files, and books were racial identifiers that leaders could use as tools for exchange and positive organizational artifacts. During a long car ride to a retreat, MOM members expressed delight and surprise that Stephen, an organizer at the SCO, defied their expectations when his radio dial was tuned to a hip-hop radio station.

The second implication of the Freirean tool kit's focus on individual development, then, is that it encouraged members of different racial groups to recognize or even highlight commonalities. Lichterman (1999), for instance, asks, "Can people make political claims *as* African-Americans or *as* lesbians without narrowing their concern for the greater good?" (101, emphasis in the original). Only by discussing issues that appeared to be racially delineated did members recognize that "race" was not the be-all and end-all of individual identity. The Freirean focus on the individual interacted with different social and political constructions of race. For instance, conversations between the Young Intellects and SBU leaders led to new campaigns documenting, protesting, and proposing alternatives to unequal access to academic counseling in two Bronx high schools. This is one way in which Freirean cultural practices offered safe means to contest color blindness.

The cultural practices described in this chapter did not only affect racial dynamics inside the SCOs, but actively shaped external political strategies. The Freirean SCOs pursued political campaigns that addressed issues disproportionately affecting racial, ethnic, or otherwise identity-based minorities, and chose to mention the concept of race or ethnicity in their political strategies.

The link between internal cultural practices and external strategies regarding issues of race has been drawn before. Gary Delgado, who worked with ACORN for over a decade and later helped to develop the Center for Third World Organizing, argues that the "centrality of race" is often ignored and that globalization, increasing diversity, and social movements have moved "beyond the politics of place" so that neighborhood-based organizing must be conjoined with other organizing principles, many of these around identity-based "communities of interest" (1994, 1998, 2003).[17] One of his earlier works (1994) ignited a spirited debate in the organizing world and helped to generate both critiques that his work makes "an assumption that there is a specific way in which race and gender issues must be addressed... [when many] issues have been subsumed by issues of class solidarity in most community organizations" (Miller 1996, 66), as well as subsequent rebuttals against such critiques. Calpotura and Fellner argue that issues like immigration belie Miller's assertions, and that there is a qualitative difference between including women of color in organizing groups and privileging their ideas and contributions, so that they help to actively shape the organizing cultures (1996).[18]

The Bronx case studies suggest that class solidarity does not always sufficiently subsume issues of race. Nor does it suggest that SCOs must identify themselves as "race-based," as People United for a Better life in Oakland does in Wood's (2002) study (see the discussion in chapter 1), in order to tackle issues of race with sensitivity and aplomb. This is partly because the Bronx education organizing campaigns did not always have obvious "acid tests," like the skinhead murder of an African American addressed in Warren's study (2001). Both the "divisive" issues, and the ways to deal with them, were more subtle.

The signature campaign issues chosen by the Bronx SCOs reflect their general approaches to issues of race in imperfect, but nevertheless significant, ways. (While each of the case study SCOs pursued a number of smaller campaigns during my eighteen months of fieldwork, I have chosen to consistently focus on their signature campaigns, the ones that consumed the bulk of the organizers' and leaders' time and the ones of which they seemed most proud. Doing this also helps me to highlight strengths and weaknesses in the SCOs' respective political strategies. Citing evidence from different campaigns would have allowed me to share a greater number of interesting stories, but it would also have run the risk of nitpicking data to conform to neatly packaged, possibly preconceived conclusions.)

The two Alinskyite SCOs pursued signature campaigns that called for adequate school funding. The locus of attention was not on equal education per se but on adequate or quality education as defined by universal criteria. More specifically, the Alinskyite SCOs tackled issues like overcrowding and the need for more classroom space throughout the area. Because they had

Table 8. Signature Campaigns of Case Study SCOs

	Alinskyite Category		Freirean Category	
	ACORN	**NWBCCC**	**SBU**	**MOM**
Signature campaign(s)	Anti-Edison campaign, No Child Left Behind	Capital plan, Small Schools Strike Back	School safety and counseling	Parent involvement protocols
Issue(s) addressed	Teacher quality, privatization	Overcrowding, poor facilities, lack of classroom space	Discriminatory practices by safety agents/counselors, inequities in quality of education	Animosity between school staff and parents, lack of grievance procedures and trust

fewer organizational spaces that mitigate tensions *between* subgroups, and because of their emphasis on fairly well-developed organizational identities that do not mention race, they also had more difficulty garnering wide support for a political campaign on race-delineated issues.

As Warren argues, "internal" discussions as well as a "relationship building around race," factors that in some ways resemble this chapter's notions of organizational space, could help "lead to a greater capacity to address the issue of racism in the public sphere" (2001, 252). The case studies of ACORN Bronx, the NWBCCC, MOM, and SBU suggest that organizer training and formally facilitated discussions, even if they come after and not before an episode of racial tension, make a difference. The backgrounds of the organizers at the four organizations suggest that while a formal college education is not necessary, some formal assistance—in the form of book clubs, dialogues about race, and organizer training exercises on diversity—deepens the organizers' understanding of racial divides among constituents, and coalition building overall.

Further, Freirean processes such as active consensus and the accompanying requisite discussions, organizational spaces in which both subgroups could meet on their own but also communicate with one another, and consistent translation encouraged conversations on themes like intersectionality (even if they did not name it that) and helped to construct widespread leader support for political campaigns tackling race-delineated issues. The Freirean SCOs pursued signature campaigns that tackled discriminatory practices and racial profiling in counseling services and school safety, raised the possibility of race-based inequities among schools, and publicized disaggregate data by race rather than by neighborhood or school district. With the Freirean tool kit, members recognized that "race" is not essentialist, but that it can nevertheless be used to build an agenda for social justice. Their campaigns reflect this.

CHAPTER SIX

WHAT THESE TOOLS CAN BUILD
Developing Capacities for Policy Making

Social change organizations (SCOs) with similar missions pursue divergent political strategies, even when these organizations face a similar political context and resource constraints, partly because their respective tool kits help to develop different strengths and capacities among leaders and organizers.

In the present study, more specifically, the Alinskyite tool kit helped the Bronx chapter of the Association of Community Organizations for Reform Now (ACORN) and the Northwest Bronx Clergy and Community Coalition (NWBCCC) to build large bases of leaders with relatively interchangeable roles, and these leadership bases held the capacity to most influence policy making when proposed policies were about to be adopted or rejected. The Freirean tool kit helped Sistas and Brothas United (SBU) and Mothers on the Move (MOM) to build somewhat narrower, but much deeper, bases of leaders with campaign- and specialization-specific roles, and these leadership bases possessed the ability to most influence policy-making by crafting new policies or making sure existing ones were well implemented. (By "deeper" leadership bases I mean that the leaders had received in-depth and multifaceted leadership training, and so organizers could call upon these members to perform complex and difficult tasks.)

The Alinskyite SCOs emphasized recruitment and organizational identity so that they could firmly stand for or against policy proposals and politicians; these SCOs' painstakingly constructed bases were then large enough to compel politicians to understand that the (usually electoral) support of these members was needed and contingent upon approval of the desired policy or program. Because leaders understood the importance of standing together, having a clear political stance, and echoing the SCOs' official positions, SCOs strategically tapped into their large membership bases to intimidate politicians.

The Freirean SCOs' tool kits facilitated issue analysis, on-the-ground data collection, varying and wide skill sets among different members, and sustained attention. Because leaders were so well versed in the city's political structures and in power and policy analyses, they could tell if the programs touted by politicians were in fact halfhearted attempts to appease constituencies. These SCO leaders strategically dove into the nitty-gritty details of policy making. They worked to reconfigure the proposals to be presented at the policy-making table, or to make sure that policies were meaningfully implemented.

The traditional policy-making cycle follows four steps: (1) problems (such as poorly performing schools in the Bronx, in this case) are presented; (2) policies are crafted and proposed in response; (3) these policy proposals are then accepted or rejected; and if accepted, these policies are (4) modified, implemented, and monitored.[1] While the traditional policy-making cycle is rarely so orderly in real life, it remains a helpful heuristic because it helps to highlight the SCOs' respective strengths and weaknesses.[2] The Alinskyite SCOs excelled in helping their constituents to accept or reject existing policy proposals, so they were most likely to intervene in the penultimate stage of the traditional policy-making cycle. The Freirean SCOs were more likely to act throughout the entire policy-making cycle. They sometimes even helped the public to understand and frame the problem in the first place, but they were especially adept at interventions in the second and last stages, helping constituents to craft and propose policies, and to modify and monitor policies as they were actually implemented. Ultimately, while the Alinskyite SCOs responded to proposals forwarded by mainstream policymakers, the Freirean tool kit helped SCOs to work toward substantively different policies and inch toward transformative social change.

The following table adds upon the previous one (table 8; see chapter 5) to include the strengths and capacities utilized in each case study SCO's signature campaign(s).

Table 9. Signature Campaigns and Capacities for Political Strategies

	Alinskyite Category		Freirean Category	
	ACORN	NWBCCC	SBU	MOM
Signature campaign(s)	Anti-Edison campaign, No Child Left Behind (NCLB)	Capital plan, Small Schools Strike Back	School safety and counseling, new small school	Parent involvement protocols
Strengths and capacities in tool kits	Large turnout at one-time events, elections, and rallies	Collection of data from various sources, large turnout at one-time events, elections, and rallies	High turnout at everyday events, wide array of skill sets among leaders, including analyses and memoranda	Continued attention to policy proposals and formulations that span a large number of meetings, wide array of leadership roles
Political strategies	Lobbying against privatization, lobbying against NCLB legislation and underfunding	Lobbying for additional funding for specific proposals in capital plan, against small school moves	Workshops with school safety agents and teachers, data collection of contrasting homework assignments and counseling advice	Collaborative discussions of parent protocols, workshops for new parent groups on issue analysis

Enabling the Clincher

The Alinskyite SCOs were best at coordinating protests, rallies, and accountability sessions. Accountability sessions are large assemblies where members rally for specific programs or policy proposals and hold politicians "accountable" via a series of yes-or-no questions, usually on what politicians will or will not support.

According to Saul Alinsky, power tends to form around the pillars of money and people.[3] The Alinskyite tool kit, with its emphasis on recruitment, focuses quite a bit on the quantitative aspect of these two pillars—that is, to fight the money-rich powers that be, low-income folks need to amass people power, and this "people power" is most easily measured quantitatively. Only with large numbers of people can they counterbalance the riches amassed by the elite few. This line of thinking suggests that, among SCOs with relatively similar budgets, the difference in policy adoption strategic capacities lies in the number of people attending the organizations' large-scale events.

While each SCO examined in the present study hosted or sponsored at least one or two events with more than one hundred people attending each year, the Alinskyite SCOs excelled most in garnering large turnouts for special events. Still, as noted earlier, unlike federal associations such as the Industrial Areas Foundation (IAF), the case study SCOs I examined work with individuals rather than congregations, which often have several hundred members each. Indeed, Bronx organizers who previously worked in groups like the IAF told me that they have gone from "turning out" and ensuring the attendance of five hundred people per organizer to turning out approximately one hundred people per organizer.

The Alinskyite SCOs' cultural practices, as described in chapter 3, emphasized recruitment as the primary organizational activity, a focus on the organization rather than individual members, and leadership development with the organizer as teacher. These cultural tools helped to yield a large turnout at special events, but they did not help leaders to become involved in campaigns in in-depth ways. Most members were unlikely to know the ins and outs of the policy issues at hand, only that a certain proposal legislative bill or program worked mainly for or against their interests. Organizers took responsibility for most of what came between these special events. As a result, Alinskyite SCOs were strongest when they pursued strategies that emphasized policy or program adoption.

ACORN Bronx: A Broad Base of Interchangeable Supporters, Ready for Action

Once it had been decided that a pending bill or political candidate worked in the interest of ACORN Bronx members, organizers and core leaders mobilized their members for large events staged to assert their support. They emphasized support for policy proposals that had already been articulated, especially when local issues or fine-grained policy questions were at stake.

ACORN Bronx's recruitment-heavy tool kit, with its language of membership and sacrifice, helped the SCO to turn out large numbers of people at major events, but this had its costs—namely, little attention to devoted to substantive leader participation on specific campaigns—so education reform in the South Bronx got short shrift among the plethora of city-wide campaigns launched by New York ACORN. Further, ACORN Bronx's numbers became less impressive when its own efforts were divorced from those of other ACORN chapters and powerful allies like unions.

Jill, who worked with a coalition of community organizations protesting Governor George Pataki's underfunding of the New York City school system, bluntly stated that she had an impression of ACORN as a "power-house," and she based her expectations of attendance upon this impression. Similarly, ACORN Bronx organizer Tara commented, "Our culture is different [from others]....We tend to think a little bigger. When we first got together on one of those retreats for one of those three-year plans for [a Bronx education reform coalition], I heard, 'How many parents can we get involved?' And some people said, 'Fifty, one hundred.' Our members said, 'Are you crazy? We can get five hundred, one thousand.' Even compared to MOM and Northwest Bronx, because we're citywide and national, we have more power to move legislation. And from our [political action committee sister organization], we're multi-issue."

ACORN indeed hosted several rallies a year that turned out five hundred to one thousand members, but none of these events focused on education reform in the South Bronx. Overall, ACORN Bronx's events were indistinguishable from New York ACORN's. ACORN Bronx therefore drew from a base of 25,000 citywide members, rather than a few thousand Bronx members, even for Bronx rallies. This diluted the attention leaders paid to specific campaigns; leaders' participation became cursory. In fact, several of the large events were cosponsored with unions, so that it was difficult to measure how much of the turnout was ACORN-specific.

ACORN Bronx exhibited a duality of quantitative success and relative qualitative weakness. In the 2003–4 school year, the only rallies that drew solely Bronx members were those for a Bronx-specific education coalition, where ACORN Bronx turnout was mandatory. Otherwise, even if the action concerned a borough-specific concern, such as a proposed stadium, housing project, or local state legislator, ACORN members from all over New York City attended. A few events were part of nationwide actions or festivities. Furthermore, the signature campaigns initiated by the SCO are not limited to the Bronx; rather, they included protests coordinated with ACORN branches nationwide against No Child Left Behind (NCLB) legislation and underfunding, as well as an older citywide campaign against school privatization.

While ACORN Bronx's Alinskyite practices helped its policy adoption strategies, its leadership development appeared to be weaker in terms of harnessing leaders for strategies for policy formulation, critique, and articulation. As another multi-SCO coalition's coordinator noted, "At ACORN, I think the key parent leaders are from Brooklyn, rather than the Bronx. Actually there, there's also a UFT [representative], who's actually [linked to people at ACORN]. . . . There, leaders . . . are very activated. [I met one of them several times, and] she doesn't ask a lot of questions; she's not like, 'Why are we protesting this person?' She sort of joins in whatever we're doing."

Large rallies or accountability sessions fit well in larger electoral, judicial, or legislature-reliant strategies. Politicians regularly mentioned what they planned to do for ACORN constituents, and how much the SCO's members' votes meant. In its signature campaign protesting NCLB, for instance, ACORN drew upon its chapters all over the country to stand against a federal policy.[4] Members were less likely to personally connected to the specific policies being addressed at any given event. Further, because NCLB as a whole was not on the U.S. Congressional table at the time, and because so many NCLB clauses varied by state and changed with implementation, ACORN Bronx did not have the capacity to change actual policy in the Bronx. The SCO's members did not possess the expertise to help to shape implementation or convince policymakers to fine-tune specific clauses.

ACORN Bronx's earlier signature campaign, and one of its successes, took place before my fieldwork period in the Bronx. During Rudy Giuliani's reign as mayor, Schools Chancellor Harold Levy invited Edison Schools, a for-profit school management firm, to take over a few underperforming schools. The relevant city charter, however, held the bar for private management rather high. Over half of eligible parents, not just voting parents, had to approve the transfer in order for it to take place. Through a series of court battles, ACORN's New York chapters won access to parents' telephone numbers and addresses, and it used its large number of organizers, members, and volunteers to join with the teachers' union in a campaign against Edison. Edison, which could not rely upon a low turnout to win approval, had to respond by getting their own message out to the media, attempting to organize parents and fighting ACORN in the courts. They were no match for ACORN's wide networks and on-the-ground organizing experience. Voter turnout was high, and Edison was defeated by a four-to-one margin.

The bulk of the organizing work at ACORN Bronx lay not in the execution of the big events or elections themselves but in the months of organizing, negotiations, research, and preparation beforehand. Because membership rituals focused more on being counted and paying dues than on leadership activities, organizers performed most of this behind-the-scenes work at ACORN Bronx. During one week, New York ACORN participated in rallies in collaboration with unions for health care on the Brooklyn Bridge, sent two busloads of parents to the state capital in Albany to protest school underfunding, and gathered a couple of hundred Bronx parents for a coalition rally. Because the events ultimately did not usually last more than two hours each, they focused on narrow, preordained agendas. According to Tara, these three events constituted "three months' worth of work, right there." The fact that Tara herself considered these events the bulk of her work indicates that they lay at the core of the organization's political strategies.

In the middle of my fieldwork period, ACORN Bronx began trying, notes Tara, "to implement a new organizing model, with less door-knocking, more flyering. Mostly, we're working on a citywide housing campaign—it's a moment when we need to start mobilizing thousands of people... [a higher-up] sent out a memo on this." This announced "change" in cultural practices nevertheless continued to focus on capacity building for large-scale events, and the roles for members and leaders remained recruitment-heavy and largely prescribed. Because the New York ACORN office's agenda focused on housing at the time, so did ACORN Bronx's agenda, and its education campaigns ended up receiving less attention.

The quantity of membership participation came at the expense of quality leadership. "Quality" participation—deep, organically developed participation—is important because it leads to more sustainable commitment among leaders, makes campaign choices more legitimate in the eyes of the leaders, makes campaigns more legitimate in the eyes of politicians, and can even lead to better campaign choices.[5] As one organizer described it, the focus on recruitment and membership that served as the foundation of ACORN Bronx's cultural practices allowed them to be "good at turning out people, but this is not organically developed. For instance, our fifty people are not necessarily fifty people who deal with schools at an education rally.... There was one instance when we got an active ACORN [Bronx] member to facilitate a [coalition] organizing committee meeting, and we just pulled her from totally different, separate activities. I think [another organizer] wasn't happy about that, and mentioned something. Because it was obvious that she didn't know anything about the issues, or [the coalition]." When a disconnect between the actual activity and the larger message transpired, the substantive content of leadership suffered in the process. Allies in the campaigns (and the politicians they were trying to target) could sometimes tell that the leaders were not really engaged with the meat of the campaigns, and the organization's reputation weakened as a result.

The Northwest Bronx Community and Clergy Coalition: The People United Will Never Be Defeated

As compared to ACORN Bronx, the NWBCCC boasted of a wider array of leadership activities. It was therefore able to attempt to pursue a wider range of political strategies involving both policy adoption and policy formulation. Nevertheless, the NWBCCC remained stronger in its policy adoption capacities and strategies. For instance, it had in the past garnered six thousand extra classroom seats in the South Bronx, roughly a 4% increase in space, and it had won Bronx schools bilingual education programs for its constituents. Its signature campaigns lay in fighting overcrowding, specifically for additional construction funds in the capital plan for part of the fieldwork period, and against the placement of small schools in large, existing high school buildings. The capital plan is the city administration's plan for all school construction and facilities budgets for the subsequent five years. To make anti-overcrowding campaigns successful, an SCO must prove that the constituents being squeezed out or left out of schools mattered and had a (potentially disruptive, attention-grabbing) voice. Correspondingly, the NWBCCC succeeded in gathering teachers, students, parents, and others in speaking out and holding press conferences about their need for "room to grow and learn." Along the way, they gathered quite a bit of media attention from both television and press outlets.

NWBCCC's focus on policy adoption correlated well with its emphasis on recruitment. To some leaders, this emphasis caused other typical organizing and leadership activities to get the short shrift. As one leader stated,

> Just two weeks before the annual meeting, Linda wants us all to go door-knocking and calling to get lots of people to come out. Two weeks, that's not enough to connect with them. If they're not coming out, just reminding them won't do anything; they won't be the excited ones. You could have a small group of people there, but if they're passionate and [on] top of it, they can make as much noise and make as much trouble as hundreds of people. And politicians are smart.... They can see if we're just there, sitting in chairs. So when Linda asked me, I said no.

To others, however, two weeks *was* enough time to convince members of the importance of an event, especially if they had been involved with the organization before. This was especially true if the event could make a difference by acting as either a signal of strength to politicians or as the exciting beginning of a longer-term relationship between members and the SCO. In conjunction with its leadership development activities, including research exercises, values reflections, and media and recruitment workshops, the NWBCCC's core leaders became well-versed enough with issues so that they could negotiate and speak with public officials even when the agenda or solutions remained ambiguous, or when organizers were not present. Mark, for example, spoke of having enough knowledge about school construction codes to bargain with authorities. According to leader and then organizer Monica, "We ultimately want our leaders to become their own organizers—leaders that can actually think for themselves....The other models aren't like that....Yeah, it may look chaotic from the outside, but these people can go from this point, and if I'm not the organizer involved, they're not going to fall apart, they can still function. And that's my ultimate goal as an organizer."

When NWBCCC leaders functioned on their own, they excelled more in policy adoption strategies than in policy formulation. Their capacities primarily lay in organizing large groups of people and in bargaining with authorities, especially regarding what the budget allowed or should allow. In the signature campaigns against overcrowding, these capacities were harnessed in arguments for more construction of schools in an existing budget and program, rather than different, unprecedented programs.

It makes sense that the NWBCCC faced more challenges in turning the Kingsbridge Armory, a former weapons storage space that takes up an entire block in the Bronx, into additional classroom space. This is partly because it could not simply demand that the Department of Education adopt use of the armory. This campaign required that the SCO make a case that the armory could be better used with small schools and a community center instead of other alternatives, such as lucrative retail space. In turn, this campaign required policy formulation efforts regarding zoning regulations, possible tenants, and other matters. While the NWBCCC's leadership development and activities included research and issue analysis as well as recruitment, the armory project demanded long-term commitment and a wide variety of skills, some of which lay outside of what is usually covered in organizing workshops. Over time, the campaign transformed from being an NWBCCC campaign to being primarily an SBU campaign. This shift may have occurred partly because SBU leaders were so enamored of the notion of small schools in the armory, but in all probability, differences in capacities also played a role.

No Such Thing As a Snap

For ACORN Bronx, "people power" was largely defined by numbers of constituents. Scale was emphasized at the NWBCCC as well, but other elements of people power also mattered. These elements include the leadership skills held by these people, the close connections and trust among them, and their collective analytical skills, vision, and passion.

The Freirean organizations excelled in policy formulation strategies. Freirean cultural practices, as described in chapter 4, include an emphasis on a variety of activities that have no immediate relevance to recruitment or even political campaigns overall, a relative focus on the individual rather than the organization as a whole, and leadership development with the organizer as partner rather than teacher. Meetings at SBU and MOM were unlikely to follow predictable agenda, even if they had standard protocols. Each meeting or activity concerned very different aspects of political campaigns, not just mobilization or recruitment, and members spent a lot of unstructured time "hanging out." This meant that issues were explored in greater depth, multiple perspectives were more likely to be explored, there was lower turnover among organizers, and because activities did not feel redundant, interest could be sustained for longer periods of time.

Because policy formulation campaigns involved so much original data and campaign-specific information (rather than public information about well-known programs like Section 8 vouchers or the Head Start program), and because they were likely to venture into uncharted territory and therefore entail less foreseeable tasks demanding varied sets of skills, such strategies drew well upon Freirean individual development and long-standing commitment. However, the plethora of activities also meant that the entire process was drawn out; those activities that were primarily handled by organizers and core leaders in the Alinskyite organizations, especially ACORN Bronx, were executed by all member leaders in the Freirean ones, especially SBU.

Sistas and Brothas United: We've Got Breadth and Depth, and the Vision Statements to Prove it

At SBU, campaigns appeared to be tied together, each a natural outgrowth of another, partly because the leaders developed them holistically. Activities for the campaign to address school safety and inequitable counseling services in schools, for example, weaved in and out of campaigns for small schools to be placed in freestanding buildings rather than in a few rooms in unsafe large school buildings, as well as campaigns to establish alliances between students and teachers. As such, when a new member joined SBU, the activities she was likely to join were of a different tenor and intensity than those that might be offered at the other three case study organizations. The tool kit meant that members followed different patterns of participation, and that they were given great leeway and independence in doing so. One leader was always involved in door-knocking and recruitment, no matter which specific campaign it was; another leader followed a specific campaign from start to finish, working on recruiting, agenda-setting, negotiating, strategizing, celebrating, and evaluating components; yet another leader specifically followed the narrower issue of facilities and overcrowding, drawing upon a set of statistics about building overcapacity, through a series of activities and campaigns. There was also so much time being spent at SBU headquarters that leaders had the luxury to pick their activities and hone skills as they wished.

The cultural practices at SBU helped members to develop as either generalists or experts; in addition, expertise could be based on organizing skills, campaign content, or both. Rather than winning adoption of ready-made policy proposals or existing programs, the signature school safety campaign launched by SBU succeeded in winning implementation of original protocols developed over long periods of time. It began with a mapping of school crime, harassment, and violence patterns from a student's perspective.[6] The resulting maps illustrated paths that diverged greatly from the beats patrolled by school safety agents. After a productive workshop with school safety officials, the leaders developed new protocols for student–school safety officer interaction.

These new protocols helped to prevent racial profiling and ameliorate tensions, leading to an entire series of professional development workshops for school safety officers and teachers. These workshops, in turn, required research and survey data collection of teacher and school safety officer preferences, protests against overcrowding, meetings with administration officials, and curriculum development by the leaders. Unlike one-day rallies or protests, each attended by a different group of members, this program involved a sequence of interrelated events that involved more than recruitment and isolated speeches, but a mixture of continued protest and collaboration by the leaders themselves.

SBU leaders drew upon their everyday experiences in the schools not just to identify potential policy campaigns for collective action but to actually shape the policies they proposed to replace current ones. Further, some of them felt so demeaned at school that they immediately latched onto a small school proposal with a pedagogical model giving them some voice in their own schooling. Sure, they wanted more, just as the leaders at all four case study organizations did—more funding for Bronx schools, more classroom space, more full-time teachers—but they did *not* simply want more of the same. To them, more funding would really make a difference only if these resources were used differently.

Just as the Alinskyite tool kit did not seem to help SCOs to build sufficient capacity for policy-formulation strategies, the Freirean tool kit may be less conducive to effective strategies that ultimately clinch adoption of the policies and programs they so meticulously developed.

The fact that members were so close to one another also allowed them to work more independently of the organizers. As noted earlier, SBU members were the ones most regularly sent in delegations at external conferences without organizers present, and MOM leaders were often the only non–staff members speaking at national conferences with other SCOs. The bonds among members also meant that even when organizers left there were still people for whom a member felt affection and emotional commitment at the organization. This way, less institutional knowledge was lost.

Mothers on the Move: We've Stuck Around, We've Learned Some Things, and We're Wiser for It

MOM leaders were proud of both their accomplishments and the travails they had overcome. As one leader noted, "I think the young members and new mothers coming in are seeing that older members are hanging in there; we can express that we've been through the things that they're going through, that they have the ability to make that difference."

At MOM, the focus on individual development with tailored leadership matrices for each member, the organizer-as-peer partnerships, and the wide variety of activities also contributed to a great degree of in-depth participation by leaders. There was little "churning" of members or organizers; those that became committed to the organization remained so for a long time. This long-standing commitment and individual attention to leaders paid off in well-orchestrated, sophisticated political and policy analyses in the SCO's campaigns. Like SBU, MOM excelled in intricate, medium- or long-term political campaigns in which leaders and organizers formulated policy proposals from scratch, introduced new protocols, or modified existing policies as they were being implemented. These sorts of political strategies demanded in-depth knowledge of existing and potential policy.

As described in chapter 4, members such as George were frustrated at the campaigns' slow pace when they first got involved; they were drawn in deeply enough, however, so that they stayed and became convinced that patience would yield worthwhile results. The intensive nature of activities at the organization was integral to this type of leadership development and organizer-member partnership. According to Michele, who had been politically active in several organizations for over three decades, "I think coming to MOM has made a lot of people attend meetings and become leaders. I think that in developing leaders, first you have to develop trust and communication with that person....It's at a slower pace, but they can do it, and they're trying to do it. People have to believe that you're really committed to doing it, that you're not just doing it to make a name for yourself. That you honestly believe in what you're doing." The rituals and conversations among members and organizers were important not only because of the political issues tackled but because they allowed the organizers to convey their honesty and commitment.

Furthermore, Michele specifically pointed to improvements in the decision-making and agenda-setting processes at MOM:

> Before, I [didn't] feel the membership was listened to by the staff on the different campaigns. It just always appeared that the staff worked on the agenda separately from the membership....Before, the staff set you up to think that you had picked the campaigns. I can tell the difference [between that and real decision-making participation] because I had the experience. They would say, "Well, what do you think of lots? We have lots of these vacant lots in our community. What do you think is the problem with these lots?" "Oh, there's rats. Oh, there's something else." And I thought, "You know what? It's cool." I can sell products, too, if I [want] to.

Such a distinction drew the line between garnering support for a specific policy already in mind on one side and shaping and forming a whole new policy proposal on the other. Whereas the Alinskyite SCOs were capable of garnering large numbers of people for a rally to turn a specific lot into a playground, especially if the playground had already been proposed by a politician, MOM's critical analysis exercises, like "Naming the Root Causes," also facilitated discussions of the histories of redlining, disinvestment, "white flight," postindustrial downsizing in the manufacturing sector, and racial and economic segregation that led to so many vacant lots in the Bronx in the first place. MOM most helped leaders to think about whether vacant lots were what they really wanted to focus on, and to consider and develop ideas for what they would like to see built there—whether it be a playground, a shopping center, a new school, a community garden, or anything else.

Along the way, the heart of political strategies shifted from standing for or against policies or policy proposals to policy formulation itself. Michele, for instance, said, "Our membership also has a voice on the campaigns and agenda for meetings—we're always contacted about it...the campaign is born differently...I go up to them." MOM's signature campaign tackled protocols for parent involvement in schools, and it attempted to redress parent-school tensions not by demanding that all school officials, teachers, and security guards be replaced but by partly replicating their own process of decision making in the school setting.

As a result, political strategies could involve entire series of tactics or moves tailor-made to the policy proposals. MOM's signature campaign grew and moved forward when the SCO's carefully considered parent involvement protocols and its reputation as a consistent advocate for new ideas about school-community partnerships resulted not in widespread policy adoption among existing schools but in the development of administrative rules and collaborative projects from scratch, implemented in a new small school as it opened. This small school both grew out of and fell in line with MOM's signature campaign regarding parent involvement. At both MOM and SBU, the creation of small schools with social justice curricula grew organically from leaders' interests, strengths, and previous experiences in SCO campaigns.

Does more participatory decision making only make a difference within the organization, or does it actually help to shape the SCO's external political strategies? In this book's case studies, an overt and explicit role in issue identification and decision making not only rendered SCO leaders more committed, but the campaigns and strategies they embarked upon were more complex and spanned greater periods of time. Furthermore, perhaps because the Freirean category emphasized the importance of means as much as ends, MOM members expressed a great deal of pride and satisfaction with the more mundane aspects of political work (writing memos, holding meetings, drawing posters) as well as the ones they called "sexy"—those that threw leaders into the media limelight, such as speeches at press conferences, surprise protests, and recruitment of peers. The less visible, mundane tasks were exactly those that built capacities in policy formulation rather than policy adoption per se.

The personal attention and development paid off in garnering commitment to reimagining policy options, but coordination of policy adoption efforts became more challenging. Although some form of all these cultural tools probably appeared in all of the SCOs, each SCO had a set of practices that it used most. Even when the goal was not recruitment per se, but simply keeping members abreast on an especially important meeting, news event, policy idea, or even staff change, the cultural tools used to coordinate large numbers of people were often those associated with recruitment and networking activities. The Freirean SCOs were not as good at these activities as the Alinskyite ones were.

Building Flexible Capacity

The previous two sections have respectively highlighted how the practices of Alinskyite organizations can be cultural tools that primarily lend themselves to political strategies aiming for policy adoption, and how the practices of Freirean organizations are cultural tools that lend themselves to strategies aiming for policy formulation or implementation. Is there necessarily a trade-off? Some of the organizers and leaders argued that while each SCO tended to have strengths and weaknesses along these lines, capacities should not be inherently construed as a zero-sum game.

SCOs ultimately aim to possess the cultural tools that lend themselves to flexible capacity—the capacity to aptly develop capacities for both policy formulation and adoption. In other words, they need to build large, but deep, leadership bases. This is no easy task.

Freirean cultural practices could sometimes be used as cultural tools for policy adoption strategies, such as a display of support for a pending bill on education. As Jill, of a multi-SCO coalition, noted, "MOM's members understand the message, the goals [of our campaign]. You can tell that Katerina spends a lot of time prepping their members, talking about why this rally is important and what the situation is. So they feel like being there is important, and know why they're involved. If I haven't called Katerina to fill her in on what we're doing, she'll call me." This testimony also suggested that, even for policy adoption strategies, mere recruitment was not enough. Jill, who was also an ACORN member, further noted, "I'm sure that ACORN [Bronx] is more than that, [more than a focus on attendance at rallies,] and that organizers, in particular circumstances, talk to people one on one, but I think that people drop off a lot. They think, 'I'm just a body.' We've lost a lot of parents that way. But I don't work with the individual parents, and I'm not sure I've gotten to know them; they do the turnout."

Still, can Alinskyite practices, which tend to emphasize the organization as a whole rather than the individual, help Freirean SCOs to build cultural tools for policy adoption strategies? One reason Freirean SCOs did not succeed in consistently cultivating the cultural tools needed for policy adoption may be that their emphasis on the individual prevented them from conveying the importance of concurrently building the organization as a whole, building the fundamental power base necessary to show that they have popular support as well as substantive credibility. Rather than doing this by focusing on organization development, however, Freirean organizations might instead attempt to build cultural tools for base building and coordination by focusing on larger visions of justice.

At MOM, so much attention was paid to developing a member's personal interests that, in addition to distributing books about everything from organizing to musicians, organizers also tried to perform tasks like arranging for child care so that one member could regularly swim at the local public pool. These practices had the potential to detract attention from solid campaign and recruitment work, and this was one reason MOM's training matrix, described in chapter 4, explicitly included recruitment expectations. Some of the capacities for policy adoption political strategies could be built by consistently asserting practices like punctuality in meetings and incorporating questions about turnout into regular meeting protocols so that expectations could then follow.

Organizers at MOM also began to focus more intensely on base-building workshops. At the same time, noted one member, "So far, the workshops have been superficial, on the media, etcetera, and very disconnected." Members themselves sometimes expressed frustration in their attempts to amend the disjunction between large-scale, long-term visions and short-term goals of policy adoption, especially given the limited options from which to choose. Organizers and leaders collectively deliberated their next steps and response to this disjunction. "We need to form a theory of change—Why do this work? Why is MOM important? What will the neighborhood look like in five years, in twenty?" These questions were the focus of a weekend-long retreat where members articulated goals, processes, desires, whims, and complaints. Rather than strengthen its turnout by appealing notions of membership per se, MOM attempted to incorporate notions of scale into its holistic vision for social justice.

Essentially, this was also what SBU did with discussion groups on notions of citizenship and what it meant to "think outside the box." SBU partly succeeded in mitigating the tension between policy adoption and policy formulation strategies through sheer effort. Not only was leadership development extensive and intensive and the variety of activities immense but the number of hours students devoted to SBU was colossal. Furthermore, one can interpret junior high schools and high schools to be akin to the congregations so important to federal organizing. In this sense, even if the schools were not official members, SBU could draw upon social networks the other organizations could not access quite so readily. While this did not diminish the significance of the capacities SBU developed, it makes it difficult to gauge the extent to which adult members can replicate the results.

The NWBCCC, described as an Alinskyite organization that boasted of a great deal of organizer-as-teacher leadership development, had a better track record in policy formulation strategies than did ACORN Bronx, but it also sometimes struggled to maintain the kind of political commitment necessary for policy formulation. According to one organizer, "After a while, it becomes too corporate... it's too Alinsky-style. There isn't enough trust.... I feel like almost all of it is bullshit. It's contrary to the movement. All those rallies with so many people, they're not into it! And the politicians, they're not stupid. They can tell. We are down to their mercy. You think that they're there and scared, but if we're not all informed, if we're just there for the numbers, they can tell."

Strategies focusing on policy formulation could only be sustained if organizers and leaders also paid attention to practices of trust and some individual development; even exciting rallies, substantive leadership development, and research activities were insufficient on their own. Leaders had to feel like they had a real stake in the policies or programs they were rallying for, and in Freirean SCOs, this was guaranteed because leaders spent so much time choosing among policy options, or developing their own proposal. The Freirean SCOs' organizer-as-partner relationship built a specific brand of trust.

The NWBCCC's ability to pursue policy formulation strategies depended on whether it could successfully enact some Freirean cultural tools. While the NWBCCC's leadership development was strong enough to harness the potential for commitment to policy formulation strategies, some leaders recounted incidents in which members were just about to quit, but a peer leader reached out to them in a new way in the nick of time, and interest renewed. In one specific incident, a new system of delegate exchanges between different neighborhood associations within the NWBCCC, alongside surveys for ideas for new policy proposals, made the SCO appealing again to certain leaders.

The 2003–4 fiscal year also marked an opportunity to influence the Capital Plan, the only official budget for new school construction. The capital plan looked like a great political opportunity to use policy adoption strategies, since it was the kind of program that responds to numbers-oriented constituency muscles, the kind Alinskyite SCOs like to flex. Yet the NWBCCC, but not ACORN Bronx, vigorously pursued the adoption of new construction programs in the capital plan budget. Why? The NWBCCC possessed more of the cultural tools necessary in developing proposals for specific construction sites or facilities repairs in the capital plan, and it was more likely to perceive the localized capital plan preparations as a political opportunity. ACORN Bronx's avoidance of school-specific organizing, rendering instead multiborough or multistate campaigns as its signature concerns, stemmed from its unique configuration of Alinskyite cultural practices, including its supraborough organizational identity and the shape of its narrow leadership-wide membership base.

ACORN Bronx remained an interesting case study because it did not boast of a wide variety of activities, and yet, it remained a powerful organization. How was this achieved? The organizational identity at ACORN Bronx was intense and marked by membership dues, as well as strong language about ownership and sacrifice. These practices lent themselves to large-scale capacities conducive to policy adoption strategies. ACORN Bronx's strategies overwhelmingly focused on holding politicians accountable via protests or elections rather than hashing out the details of policy proposals. When showing support, they still involved a series of rallies. As most of its political campaigns dealt with citywide or statewide issues, the work benefited from some—but not extensive—input from its large base, nor did it suffer when the base was stretched thin across many campaigns. A small percentage of core leaders was sufficient for most meetings and policy formulation strategies. Division of labor also helped.[7] Staff and organizers coordinated events, conducted research, and helped to investigate the policy and program proposals advocated by the SCOs. In addition, certain choices were made between local and citywide work. ACORN Bronx succeeded because it focused less on local work, so that it could rely on the same leaders and expert staff to work on different political campaigns, especially if these campaigns involved some policy formulation and research.

Swarts (2007) describes somewhat similar dynamics at national ACORN. She writes about the ways in which a willingness to take advantage of political opportunity structures and centralized leadership helped ACORN achieve a scale and build the capacity to push national-level policies that eluded other networks, such as the IAF and the PICO National Network. Drawing from both the Bronx case studies and the work by Swarts, then, a key question lies in the extent to which a single network can concurrently and *substantively* engage constituents at the local, regional, and national levels.

Still, the Bronx case study suggests that if no politician or federal program offered a palatable policy proposal or solution at a given point in time, ACORN Bronx was caught in a bind. Given the poor state of public schools in the Bronx, however, Alinskyite organizations had enough clearly needed campaigns, like those asking for funds for the programs already on the slate, to keep their hands full. Concurrently, Freirean SCOs can work to ensure that, when proven ineffective, the same policy proposals are not churned and spouted again and again. In the eyes of the storms of policy making, Freirean SCOs can also negotiate new policy proposals when opposing proposals seem to be intractable.

Finally, as mentioned earlier, leaders and members of MOM and SBU were much more likely to describe themselves as "activists" and to claim that they had remained committed to their respective SCOs because of the mission and its ideas about social justice. In contrast, members of ACORN Bronx stated that they had remained committed to the SCO because of the victories gained, and as a whole, interviewees from the NWBCCC did not appear to fall into one category or another. SBU and MOM leaders were also concerned about effectiveness, of course, but they were more willing to stick with their SCOs, through thick and thin.

Notably, MOM members also stated that they did not stay with the group only because of victories but because they were emotionally committed to the organization and each other. This has major implications. First, in an analysis of several social change organizations on both the left and the right of the political spectrum, Stephen Hart argues that right-wing organizations have become much more willing and therefore successful at bringing explicitly moral values into the discourse in their mobilizing efforts, while leftist organizations have focused on pragmatic issues around success and effectiveness (2001). According to Hart, this type of discourse limits the leftist organizations' ability to draw people in and make strong cases for their causes.

Further, the labels "activist" and "social justice" are in some ways connected to what Lichterman calls a "life-way" of political work as an entire lifestyle, in which a person's political activities are associated with the individual's self-perception and identity (1996). This is contrasted with a "life-way" in which political work is not "personalized" but a discrete, separate activity from the rest of the individual's family, recreational, and work life. According to Lichterman, a personalized lifestyle is correlated with predominantly white SCOs whose members have are correlated with higher socioeconomic status and education levels. If true, then the fact that MOM and SBU helped low-income, primarily African American and Latino residents to participate in personalized politics is significant. They empowered these leaders to utilize a style of politics usually off limits to them, one that largely remains the purview of socially and economically privileged, white activists.

Second, personalized politics allow SCO participants to sustain work for longer periods of time, to better engage in different aspects of policy making, and to aim for truly substantive social change. They also belie the myth that individual fulfillment comes at the expense of the common good, or vice versa. As such, personalized politics may help SCOs to minimize what Shirley (2002) calls the "hidden costs of social capitalization." He analyzes a case where teachers burned out on working on campaigns and began to begrudge the Texas IAF, mainly because of their "additional workload, distraction from an academic focus, and uncertainty of results" (2002, 62). Teachers there specifically resented the fact that "Industrial Areas Foundation organizers, in line with...the notion that one should never do for others what they are capable of doing for themselves—often move on to another site quickly after organizing one school" (2002, 54).

The cases of MOM and SBU suggest that leaders and teachers might be less likely to burn out if they feel supported along the way, if campaign work yields social as well as political rewards, and if politics are personalized. Indeed, while the United Federation of Teachers union worked on specific campaigns with a coalition that included ACORN Bronx and the NWBCCC, individual teachers collaborated with SBU and MOM in longer-term projects and signature campaigns partly because the leaders there had developed personalized, context-specific policy proposals that incorporated teacher input. Rather than finding ready-made common goals, they formulated and implemented them.

The next chapter ventures away from capacities and their logical consequences in political strategies, arguing that strategies are also partly shaped by the embedded preferences developed in the SCOs' tool kits.

CHAPTER SEVEN

FAVORITE HITS

Embedded Preferences for Confrontation or Collaboration

Tool kits do more than help social change organizations (SCOs) in deciding on their approaches to issues of race and their capacities to influence different stages of the policy-making process. Their significance is clearest in the SCOs' embedded preferences for collaboration or confrontation, since the organizations tend to stick to their respective repertoires of political strategies, even after campaign "failures" as well as "successes." Here, confrontational strategies are those that chiefly pit the SCO in *opposition* to policy makers and the state, usually represented by a public official or the Department of Education. As in a court case in the American adversarial judicial system, there are clear losers and winners, and SCOs attempt to "win" in an argument, whether by outshouting the targets, outwitting them, or winning them over. Collaborative strategies are those that generally ally the SCO *with* policy makers and the state, as if they were members of the same (sometimes amorphous) team.

Collaboration and confrontation do not have to be dichotomous. Indeed, just as SCOs aim to develop the capacity to influence politicians at different stages of the policy-making cycle, SCOs would also become more efficient if they nimbly combined or alternated between political strategies.

Why, then, do SCOs rarely change course when a political strategy falls flat? By that time, leaders and organizers in the SCOs have formed habits that cannot be easily broken. Further, the strategies that they do pursue yield a sense of satisfaction that mitigates the disappointment of a campaign setback. Via a dialectic of self-selection and personal transformation, leaders either choose to opt out or become ever more invested in the tool kits and respective political strategies in which they participate. This chapter emphasizes the nonmaterial rewards of leader participation in SCOs.[1] It examines the ways in which the Alinskyite and Freirean tool kits lead to political and emotional commitment to certain political strategies, and how each SCO attempts to strike a balance between confrontation and collaboration.

A brief analogy might be helpful here. If the SCOs' organizers and leaders are like musicians, then we can imagine the Alinskyite SCO leaders playing music like a big, well-disciplined orchestra, working under the direction of an organizer-conductor. Their rehearsals are heavily structured. By contrast, Freirean SCO leaders are more used to working with each other and feeling out each member's style and strengths along the way. As musicians, they might often riff off each other, one picking up on a harmonic theme where another left off. Their practice meetings are less like rehearsals per se, and more like jam sessions. It makes sense that with different styles of training from different tool kits, these leaders also end up developing embedded preferences for different musical styles. Whereas the Alinskyite leaders might prefer to astound and maybe even intimidate audiences with their virtuosity, playing classical symphonies as if with one booming voice, the Freirean ones might feel like they are most in their element while playing improvisational jazz. They might take turns playing solos rather than follow a conductor's directions or stick to a musical score, and they might even ask for audience participation along the way. In the end, a pianist might aspire to play a wide variety of styles, and a skilled one can probably adapt to playing Frédéric Chopin's concertos as well as Thelonius Monk's jazz pieces, but it is quite difficult to switch back and forth, and to skillfully launch into whatever style the occasion requires. This is especially true because eventually the pianist might be more emotionally moved by some pieces than others. Depending on how the pianist has been empowered, she will also have different dreams of grandeur.

As with these hypothetical musicians, the internal tool kits of the different case study organizations helped to determine the leaders' embedded preferences for the SCOs' external political strategies. The largely organizer-coordinated activities of the Alinskyite tool kit, which help to build strong organizational identities and a sense of mission and unity, encouraged leaders to revel in more confrontational political strategies. The teamwork-oriented activities of the Freirean tool kit—which emphasize individual development and, in turn, multiple perspectives on the same issue and the creation of alternative institutions and lifestyles—allowed leaders to excel in, and to consequently favor, collaborative strategies. In each case, the SCO's internal tool kit provided some fodder for the leaders' embedded preferences for certain external political strategies.

Deciding on external political strategies is not easy. Figuring out what to do for school overcrowding, for example—choosing between negative or positive pressure, between figurative carrots and sticks, and among press conferences, marches, rallies, boycotts, and petition deliveries—raises the point that either collaborative or confrontational strategies can be romanticized. Further, the same tactic—say, a press conference or a publicized letter delivery to city hall—could be either confrontational or collaborative, depending upon the larger strategy pursued by the SCO. In the case studies, the underlying tone of the SCO's political tactics of strategies mattered as much as their overt content.

In addition to helping leaders and members choose between different political strategies, cultural practices helped to shape strategies by providing the underlying themes, moods, and key messages for any political strategy. This was true even when the same tactic was used by different SCOs. For instance, all of the case study SCOs held accountability sessions with several hundred members rallying in front of a politician, holding him "accountable" to SCO constituents. Such accountability sessions had different tones when executed by Freirean or Alinskyite SCOs, however. They projected different underlying messages, and were integral parts of different larger strategies.

It is significant that these SCOs are specifically working in education organizing. The Alinskyite case study SCOs have primarily worked on housing campaigns in the past, but both leaders and organizers state that education is a different ball game. As one organizer stated, it is "harder to identify one clear-cut 'target,' given that the education system involves a web of relationships with different kinds of decision-making power. For example, at the school level, the principal; the teacher in a classroom; the teacher's union; and the superintendent or community board who calls the budgetary shots, etcetera." Further, education reform overtly demands nuanced political strategies that simultaneously work within the school system and challenge it. This is partly because real education reform requires both continuous monitoring and good rapport with would-be "targets." While teachers and administrators constitute the official targets of education SCOs' political campaigns, it is much more difficult to elicit policy changes from vilified teachers than it is from slumlords.

Beyond reducing overcrowding and improving facilities and funding, it is difficult for Bronx SCO parents and leaders to agree on the pedagogical policies they would like to propose (Mediratta 2001, 42). Freirean organizations that provide social services, such as tutoring, must translate these services into political and power issues. The embedded preference for collaboration built by the Freirean tool kit nicely dovetails with strengths in policy formulation, providing SCOs with a means to work toward meaningful social change within the mainstream policy-making process. Alinskyite SCOs largely bypassed such pedagogical issues; they employed confrontational strategies to intimidate public officials into allotting more funding for Bronx schools in the city or state budgets.

In the end, the SCOs would like to adroitly pursue both collaborative and confrontational strategies. Mothers on the Move (MOM) and Sistas and Brothas United (SBU) were more likely to achieve this, partly because of the context in which they operate. Because Alinsky's legacy looms so large in American community organizing, the Freirean SCOs have tasted bits of the excitement that comes with confrontational strategies, and when push comes to shove, they can execute them, too (though probably not with the same refinement as the Alinskyite SCOs). Because organizers in all four case studies have been employed in Alinskyite organizations or gone through training in Alinskyite practices, the Freirean SCOs I examined were more familiar with confrontational political strategies than the Alinskyite SCOs were with collaboration. While I emphasize the Freirean SCOs' collaborative strategies here, it is important to note that in reality these case studies' strategies were collaborative *by comparison*. Across a longer, more diverse SCO spectrum, all of the case study organizations in this book might be closer to the confrontational end of the spectrum.

Both Alinskyite and Freirean SCOs attempt to build power and leave room for questioning authority. Still, the Freirean tool kit's teamwork-oriented activities and emphasis on the individual ultimately lead members to question institutions in a way the Alinskyite category does not. Because its tool kit bases its activities on institutions its members forge outside of the political system (through meditation, ball games, peer tutoring, and spoken word and music workshops), it encourages members to tie political ends to alternative social institutions as well as more Alinskyite strategies focused on elections and political parties, even when they come face to face with policy makers. While social institution building sometimes includes social activities that are not always construed as civic engagement, it also sometimes leads members to question the political system as a whole.[2]

Table 10 builds on table 9 (see chapter 6), drawing upon the four case study SCOs' signature campaigns to link the tool kits described in chapters 3 and 4 to embedded preferences for collaborative or confrontational political strategies. Components of the analysis discussed in this chapter are introduced in the second row of the table.

Shouting Truth to Power

This section analyzes the ways in which leaders and organizers at the Bronx chapter of the Association of Community Organizations for Reform Now (ACORN) and the Northwest Bronx Clergy and Community Coalition (NWBCCC), both of which subscribe to key practices of the Alinskyite tool kit, became politically and emotionally committed to primarily confrontational strategies. Because the Alinskyite tool kit includes so many organizer-coordinated activities, members were accustomed to receiving directions or guidance from organizers. Sometimes their steadfast allegiance to a particular stance also led to language that pitted "us" against "them," with "them" including anyone who was not a member of their SCO. The leaders were fed by the adrenaline of confrontational rallies and accountability sessions, where as a collective, they finally felt more powerful than the powers that be.

Because ACORN Bronx and the NWBCCC's internal Alinskyite tool kits have been thoroughly dissected in previous chapters, this section concentrates on how they resulted in more confrontational strategies.

ACORN Bronx: A Whole Greater Than the Sum of Its Parts

Organizers and leaders at ACORN Bronx quickly became used to confrontational strategies—namely, a series of "hits" meant to catch target politicians off guard. After a while, such surprise protest actions became an automatic rather than a considered strategy. Even when the SCO's capacities for different political strategies were not in question, the preferred strategy's strengths were assumed, and its weaknesses were not weighed nearly as heavily. The organizers and leaders became emotionally wed to the dynamics of large gatherings, and to the power they felt in intimidating policy makers, and making sure that others listened to what they had to say.

Leaders' stories of their first encounters with ACORN Bronx describe processes of both self-selection and personal transformation. From the

Table 10. Signature Campaigns and Embedded Preferences for Political Strategies

| | Alinskyite Category | | Freirean Category | |
	ACORN	NWBCCC	SBU	MOM
Signature campaign(s)	Anti-Edison campaign, No Child Left Behind (NCLB)	Capital plan, Small Schools Strike Back	School safety and counseling	Parent involvement protocols
Preferences/embedded preferences from tool kits	Excitement of participating in major events/happenings, "turning up the pressure," being part of a large SCO	Seeing concrete changes in the immediate future, participating in major events/happenings	Display of knowledge and substantive credibility, mediation, friendship building	Doing everything from the bottom up, proving grass-roots credibility, display of knowledge, utilizing hard-won relationships
Results	Defeat of Edison contract, less public support for NCLB (difficult to measure)	Additional funding incorporated into capital plan, city council funding on specific proposals	New school safety protocols adopted, involvement of teachers, counselors, and others in campaigns, new school	Opening of new school using policies developed and monitored by MOM members

beginning, Sylvia, a leader at ACORN Bronx, knew that participation in the SCO would be exciting, and it was something for which she either had or developed a preference. Sylvia described her initiation into the SCO this way: "When I found out about ACORN, I was taking English classes at the community college. I heard screaming in the cafeteria, all this noise. I thought there was a fire.... Then I heard, 'You have to vote!' I asked someone who worked at the cafeteria what was going on, and she said, 'That's ACORN. They fight for social justice.' And I was very interested, so I signed up and went to the meetings." Later, as Sylvia developed leadership skills via ACORN Bronx workshops, she gained confidence in herself, and in ACORN Bronx's vision. ACORN Bronx was her main exposure to the SCO and activist worlds, and the organization's campaign messages helped her to further articulate her inchoate feelings about the need for social justice, and so the SCO's language became her own. In this way, her politics were both dynamically informed and partly shaped by her involvement at ACORN Bronx.

Sylvia's sentiments fed upon themselves so that her preferences for certain political strategies were akin to those she first formed in her introduction to ACORN Bronx. Again and again, the stories relayed by leaders inevitably exhibited the same components: a large number of actors, crowds of people, recognizable antagonists, and endings that emphasized the power of raised voices. One example was Sylvia's tale about a protest at 110 Livingston Street in Brooklyn, then the site of the Board of Education offices: "If I'm in the front and they tell me, 'You're making too much noise! You have to quiet them!' I tell them that I can't quiet them. There are too many people! And they ask, 'Who's the leader?' 'All of us!'" Sylvia was clearly exhilarated by the experience, and to her, the collective identity of 'all of us' was surely greater than the sum of its parts.

The leaders' introductory experiences were then replicated, explicitly encouraged in later campaigns, and fueled by the SCO's internal tool kit. The leaders did not know each other well, but organizers helped them to understand their roles as ACORN Bronx members and political constituents at rallies and accountability sessions. These confrontational strategies fit well with other, similarly structured activities at ACORN Bronx.

Tara, an organizer, recounted an instance in which several local SCOs gathered for a brainstorming session on potential political strategies in several hypothetical situations. In one, the local parents felt that there was a need for an additional safety bump or crossing guard in front of a local school. The ACORN Bronx leaders were more comfortable projecting themselves as a collective of ACORN Bronx members than as individual stakeholders, and they did not necessarily have the training to represent themselves in policy-making meetings. "We wanted an action at City Hall," recalls Tara. "The [other] people said, 'When we [had a demand], we just wrote a letter asking for it!'…We're more militant than the other groups," she added, smiling. Via such interactions, leaders heard the benefits of confrontational strategies again and again. Variations in capacity could not be divorced from questions of preferences in political strategies; these were mutually reinforcing. In other words, leaders sometimes chose to pursue political strategies they knew they were good at, even if the situation might have called for something different. Even when capacities for alternate strategies (such as multiple rounds of negotiation, beginning with a letter of request) existed, cultural practices helped to shape embedded preferences in choosing the default strategy.

Thus, in ACORN Bronx's two signature campaigns, the thrill of confrontation clearly pervaded. In the anti–school privatization campaign, the Edison company proved to be a nemesis with moves that demanded loud, confrontational responses at each step along the way.

The signature campaign against No Child Left Behind (NCLB) legislation, however, was more complex. The legislative bill includes so many provisions, some of which could have been used to ACORN Bronx's advantage, and many of which varied by state. Because ACORN Bronx leaders had not conducted the sort of research performed at the other case study SCOs, they had no desire to negotiate with policy makers. Instead, they revealed embedded preferences for strategies that put the policy makers on their toes; they hoped that this would compel the policy makers to then do the right thing. In this signature campaign, ACORN members from around the country delivered a letter of grievance with confrontational flair. Hundreds of protesters expressed dissatisfaction with the legislation not by asking for certain changes but by staging a large protest in front of the national Department of Education headquarters in Washington, D.C., outside then secretary of education Rod Paige's office. While most of the leaders had not had the opportunity to study the full legislative bill and therefore found it difficult to follow specific statements about it, they got the gist: The law was no good. They eagerly joined organizers in chanting prewritten mantras and demanding that Paige come down from his office and meet them outside. The action felt emotionally satisfying because it was exciting to be there with so many other people, and it seemed like a smart political move, since it forced Paige to pay attention to them. Processes of emotional and political commitment were bound together.

The emotional stimulus organizers and leaders associate with crowded protests explains their embedded preference for confrontational political strategies. Edgar, for example, recounts an especially relished victory from years before: "There's no better feeling, than [when] those people announce that you can stay, nothing like the pain that I felt when everyone is crying and smiling and jumping on me and pinning me down, chanting, 'We won! We won!'" The fact that Edgar continued to point to that event points to its power as a rallying symbol.

The leaders' sentiments and the confrontational political strategies corresponded well with the SCO's cultural practices, which emphasized recruitment as well as activities that focused on the organization as a whole. In turn, leaders felt most comfortable with activities coordinated and arranged by organizers. Collaboration, by contrast, often requires slow deliberation, individualized research and preparation, often culminating in long tête-à-tête meetings that require the presence of just a handful of leaders. Such collaborative strategies came to be seen as boring, wimpy, and indecisive by ACORN Bronx leaders.

Further, there was a subversive and righteous pride in ACORN Bronx's culture of sacrifice. Some leaders felt such allegiance to the SCO that they viewed nonmembers, including activists at other SCOs, with suspicion. An implicit message was, "This ain't pretty, but it's what we need to get things done." By "not pretty," organizers and leaders meant that ACORN Bronx members should not be docile; they should risk being seen as troublemakers in order to capture the attention of politicians. All of this also contributed to a political vision of social change via defiant confrontation. In turn, repeated or familiar suggestions were met by immediate signs of recognition—nods of heads, smiles, and applause—whereas new or different ideas were met by considered silence or confusion.

ACORN Bronx's political strategies worked during the Edison anti–school privatization campaign, but they yielded mixed results in the more complex NCLB campaign. The latter was implementation-dependent, full of unfunded mandates that varied across states, and required local action and negotiation as well as confrontational flair or electoral clout. As mentioned earlier, ACORN Bronx's local campaigns were generally pursued in a more cursory manner.

The Northwest Bronx Community and Clergy Coalition: Infusing Politics with Drama and Verve

At the NWBCCC, leaders engaged in a wide variety of activities, such as research and outreach for different campaigns. These activities gave leaders a wide degree of latitude. Although a fairly large number of key NWBCCC leaders were well-versed in policy, many other members were not quite so active, and these largely relied upon organizers to help them interpret their positions on specific policies, politicians, and other matters. Organizers largely acted as guides and helped leaders to work in conjunction with other members as parts of a larger whole.

These wholes came into sharpest relief when the SCO pursued confrontational strategies. At those moments, all members assumed a united stance vis-à-vis public officials and experienced the exhilaration of collective action. In each NWBCCC campaign, the cause also became more honorable and the confrontation more attractive to leaders because of their participation in NWBCCC activities, and because these activities emphasized group identity and recruitment.

This had as much to do with the acquired preferences of members as it did with their capacities. Leaders at these organizations readily admitted that some political strategies were considered "sexier" than others, and different SCOs had different notions of what strategies were sexiest. The NWBCCC's annual meeting, for example, is traditionally the SCO's biggest gathering each year, and often a new member's first real exposure to the full array of its campaigns. Each year the meeting is immediately followed by some protests, and in the weeks afterward, leaders hear of the impact they made that day. Leaders quickly took a liking to such strategies. They also believed in their SCO's vision of social change. Subsequently, rather than considering all the factors specific to a situation, leaders looked forward to those situations where they could pursue their favored political strategies.

At one NWBCCC annual meeting, the exhilaration was palpable and contagious as leaders chanted outside Governor George Pataki's mansion in Garrison, New York. They argued against overcrowding and for greater funding for classroom space and city schools. The willingness of leaders of all ages and religious backgrounds to participate and chant vigilantly, even after police arrived and threatened arrest for trespassing, is significant because it was highly unlikely that each of these individuals would have felt similarly on her own. Their feelings of solidarity had been cemented at the annual meeting from which they had just come. This annual meeting included a retrospective of thirty years of NWBCCC work and spoken-word chants such as the following:

Soldiers of society trying to keep their eyes on me
In their hands is my education
And I blindly search for academic salvation
Though I have no books to read, no chairs to sit in, no room to breathe

And y'all say, "keep your head up"
Well, to tell you the truth, I'm fed up
Even the Governor says we don't need college
All we need is an eighth-grade education?
Yeah, that's enough knowledge...
Why does the government fail to realize the importance of our youth?
Governor Pataki, I have some things I'd like to say
But they would be inappropriate
So Jeremy, it's your turn to play...

In its signature campaign for more school construction in New York City's capital plan, the NWBCCC worked to present a cohesive set of demands to both the School Construction Authority and to elected officials; it then pursued confrontational political strategies in how to lead these demands to be met. First, the NWBCCC gathered teachers, leaders, and students to list their grievances. They knew that the state constitution included a provision that all residents be guaranteed an "adequate education," and that Governor Pataki had argued in court that this meant that students should receive a decent education through the eighth grade. They knew from court decisions the amount of money they officially deserved from New York State, and they knew from student enrollment rates and overcrowding the amount of additional classroom space they needed. Together, they put pressure on New York City Council members to successfully garner money in the capital plan budget or, using individual politicians' discretionary powers, in other city administration budgets.

Two months after the annual meeting described above, the campaign was already yielding results—members mobilized around the issue, more leaders had learned about how school funds were distributed in general, and the latest capital plan budgets allocated more funds to Bronx schools. The leaders were partly motivated by their conviction in the importance of public schools, but they were also fueled by the excitement of participating in press conferences, especially ones that were covered all over the news media.

At another NWBCCC protest a similar kind of anticipation and restlessness could be given credit for the leaders' stamina, even when the protest location changed at the last minute. NWBCCC leaders picketed against the relocation of a small music-focused high school into an already overcrowded building, one where students were already scrambling for classroom space. They looked forward to speaking to major network news crews and confronting officials about the resentment and anger they felt about the impending move. In fact, the political strategies pursued by the NWBCCC were so confrontational that some constituents perceived the SCO as pitting small schools against big ones, and the NWBCCC later altered its language to include both big and new small schools in a fight against overcrowding overall.

Embedded preferences for confrontational strategies were developed partly because protests are essentially dramatic, and some are the stuff of legends. They emphasize the "all for one, and one for all" nature of Alinskyite tool kits, as well as a political vision that appears to challenge mainstream political structures by choosing specific politicians as targets. Logistically, confrontational strategies require good coordination among leaders, but leaders do not always have to be incredibly well versed in policy to participate. Leaders often stated that after participating in one protest, they were hooked. Mark, a member of the NWBCCC, recounted the time when he and an entire team of NWBCCC leaders approached the campaign staff of Republican Senate candidate Rick Lazio, pretending to be students from Lehman College (the City University of New York senior college located in the Bronx). They professed that they wanted to volunteer for the Lazio campaign, and they were warmly received, with Lazio campaign buttons, hats, T-shirts, and other paraphernalia. When they arrived the next day and entered the office en masse, Lazio's staff did not realize until too late that these NWBCCC leaders were in fact shedding their Lazio gear and executing a surprise protest at the campaign office.

During the present study's fieldwork period, the political context had changed. Lazio was not in the picture, Hillary Rodham Clinton had been elected, and the original target of the confrontational strategy (the junior New York State Senator) had nothing to do with the school reform campaign at hand. Nevertheless, NWBCCC leaders recommended the same strategy of surprise and humiliation in their campaign for more funding and against overcrowding. Months later, a representative from a coalition of various school reform SCOs expressed awe at Mark's story, and dismay at his suggestion that they employ a similar strategy for other politicians. Yet, simply in the retelling of the story, the NWBCCC's confrontational strategies garnered a lot of attention, and its image as a go-getter of confrontational strategies was reinforced.

On the downside of steadfast adherence to cultural practices, one NWBCCC leader, Daniel, stated that the SCO's Alinskyite emphasis on numbers and noise prevented it from adopting flexible political strategies: "I was having a conversation with [an organizer], and I said, '[NWBCCC] has become too pussy.'[3] And he said, 'Pussy how?' I don't believe in formal speaking. We aren't willing to really push things—Yeah, we fight for social justice and all that, but we are still trying to get to the same politicians and only working within social norms. And sometimes, social norms aren't right. We aren't opening the lines of communication and trusting our organizers, our leaders."

According to Daniel, confrontational strategies might help SCOs to cultivate a radical reputation, but in reality, they also often help to reinforce and legitimize the very forces they wish to challenge. Without deep, meaningful, bottom-up participation, SCO campaigns in fact operate in the same top-down manner as the official policy makers and politicians. By gathering large crowds to intimidate a certain politician, for instance, an SCO hardly subverts the local electoral system. Worse yet, if these large crowds are not well versed in the policy proposals at stake, the politician might not even get truly intimidated—the politician knows that she can, in the end, get away with whatever was first intended.

Further, Daniel suggested that SCOs sometimes stayed the course even when the political strategies pursued were not fulfilling their original purpose of scaring or intimidating politicians into acquiescence. Preferences for certain political strategies could therefore become so entrenched that individual leaders' ideas for innovation and change became stifled. This was particularly the case in the Alinskyite SCOs because their tool kits focused on the organization much more than the individual, and because organizer-coordinated activities sometimes left less room for in-depth input by leaders. It might have been riskier to pursue a wider variety of political strategies, improvise, and let key leaders possibly go into different directions, but to leaders like Daniel, the higher risks would also yield better results. This left less room for potential strategies that deviated from the official line.

From the NWBCCC's perspective, leaders developed embedded preferences for confrontational strategies because they worked. This was by far their best bet in engaging in pluralist politics, whereby most groups win "some of the time, but no one wins all of the time." Via their participation in the NWBCCC, these leaders won more often. Leaders came to see protests and rallies as a means for social change, and they were emotionally galvanized by them. Indeed, the NWBCCC garnered its constituents wins in impressive signature campaigns, like the one for more funds to Bronx schools in the capital plan.

Rebellious, Yes; Rebellion, Maybe

Large-scale, confrontational events helped leaders to feel as if they were members of a collective, building nicely upon the cultural practices inside

Alinskyite SCOs. Because these confrontational strategies also worked best when there were short-term goals at hand, the resulting victories reinforced leaders' preferences for them. The SCOs' confrontational strategies thus provided comfortable venues for new leaders to participate in visible and relatively accessible ways.

Ironically, such political strategies also made it harder for leaders to infuse the policy-making process with new ideas for social change. These confrontational strategies did not require leaders to know one another well. In fact, to assert one's individuality at this stage would have seemed fatally divisive. The large-scale events hosted by these SCOs were primarily associated with electoral strategies (to either reelect the politician, or vote him out) rather than other forms of mass resistance, such as riots, boycotts, sit-ins, or strikes. To the extent that the electoral system assumes participation in established institutions, these SCOs' confrontational strategies continued to uphold to primacy and power of electoral politics and organizational identity—whether in the name of an SCO, a political party, or a socioeconomic class. In their confrontational strategies, SCO organizers and leaders nurtured their standing as rebels, but they did not necessarily stage rebellions against traditional electoral politics. Politicians certainly paid attention, and that was a feat, but they did not necessarily tremble. They knew no coup was coming.

Negotiating Truth to Power

The two Freirean SCOs, Mothers on the Move (MOM) and Sistas and Brothas United (SBU), were more likely to pursue collaborative political strategies as well as confrontational ones. (As stated earlier, this chapter gives short shrift to SBU and MOM's confrontational strategies in order to highlight their more distinctive embedded preferences.) In these SCOs leaders underwent intensive and individualized leadership development and formed lifelong friendships with people they previously thought to be unlikely allies. They developed complementary strengths, were accustomed to designing and coordinating campaigns themselves, and were eager to put their newfound skills to use.

Many of these leaders were also so taken with their experiences inside the SCOs that they sought to translate the teamwork-oriented processes of conflict resolution and negotiation they had experienced with each other into external, collaborative strategies with policy makers. Further, they were encouraged to develop as individual leaders, to value and draw upon their own experiences in becoming activists, and to pursue interests even if they veered off in unexpected directions. Their brainstorming sessions and research led them to formulate visions of school reform that differed from those being batted about by elected politicians. Finally, some of them saw that even when protests had gotten them the attention of policy makers, negotiations were sometimes necessary for longer-lasting influence. Leaders at these SCOs developed embedded preferences for collaboration, working to broaden or reconfigure visions for social justice in mainstream politics.

Sistas and Brothas United: Welcoming the "Other" as One of Us

At SBU, the link between cultural practices and political strategies was clear. Via teamwork-oriented activities like peer tutoring, hanging out, spoken-word workshops, sharing music, brainstorming sessions on vision statements, gathering oral histories, and working with organizers as partners, leaders learned about and reaped the rewards of cooperation and friendship. By crafting policy proposals together, they had become incredibly close to people with whom they had never thought they would get along, and though they were not so naive as to think that they would actually become friends with policy makers, they were nevertheless eager to replicate something like the personal transformation they had experienced. At times, this came down to something as simple and real as unabashed enthusiasm, manifest in the tone in which leaders talked to one another and to policy makers. Such a demeanor was encouraged at Freirean SCOs. It was seen as proof that these students and parents care, belying images of poor African Americans and Latinos in the inner city as neglectful on issues of education. Further, the leaders forwarded a positive vision with which they could they could replace the status quo.

In keeping with the Freirean category, cultural practices were more about individuals and teamwork-oriented cultural exchange than about set routines used to advance existing campaigns, such as flyering. Rather than gathering and pressuring policy makers via confrontational strategies, SBU leaders developed a preference for gathering many different viewpoints and ideas from leaders, teachers, and policy makers, and collaborating with politicians to come up with new policies. While staff members at all of the case study SCOs used statistical data, leaders and not organizers or expert staff most consistently gathered such data at SBU and MOM. These groups were also more likely to consistently draw upon qualitative data (and political strategies) to complement quantitative work.

According to the leaders, the policy makers need to experience firsthand a glimpse of what they as students experienced every day in order to empathize, and to fruitfully collaborate on policy proposals. When SBU wanted to address the issue of disparities among leaders' schools and educational experiences in its signature campaign regarding access to counselors and a sense of school safety, leaders recited statistics to bolster their complaints of classroom overcrowding, inequities in access to counseling services, and disparities in disciplinary rates and responses to violence at the schools. At the same time, they were most excited about the politicians experiencing firsthand the crush of teenage crowds and long lines of irritated students in guidance counselors' offices, so that these policy makers could feel the tension of imminent violence themselves. SBU leaders also solicited evidence about the lived experience of students at overcrowded schools, through details like girls' bathrooms without stall doors, third-story floor-to-ceiling windows missing glass panes and bars, and strange smells and powders emanating from classroom closets, again so that the politicians could feel the dangerous conditions for themselves. SBU activists believed that this sort of personal observation of the contrast between "uptown" and "downtown" planted the seeds for collaborative, productive discussions and campaign success.

SBU leaders possessed the capacity to successfully execute collaborative strategies; more than that, though, they actively sought opportunities to sit down and force leaders in disagreements to air their disputed opinions or conflicting perceptions of the situation. They enjoyed it. As described in chapter 4, in the process of becoming friends with leaders they would not have gotten to know otherwise SBU members not only learned about but became invested in rituals of conflict resolution, negotiation, and exchange of favorite music and books. Having gone through the process of sustained teamwork inside the organization, SBU members were clearly enthusiastic about applying similar principles to their external political strategies. At one meeting with a citywide Department of Education official, the chair of the meeting, a student, encouraged people in the room to speak up about their grievances and ideas about the public school system; potential follow-up steps were discussed for each grievance. This differed greatly from the protocol in a confrontational meeting or accountability session, where public officials were primarily told to simply answer "yes" or "no" to each demand, grievance, or question, and where anything else was seen as equivocation rather than nuance.

Because it proved to be so meaningful and rewarding for the leaders, this emphasis on solidarity and teamwork applied to SBU's vision of school, too. That is, the tool kit helped SBU leaders to form not only their external political strategies but even the content of their campaign proposals. SBU's signature campaigns, such as their small school proposal, included not only social justice curricula but elements of negotiation, collaboration, and set procedures for students to get involved and build a sense of community.

Just as organizing activities at SBU varied greatly, the SCO's leaders' list of schooling issues was impressively wide in scope. While most of the SBU campaigns continued to address traditional educational issues like poor facilities and teacher quality, it was clear that these students did not think that activities such as sports or pep rallies as auxiliary or superficial. Nathaniel, who had lived in Pennsylvania for a year, spoke breathlessly about how different it was there:

> They had a good sense of community in the school, too. They had Homecoming…they had concession stands, they had Pajama Day, when you wore your best pajamas there, they had Halloween parties, Christmas parties, parties all the time….These things made a *big* difference because schools are kind of like a home; you're there most of the time….I never knew what field hockey was until I got there. I was like, "What is that?" I thought it was a new sport they just made up when I got there….I felt like there was better education out there. They had resources….Money problems…I don't think they had money problems. Like when it comes to science class, you actually get to do science experiments. Now, we just take notes….We don't have science labs; we don't have any of that stuff.

SBU leaders like Nathaniel drew upon their own experiences to articulate what they were missing in their schools, and what was missing in typical proposals for school reform, which tended to emphasize standards reform more than the science labs and cultural programs that they held so dear. These leaders knew to draw upon these experiences and insights because this was what they did within SBU, and their experiences there inspired them to craft new policy proposals, with policy makers and administrators from the Department of Education, in similar ways.

The SBU leaders' preferences for collaborative strategies also grew because of their love for artistic expression as a tool in organizing. While chants are ubiquitous at most grassroots rallies, several SBU members also described how spoken word shaped their work, and how cultural symbols in the campaigns, like certain musical traditions, fit into their larger political visions. As Lisa told it, SBU's focus on individual development compelled other leaders to take an interest in her passions and her writings:

> As soon as I found that I could write, and [one of the organizers] could help me, we just clicked immediately....We mainly talked about how things are so unequal in our society....And music in general, not so much the music that we listen to, but agreeing that commercialism has taken over....He showed me that there was poetry, that was kind of boring to me because it didn't rhyme or tunes to it, but I love rap, and when you find spoken word, which is right in the middle of the two, where you can talk about issues that will blow people's minds! You're talking about social equality, racism, anything.

Cultural practices like spoken-word workshops helped to shape Lisa's embedded preferences for collaboration because they allowed her draw creatively upon her experiences in her attempts to impress policy makers, much in the same way that she first sought to impress and work with peer leaders within SBU. Like Lisa, several other SBU youth worked extensively on spoken word projects in addition to public speaking, chairing meetings, and other skills commonly described in stories about organizing.

The unspoken tendencies toward confrontation or collaboration were so far reaching that SBU leaders changed the content of their written speeches or poems for events sponsored by the NWBCCC rather than SBU. The spoken-word pieces written for SBU-specific meetings were decidedly more collaborative in nature. Whereas pieces recited at NWBCCC events (like the one above) mostly emphasized negligence on the part of policy makers, the ones performed at SBU events emphasized each participant's perspective, and the possibility that they ultimately had common goals. At the inaugural meeting of a student-teacher working group, for instance, an SBU leader performed the following:

> There's many problems with our education...
> Is it the students' fault? Just try and *think* about their status:
> Got books from when the colony's first established...
> Constantly treating them like a statistic, treating them like lab mice.
> Scantrons mess up and lower scores, and *students* pay the price.
> Well, if we say it's not the students' fault, let's look at a new vision.
> Are the teachers to blame? Now let's just look at *their* position...
> Forced to teach us student from...disengaging, irrelevant books,
> Forced to teach 30–35 students, and feeling like they have no weight.

Stressed while teaching, and the check ain't even that great…
They're raising standards for us, and it sure ain't fun,
And who's responsible for raising standards for all of them?
To make up for their mistakes, they try to keep us going at a fast pace,
With not enough resources to keep us on track in the first place…
In order to beat the powers that be, we got to try to work together with
   all our might…

Likewise, partly because the internal cultural practices at SBU let individual leaders develop personal interests, the creative expressions of leaders were allowed to veer off into unique directions, and they were not assumed to fit with a single party line. It seems apt that as SBU leaders reviewed chants for an NWBCCC protest, one member constantly made quips like, "Man, these lines are lame! Who cares if we get everyone together if this is what we're chanting! We have got to write new ones for them before next time…." For SBU leaders, a set of well-crafted, customized messages was preferable to any single, cookie-cutter line about social justice.

Consequently, in alliances with teachers or school safety officers, SBU leaders began every campaign with a survey of the preferences, opinions, and habits of all participating parties rather than with a set of demands or a presentation of the students' self-interests. This type of approach attempted to validate the views of everyone involved. Via their interactions with each other, they had learned that with work, radical revisions of school reform could eventually incorporate everyone's interests in a more equitable manner. The leaders hoped that collaborative strategies with policy makers would help them to generate similar results, albeit on a larger scale. The youth's school safety campaign, for instance, involved a forum whereby school safety officers and SBU youth formed respective teams and performed skits about how they perceived the others. In this way, the signature campaign addressed issues of racial profiling in the schools, an aspect of school security often overlooked or avoided in community organizing campaigns. Later in the forum, the youth and school safety officers came up with a new, official protocol for respectful, "open-minded" interactions in schools. In their understanding, power was not a limited resource; SBU leaders did not want to take power away from school safety officers as much as force everyone to reconsider their sources and uses of power.

Likewise, the guidance counselor reform proposal described in chapter 4 was the result of a collaboration among the Young Intellects (the group of young Muslim women who sometimes worked with SBU), SBU, and school officials. Each group pitched in resources and provided information, so that together they constructed a clear picture of inequalities in access to school counseling as well as what could be done about it. After consulting with education experts from local think tanks and universities, the leaders took to extensively documenting every homework assignment to illustrate that they were not being prepared, challenged, or evaluated at grade level. They also documented every failed or successful attempt to reach a guidance counselor in order to illustrate unequal access to counseling services in their schools. They found that the Young Intellects, who were mostly African or South Asian, were contacted by their guidance counselors and saw them several times a year, while SBU members could never reach their guidance counselors, even after many attempts at making appointments. Although the conclusions were not surprising, the fact that they conducted the study in a transparent manner, asked for advice throughout, and shared their findings made their resulting policy proposals more legitimate in the eyes of policy makers.

After its campaign on inequitable guidance counseling succeeded in making administrators increase access to counseling services by African American and Latino students, SBU decided to expand the campaign by initiating a similar process with teachers. Along these lines, SBU proposals took a considerable period of time to fully develop policy proposals with the teachers. They did not just come up with a list of demands and see whether the teachers agreed. Their collaborative efforts drew on individual leaders' strengths and on their passions. When students and teachers expressed their respective frustrations with overcrowding at a meeting, the students who had studied quantitative data analysis eagerly recited relevant school construction codes and bylaws. When small disagreements transpired between SBU leaders and policy makers, leaders immediately adapted informal SBU conflict resolution protocols to the campaign.

Sometimes it was difficult for SBU leaders to let go of their internal cultural practices, or "the way [they] do things," in external campaigns, even when the campaign work called for different strategies. For example, SBU members had some trouble collaborating with external experts in creating certain policy proposals, such as the small school application, precisely because their Freirean cultural practices valued everyone's opinion equally, with the organizer as partner rather than teacher. While these cultural practices mostly helped SCOs to engage in collaborative strategies because they encouraged compromise and negotiation, they also attempted to establish a level playing field.

Some of the pedagogical experts SBU consulted felt that their authority was being challenged and disrespected by these cultural practices. Campaigns sometimes required that SBU leaders defer to experts, and at least one person stated that this type of institution building was very difficult for the students. According to an SBU staff member, the SCO's earlier small school proposals were not rejected "because of the youth empowerment component, like they keep saying, but because [SBU's earlier draft application for a social justice–themed school] was a poor proposal without an educator helping them out. I don't think anyone has had the courage to face them and tell them that."

Partly because they acted as partners with the organizers and worked intensively with one another, SBU leaders grew to revel in close collaboration with policy makers as well. It also led to the sort of innovative policy development examined in chapter 6. Nevertheless, the leaders sometimes also found it difficult to defer or delegate campaign work to outsiders or experts even when it might have been a good idea. Doing so was especially difficult for these leaders because SBU campaigns are the one place where their voices matter, where they are not always being instructed to follow others' directions.

Mothers on the Move: Reveling in Face-to-Face Negotiations

MOM leaders also developed embedded preferences for certain political strategies via iterations of self-selection and personal transformation. Some of them had seen MOM's campaigns falter when only confrontational strategies were pursued. Over time they became accustomed to participating in important decision-making and governance at the organizational level, often chairing meetings and representing MOM at conferences with other SCOs. They enjoyed these processes and were eager to display their breadth of knowledge, and to similarly participate in actual policy making themselves.

MOM's tool kit included teamwork-oriented activities and encouraged leaders to resolve disagreements via research and dialogue. It also emphasized a wide variety of trainings and retreats, accessible binders and archived documents, and individualized plans of action for members. These practices helped to build a system of accountability in the SCO that, in turn, persuaded leaders to hold policy makers accountable in analogous ways.

MOM had been cultivating such cultural practices in the years right before my fieldwork period in the Bronx. While MOM was previously known to engage in one protest after another, many of them surprise "hits" at politicians' homes, both leaders and organizers readily admitted that the SCO had a bit more trouble keeping the policy makers' attention and working with public officials in a sustainable way. As one leader put it, "[B]efore…we would go out and campaign against [public officials], put a hit on them. But now…MOM has already made a statement of who we are, and how far we're willing to go to bring about justice.…So agencies are more apt to sit at the table with us than they originally did twelve years ago." With an automatic seat at the policy-making table, MOM developed new cultural practices to help leaders decide when to sit down and when to walk away. In the past, MOM had helped to oust hostile officials through confrontational strategies, only to fail in winning campaign proposals from subsequently elected officials because it had not yet learned effective collaborative strategies. Because of this history, some leaders had since developed preferences for taking as much advantage of political opportunities as possible, through collaborative strategies.

Ideally, MOM wanted to pursue just enough confrontational strategies so that politicians feared them, but also enough collaborative strategies so that their ideas were incorporated into official public policy. By focusing on individuals and demanding accountability, extensive documentation, and negotiations at the microlevel, MOM leaders aimed to become more flexible in their external political strategies.

At a press conference with several state legislators, parents and public officials presented typical testimonials about poor school conditions and their joint desire to improve education, and MOM leaders presented "grades" on the progress each legislator had then made toward school funding goals. These grades were not meant to disgrace the officials, but to encourage them to get "better grades" next time; the fact that none of the politicians failed is significant because it showed that even as MOM tried to shame the officials into improving their grades it had no intentions of completely alienating them. It is also noteworthy that these events were officially cosponsored by MOM and other groups in a statewide coalition. For MOM's own political strategies, leaders appeared to revel most in collaborative strategies that specifically relied on honest criticism in intimate settings.

While accountability and confrontation existed in MOM's political strategies, they had important but nonetheless limited roles in larger, collaborative strategies. MOM's leaders developed embedded preferences for this because they had experienced teamwork-oriented decision making firsthand, and they wanted to experience hands-on policy making as well, and to see their policy proposals come to fruition. For instance, the SCO's signature campaign regarding parent involvement protocols sometimes included somewhat confrontational tactics, like group protests, especially after specific incidents in which MOM leaders were egregiously mistreated in the schools. Yet, MOM leaders also incorporated lessons from these incidents in creating newer institutional procedures and considering what their ideal school would look like. Along the way, accountability sessions resembled not confrontational protests with ultimatums but give-and-take informational sessions about potential levers of power for parents in all levels of government. Such sessions focused on parents' rights in legislation from NCLB to Mayor Michael Bloomberg's Administration's Children First.

MOM leaders asserted that calculations on political strategies could not be reduced to "confrontation equals rebellion" and "collaboration equals co-optation." Confrontational strategies can bolster politicians' standings by giving them attention, and collaborative strategies can keep politicians accountable by making them take notice of alternative visions for school reform in actual strategizing sessions, and by making sure that politicians deliver on their publicized promises.

MOM therefore attempted to couch confrontational tactics in larger collaborative strategies by drawing upon the kind of leader-to-leader interaction present in the Freirean tool kit. In mending rifts between different leaders and in successfully mediating conflicts at schools along the way, MOM leaders believed that the SCO developed both the credible reputation and the substantive policy proposals necessary to successfully pursue collaborative political strategies. Leaders conducted research and built lasting relationships with parents, students, and sometimes principals and teachers at individual schools, and they used teamwork-oriented activities as a foundation upon which they could, together, launch new programs and their own school.

MOM's leaders came to deeply value the power of dialogue. When a member recalled hearing disparaging remarks about residents in a new homeless shelter nearby, another member responded, "If something like that is going to be built, we need to meet. People don't say things like that face-to-face." Such a response contrasts the scenario described in chapter 3, whereby an ACORN Bronx leader's description of homeless men who "are [*sic*] AIDS" went unchallenged.

This is not to say that MOM leaders and organizers were rarely confrontational. At one demonstration, a MOM organizer addressed a politician's staff members by chanting "alcaguete," a colloquial term that means "shameless" but, according to leaders, roughly translated to "ass-kisser." The mood here was different that that at an Alinskyite SCO's demonstration, however, in that chants were less likely to have been developed beforehand and distributed; rather, emphasis lay on a diversity of styles under a single banner. MOM's signature campaign may have included protests against public officials, but these protests then became part of a larger strategy that included both collaboration and confrontation.

In this study, MOM and SBU were the SCOs that successfully sponsored and opened functioning small, social justice–themed schools. Interestingly, concerned teachers and other community-based organizations approached MOM, rather than the other way around. To the remaining older members, this strategy was not "selling out," but the expenditure of political capital they had painstakingly built over the years.

At the same time, these leaders remained wary of the fine line between legitimacy and co-optation. Collaboration, when superficial, allowed SCOs to become highly vulnerable and run the risk of being "strung along." MOM's challenge, then, was the transition from protest and the building of alternative institutions from outside the system, to the insertion of alternative, truly innovative policies into the system. MOM's leaders and organizers believed that as long as they kept one another in check along the way, they would not lose sight of their substantive visions for school reform.

Fair-Weather Friends

The term *fair-weather friend* is usually pejorative, describing a person whose selfish aspirations give loyalty the short shrift in friendships. In education organizing, members and organizers remain loyal to one another (in Freirean SCOs) or to the organization (in Alinskyite SCOs), but they aspire to be fair-weather friends of all external parties. For an SCO, to stick with a specific politician through thick and thin is not so much being fiercely loyal as shooting oneself in the political foot. As smart strategists, leaders from all four Bronx groups attempted to be efficient fair-weather friends.

SCOs aim to place pressure on elected public officials and engage in confrontational tactics when these officials pursue ill-conceived policies, but they try to win these same officials over when they have a chance to shape or push new policy proposals. It makes sense that elected officials attempt to downplay the efficacy of confrontational strategies since such strategies tend to cast politicians in a negative light. Interviews with both current and past Bronx borough presidents, for example, suggest that SCOs' confrontational strategies were generally looked down upon. Adolfo Carrion, who has served as Bronx borough president since 2001, stated that protests are rarely productive; at the same time, his expressed contempt suggests that the protests were incredibly successful at getting his attention. Indeed, this fits well with the notion that, among the less powerful, the threat of disruption is an SCO's greatest weapon.[4]

Likewise, Fernando Ferrer, who served as Bronx borough president from 1987 to 2001, dismissed the idea that MOM's protests led to the ouster of racist Bronx District 8 Superintendent Max Messer in the late 1990s, asserting that then schools chancellor Rudy Crew would not have let him come back, anyway: "[Messer] wasn't ousted; he retired. [Crew] would not let him come back in because what Max Messer was running was a plantation shop. Now, among the groups that were working against him was Mothers on the Move.…And, by the way, would not let [the administration] install his handpicked number two. And Mothers on the Move was important at that stage, that his number two couldn't be put in. They were helpful there. They got Betty Rosa. Betty Rosa was a terrific educator. Just first-rate." From MOM's perspective, however, Messer's long tenure suggested that unless outside groups put quite a bit of pressure on both the administration and Crew, either Messer or "his handpicked number two" would have been allowed to continue serving as superintendent. Further, their job included more than the ouster of policy makers they thought ineffective or malevolent; it also included making new policy makers accountable to the demands of constituents.

Leaders at the different organizations all saw that protests captured policy makers' attention, just as they also saw that negotiation could also yield results. Balancing collaboration and confrontation is tricky for education reform SCOs since, as the case studies in this chapter suggest, tool kits help to shape not only the SCOs' strengths in political strategies, but also the strategies their leaders *enjoy* pursuing. Overall, the Alinskyite SCOs were more likely to pursue confrontational strategies, and the Freirean SCOs were more likely to pursue collaborative strategies.

SCO leaders had an affinity for political strategies that replicated their internal rituals and cultural tools, in a way that later rendered certain strategies more automatic and reified than others. For example, MOM press conferences and accountability sessions were more likely to be informative, include back-and-forth discussion, involve debates between public officials from different political parties, and be part of larger collaborative strategies than those sponsored by ACORN Bronx. When ACORN Bronx representatives met with public officials or the teachers' union, these meetings were usually part of a larger confrontational strategy, such as an electoral campaign against a third party. In the meetings or rallies most frequently staged by ACORN Bronx or the NWBCCC, members emphasized their organizational membership, felt the excitement of collective action, and focused on a specific, short-term goal, such as victory in an upcoming election.

Ultimately, while all of the SCOs have their favorite strategies, the Freirean SCOs proved to be more adept at mixing collaboration with confrontation, for two key reasons. First, as mentioned earlier, Freirean SCOs were still somewhat familiar with Alinskyite cultural practices. Second, the Freirean tool kit's attention to individual development and organizer-leader partnerships allowed more room for leader-driven innovation in political strategies, and for more quirks in their preferences for certain political strategies. Although these quirks were not to be indulged haphazardly, Freirean SCOs had the chance to draw upon more varied preferences for political strategies than Alinskyite ones.

The Alinskyite SCOs' narrower range of embedded preferences for political strategies partly stemmed from the structure of their tool kits. Their confrontational strategies may have been informed by leaders' concerns, but paid staff often coordinated them in a top-down manner. Out of the four groups in the study, ACORN Bronx is the one that most consistently pursued confrontational strategies, and it prided itself on this pattern. If a number of members reported grievances concerning truck traffic in school zones, for instance, an organizer arranged for a rally to be staged at the Department of Transportation.

The Alinskyite category's emphases on recruitment and leadership development with the organizer as teacher lent themselves to large-scale events, where confrontation, demands, and questions with yes-or-no answers were more likely to dominate and in-depth discussion less likely. Leaders at all four organizations, but at ACORN Bronx most of all, expressed great enthusiasm for the exhilaration inherent in large, confrontational events, where they listed their demands and forced public officials to give clear answers. They conveyed confidence in the power they felt as "many in the face of one," no matter how powerful this one public official appeared to be just moments before. The cultural practices inside the organization encouraged members to identify with the SCO. With little interaction among leaders, these members felt most exhilarated with strategies that pointed to clear allies and targets.

To the extent that negotiation was also less predictable and usually involved several exchanges of information, members of Alinskyite SCOs, especially of ACORN Bronx, might have felt uncomfortable with strategies that could not be scripted. At one small meeting between ACORN Bronx leaders and a politician, an SCO member read a speech outlining her demands for education funding. The politician responded by asking how many of the schools and parents involved were located in his district. The parent, unable to answer the question, ignored it and simply picked up where she had left off in the speech. The anecdote is also revealing in how the leaders later reacted to the meeting: some felt that the meeting was a disaster, and others felt that it had been a learning experience. Cultural practices helped to shape not only capacities, but preferences for and reactions to different strategies.

Although the NWBCCC's stories about sabotaging Rick Lazio's campaign was just one piece of evidence belying ACORN Bronx's assertion that it was the *only* confrontational SCO in the borough, the SCO's self-perception was at least as important as reality. According to one organizer, even as "direct action is special for ACORN ... [t]he other groups you're working with are not into direct action," those in the SCO also "understand how important UFT is in New York City. We understand that when we work with a group like the UFT, there are things that may not look all the well to the membership, but the fact of the matter is that they're a powerful group." With such a self-image, organizers were much more likely to help leaders participating in confrontational strategies than collaborative ones.

Shirley and Evans (2007) provide an alternative view of ACORN via a case study analysis of its Chicago chapter. There, organizers had read research concerning teacher quality and used Section 1119 of NCLB legislation to stabilize the teaching force in the city. At the same time, they protested the underfunding and punitive aspects of NCLB, including its school choice provisions and proposed de facto privatization of underperforming schools (which, of course, tended to occur in poorly resourced neighborhoods and cities), as part of a national ACORN campaign. Thus, although ACORN Bronx has chosen to focus on the confrontational, the Chicago case study highlights the ways in which NCLB is a complex piece of legislation, with some opportunities for collaboration as well as confrontation. Perhaps something about the Chicago context encouraged ACORN there to pursue different political strategies; I would suspect that its configuration of the Alinskyite tool kit, with its own blend of research and leadership development practices, may have also made a difference.

When collaboration was clearly needed, ACORN Bronx mitigated the tension between confrontational and collaborative strategies through division of labor. It sent its parent organization's affiliate political action committee representatives or staff researchers to high-level meetings with the teachers' union, for example. This delegation of strategies also allowed ACORN Bronx to, for the most part, maintain the militant image it so carefully cultivated. Staff-driven collaboration, however, was more limited than leader-driven collaboration. Experts and staff were less likely to draw from "local knowledge," such as school- or teacher-specific information, or from the varied experiences they had as parents.

By contrast, the Freirean SCOs' attention to individual leaders' varying preferences and strengths allowed more room for innovation. SBU, for instance, managed to have it both ways. It was sometimes a fierce, confrontational SCO, especially when the leaders felt that officials might be dismissing them because of their status as minors. Yet it was also a conversant, collaborative one, partly by playing its affiliation with the NWBCCC up or down as it saw fit. Finally, MOM both contributed to coalitions, through which it participated in large rallies, and continued to ride on its past reputation as a confrontational SCO capable of disabling politicians when it needed to. It also launched and hosted candidates' forums, evenings in which MOM leaders asked political candidates tough questions that demonstrated the SCO's potential electoral power. These differed from Alinskyite accountability sessions, however, in that they were less scripted, questions were unlikely to have yes-or-no answers, and their intimidating nature stemmed as much from leaders' informed questions and eloquence as from the size of the audience.

Rightly so, MOM, the NWBCCC, and SBU leaders were also proud of the significant bodies of knowledge they had acquired on the different strengths and weaknesses of various school reforms and policy proposals, and they were keen to show off this knowledge, brainstorm, and engage in the nitty-gritty of policy making. MOM and SBU went further than the NWBCCC in using such policy analysis to form alliances with educators and open social justice–themed public schools. Even among Freirean category SCOs, however, embedded preferences for collaborative strategies were qualified; SBU's experience in developing a small, themed school suggested that to such SCOs, collaboration in which leaders must defer to so-called experts did not necessarily constitute true collaboration at all.

Further, the Freirean SCOs' relatively stronger preferences for collaborative strategies gave them an advantage here because education reform demands more collaboration than community organizing campaigns dealing with other common issues, such as housing. As compared to labor or housing justice issues, education reform requires greater attention to what happens *after* a new contract is won and written, or after new infrastructure is built or repaired. SCOs need the buy-in and cooperation of teachers and principals for successful implementation of political strategies, even after promises are made and deals signed, in a way they do not from "slimy" politicians or greedy slumlords. After all, continued interaction among parents, educators, and students takes place over at least nine months out of every year.

SCO leaders were careful to note that they were not so close to teachers and principals that they treated them like family, because in *those* relationships, "you let things slide." Still, they noted that they needed some collaborative strategies to effectively keep "street-level bureaucrats" like teachers accountable. To constantly maintain a confrontational stance would have been counterproductive, since educators can sometimes take this antagonism out on the kids.

While the confrontational strategies held sacred by Alinskyite SCOs, but especially ACORN Bronx, remained incredibly useful, they did not necessarily lead to substantive social change. This is because education reform inevitably involves long-term, fine-grained, collaboration-heavy implementation work, and because radical change also requires alternative visions of schooling not easily found in the political mainstream. In order to inject such alternative visions of schooling into the official policy-making process, SCOs must sit at the policy-making table or really have the ear of someone who does. Leaders at Alinskyite SCOs reveled in traditional forms of civic involvement, such as voting in elections, rallies, and letter-writing for or against a bill. They ultimately helped to win more resources for severely underprivileged communities. To make sure that these resources were used properly, and that they were neither wasted nor funneled to schools or programs that were already relatively privileged, Freirean SCOs worked with policy makers to see what potential policies really were best for the students, what a vision of truly good schooling looked like, and how teachers, administrators, parents, and students could work together to realize this vision.

Leaders at Freirean SCOs interacted with each other extensively, grew close, and were more likely to view organizers as partners. With everyone participating in the SCO in different ways, there was less likely to be a single mantra, chant, or slogan that applied to everyone. While leaders at SBU and MOM also got excited about rallies and protests, they nevertheless expressed a strong desire for collaborative strategies, and to come to mutual understanding with politicians in ways akin to how they came to work with one another. Lest this be perceived as "sleeping with the enemy," they were careful to note that true accountability requires honesty and knowledge that only comes with relative intimacy and collaboration as well as confrontation.

Such collaborative strategies can eventually help Freirean SCOs to expand their repertoires overall. To the extent that their strategies were a bit less based on calculated moves and countermoves, it follows that their strategies as well as their policy proposals hold the potential to incorporate the idiosyncrasies of various players and innovate. Critics would contend that Alinskyite tool kits yield more victories; in response, Freirean organizers and leaders would retort that their victories may be fewer in number, but they are sweeter. When successful, they will ultimately help to not only change the balance of power in a policy-making community but alter the ways in which power is henceforth distributed.

Chapter Eight

Commitment and Commencement

All of the social change organizations (SCOs) in the present study sowed and reaped rewards for their efforts in local education reform, and all of them received media attention for it. Outlets as varied as the *New York Post,* the *New York Times, City Limits,* the *Christian Science Monitor,* and National Public Radio chronicled various campaigns for greater funding, better teacher training, and greater parental voice in school governance. A quick glance at these articles would suggest that the Bronx chapter of the Association of Community Organizations for Reform Now (ACORN), the Northwest Bronx Clergy and Community Coalition (NWBCCC), Mothers on the Move (MOM), and Sistas and Brothas United (SBU) performed similar work, and indeed, some of their campaigns overlapped. Further, a lot of the keywords used in these articles were the same: *accountability, education reform, school reform, social justice* for the Bronx, and so on. A closer look, however, yields faint hints of some of the lessons covered in this book—that these organizations tackled different aspects of school reform, that they utilized different strategies in their campaigns, and that, ultimately, their campaigns eventually led them to different ends as well as different means. Through an investigation of their tool kits, this study has examined how and why this happened.

The practices that marked commitment and participation in Alinskyite and Freirean SCOs, primarily described in chapters 3 and 4, formed distinct tool kits. When put into action, these tool kits revealed different capacities for policy formulation–oriented versus policy adoption–oriented political strategies, different embedded preferences for collaboration or confrontation, and different ways to address (or gently tiptoe around) issues of race and ethnicity. Through dynamic activities like extensive recruitment or conflict resolution, intense shared experiences like accountability sessions or deeply personal conversations, and high dues payments or peer tutoring and media literacy classes, the four Bronx education organizing groups revealed not only disparate cultural practices, but different assumptions, preferences, and strengths in their political campaigns.

An Ever-Changing Epilogue

In the months immediately following this book's fieldwork, ACORN sponsored large-scale events regionally and nationally. While the 2004 presidential election results were disappointing for the organization, which endorsed the Democratic Party candidate via its political action committee affiliate, ACORN succeeded in registering over one million new voters, hosting numerous rallies, and helping to approve a referendum raising the minimum wage in Florida.[1] Locally, ACORN Bronx continued to contribute to citywide campaigns for affordable housing and regional alliances for New York City school funding. However, ACORN also gathered some negative attention, with articles about its tenuous role as both a Department of Housing and Urban Development–sponsored landlord as well as a tenant activist organization in media outlets such as the *New York Times*.[2] In some ways, this mixed media coverage echoes lessons found in this book, that in its quest for a large support base and political power, ACORN Bronx struggled to navigate nuances in the terrains of substantive leadership-driven initiatives, education policy, and radical social change.

The NWBCCC continued to integrate its education and immigrant campaigns across neighborhoods and official issue categories, scoping out and promoting community-based land use on vacant lots and at the Kingsbridge Armory. Although the plan it developed with architects and planners from the Pratt Institute was ultimately rejected, policy makers cited pressure from the NWBCCC as one of the reasons they finally made an official call for proposals for the armory's redevelopment.

The NWBCCC also expanded its campaign against overcrowding, and for adequate funding and school construction under the city's capital plan. For example, after a small, music-themed school was forcibly moved from one large high school building to another without notice, the parents contacted the NWBCCC to help them negotiate for a permanent, adequate space for the students, who take upright basses, cellos, and other instruments to and from school every day. The NWBCCC helped the parents at the Celia Cruz Bronx High School of Music to join forces with other parents, at both small and "regular" comprehensive high schools, in fighting overcrowding overall. This received coverage by all of the New York television network news organizations, as well as major periodicals.[3] The NWBCCC also expanded its efforts to collaborate with other SCOs, including its affiliate, SBU.

During this time, ACORN Bronx and the NWBCCC also worked with other Bronx groups in the Community Collaborative to Improve District 9 Schools (CC9) coalition, working in what was formerly Community District 9, in close collaboration with the Institute for Education and Social Policy at New York University. Participation in the CC9's campaigns constituted the bulk of ACORN Bronx's work on local education reform. This coalition managed to secure a lead teacher program for its schools. The program, which gave $10,000 bonuses to master teachers mentoring less experienced ones, received several hundreds of thousands of dollars from private foundations, in addition to $1.6 million from the Department of Education. Most important, it earned the relatively new coalition a reputation for substance and success in the city. In 2005, the coalition expanded its geographical focus from District 9 to all of the Bronx, was joined by MOM in its efforts, and became known as the CCB. SCOs often ally on short-term campaigns, but rarely work in close collaboration for long periods of time; the CCB therefore promises to be an interesting case study in itself, as it helps different SCOs, with dramatically different tool kits, to work together on long-term campaigns.

SBU continued to work on its small school proposal, got it approved, and helped to open its Leadership Institute in September 2005. As one SBU leader explained it, the school focuses on SBU's three central themes of "leadership, social justice, and community action." Several SBU leaders got together to write about their experiences working on the school; they described the ways in which the curriculum is aimed at giving students the courses they need to attend college (something absent from many high schools in the Bronx) along with organizing skills, like issue identification, policy analysis, and the practices needed to "unite the members of [the] community to work towards fixing the issue at hand" (Carlo et al. 2005, section 2, para. 4).

In the meantime, SBU also continued its larger education reform campaigns, including its work with a student-teacher alliance. For these campaigns, it forged collaborative teams via tactics like conducting neighborhood tours for teachers, showing them both local resources and social gathering places. They were also able to gain official participatory roles in new decision-making groups at several Bronx schools. This was no small feat. At a time when Education Councils wrestled with the administration of Mayor Michael Bloomberg for a semblance of school-level decision-making powers, high school students managed to reach the ears of top officials.

At MOM, new members took leadership roles in all of the events and roundtable discussions covered by the media, and the small middle school cosponsored by MOM opened in September 2004. After a public official admonished the school principal for daring to submit a proposal as "radical" as parent-teacher home visits, MOM and the school were able to secure funding for the "radical" program. MOM's next major development in its education campaigns, completed a full year after the end of the present study's fieldwork period, was a comprehensive "Platform for Excellent Schools" that confirmed a strength in policy formulation, as articulated in chapter 6. For example, rather than opposition to No Child Left Behind legislation, the platform argued for an overhaul of certain provisions, such as the military recruitment clause in public schools. The platform also echoed other Freirean themes in its calls for "cultural competency training," better use of city administration institutions such as "C-30 committees," parents and teachers as coeducators, and schools as community centers, so that education reform would not be a campaign topic deemed mutually exclusive of other community issues.

Despite these concrete results it is impossible to precisely gauge the *full* impact of these SCOs right away, especially because so many members are transformed into lifelong activists. These activists, partly because they commit themselves to large-scale social change, do not always stay committed to a single organization. For example, many of the leaders at MOM have since become paid staff members at other SCOs, most of which work on issues other than school reform. Some rose to top positions, such as executive directorships. Again, this is remarkable because these leaders were in some ways among the traditional "hard-to-serve" population—including single mothers on welfare who, at least at first, lacked the confidence and "official" expertise expected of SCO activists.

These developments suggest that the Alinskyite SCOs have helped to mobilize their constituents and increased their civic participation in the current political system, but that the Freirean SCOs have also helped these constituents to articulate a new vision for their schools, and to eventually work toward greater social change. While ACORN Bronx contributed to national efforts by ACORN to mobilize constituents in the electoral process, the NWBCCC continued to put the Bloomberg Administration under pressure for adequate classroom space in via the city's capital plan. SBU and MOM continued their efforts to change how Bronx schools are run, and to battle inequalities within the school system, and they have managed to get their own schools open and running.

The importance of tool kits is often lost if we solely focus on how structural determinants, such as levels of funding and the larger political context, affect the political strategies of social change organizations. The case studies in this book show that, even when SCOs face the same constraints, the tool kits of individuals involved—organizers, leaders, members, students, parents, educators, and allies—collectively make a significant difference.

Regaining a Sense of Agency

Funding and political contexts cannot be ignored, but they are not the be-all and end-all of strategic planning. If anything, the analysis here should instill hope in leaders and organizers at social change organizations: by paying attention to tool kits, organizers and leaders can make their organizations more powerful and work toward more meaningful social change, no matter what circumstances they face next.

Embedded preferences for political strategies play a large role in this book's cultural analysis; at the same time, cultural practices should not be construed as so petrified as to constitute yet another structural constraint. Rather, the cultural practices described in this study are like old habits; they are ingrained by ultimately remain mutable. They are not simply reflections of organizational histories; nor are they necessarily ossified.

A sense of agency is best enacted when it helps social change organizations address and bridge racial divides and strike a balance between collaborative and confrontational strategies as well as those of policy adoption versus policy formulation. There is a consensus that no single set or narrow repertoire of strategies—whether confrontational or collaborative, for example—is in the organization's best interest. Although these tensions exist for all SCOs, they are highlighted in the field of education organizing, which requires long-term monitoring and sustained, in-depth political involvement.

ACORN Bronx was more likely to attempt to striking a balance between different types of political strategies via division of labor, and MOM and SBU were more likely to alternate between political strategies. While the NWBCCC's practices fit within the Alinskyite category, it differed greatly from ACORN Bronx, and exhibited some political strategies like those of SBU and MOM. Overall, however, the Alinskyite tool kit develops capacities for policy adoption strategies and embedded preferences for confrontational strategies. It tends to encourage large-scale events, with limited participation by large numbers of people.

The Freirean tool kit develops capacities for policy-formulation strategies and some embedded preferences for collaborative strategies. The category's practices tend to facilitate intense, deep, sustainable, and even lifelong participation by what turn out to be, for the most part, smaller numbers of people. Still, because all four case SCOs were familiar with Alinskyite cultural practices, the Freirean ones were able to pursue a wider variety of political strategies than the Alinskyite ones. In reality, SBU and MOM's tool kits also incorporated some Alinskyite practices, but looked quite Freirean by virtue of their contrast to the ACORN Bronx and NWBCCC tool kits.

The SCOs' cultures were not defined only by demographic makeup, ideology, or overriding mission, regardless of whether the SCO was "faith-based." Rather, the SCOs' cultures were best defined by patterns in the activities, meetings, services, and rituals that formed their tool kits. The notion that real power for social change lies in the organizations' tool kits might sound somewhat pedestrian at first, since changing them does not *necessarily* require a great deal of new funding nor a once-in-a-lifetime charismatic leader. Therein lies their strength: tool kits are real, accessible, and moldable. By considering them carefully, SCOs can reinfuse agency into their internal work.

ACORN Bronx's constant "churning" of organizers and members was disheartening. Yet it is reminiscent of larger trends in social change organizations, whereby civic participation exists primarily in the form of "mail-in membership" in tertiary associations, requiring "no active involvement on the part of their members" (Berry 1999, 389). Since SCOs often provide everyday citizens with their first taste of democratic politics, it is imperative that they be given meaningful roles. As Fisher (2006) writes in a study on canvassers for progressive organizations, "It is misguided to assume that hiring people to knock on doors, stand on street corners, and make phone calls can strengthen a failing or nonexistent political infrastructure on the left.... [A] standardized model to train them quickly and get them out on the streets as soon as possible raising money for their causes...assumes that these idealistic young people have nothing beyond their time and their bodies to add to progressive campaigns." (107–8).

Like these canvassers, ACORN Bronx's organizers and members were expected to support a wide variety of well-scripted campaigns. While the SCO did a commendable job of representing the overall interests of low-income constituents in electoral politics, its campaigns lacked the nuance of campaign- or locality-specific deliberation. As a result, there was less innovation in ACORN Bronx's campaigns; ultimately, this may have rendered policy makers and advocates less connected to their members and constituents.

If ACORN Bronx would like to have less churning of organizers and leaders, it could better sustain policy formulation strategies by devoting more individualized attention to leaders and incorporating a greater number of workshops that deal with skills other than recruitment. The dues-paying system and ownership model were remarkably efficient means of encouraging quick emotive investment in the organization. This is less likely to be sustained, however, unless leaders have other consistent means of participation. While its strategies worked well for large-scale, occasional events such as elections or referenda, ACORN Bronx faced greater obstacles in local education organizing.

The NWBCCC, an Alinskyite organization with a dramatically wider variety of activities and more nimble tool kit, appeared to be in a state of transition. Its Thanksgiving services, research groups, faith-based reflections, and individually focused activities had greatly expanded just before and during my study in the Bronx. While its housing campaigns were incredibly successful, its most impactful education campaigns focused more on macrolevel issues, and it was trying to tackle more microlevel education issues as well. Overall, the SCO appeared to be succeeding in its attempts to develop diverse and balanced cultural practices. Although some leaders continued to criticize the organization as "too Alinskyite," the organization also exhibited strong practices of self-evaluation, and leaders were open to change.

MOM and SBU were most successful in tackling issues of race, and they did this by offering opportunities for members to confront one another as individuals rather than representatives of racial groups. Partly by being "race-conscious" rather than colorblind, these SCOs successfully developed ways to dissolve tension and racial divides among leaders. These two organizations also built impressive practices of trust and commitment building.

Yet they continued to struggle with building capacities for large-scale, intimidation-dependent strategies like walkouts and rallies. Mothers on the Move addressed this through new political strategies like its candidates forum, which allows a relatively large audience, though not necessarily on the scale of some Alinskyite organizations, to ask multiple and competing political candidates in-depth, hard-hitting questions before an election, as in a town hall meeting. Such an event differed from the typical accountability session, but it nevertheless worked to build on Freirean category strengths in a way that dovetailed with electoral strategies usually associated with Alinskyite category organizations. Notably, MOM also succeeded in helping to open a small, themed school with remarkable ease and speed; the entire process took a few months. In comparison, several other organizations took several years to propose, win approval, secure funding, negotiate logistics, and help to open a small school.

Ultimately, the demonstration of the threat or potential of confrontation is essential to all of the SCOs. Collaboration is a bit more difficult to execute, since the mere pretense is not enough. In addition to alternating between collaboration and confrontation, organizers and member leaders also cope with all the work to be done via division of labor. Such division of labor could run along the lines of staff versus leader, as is done in ACORN Bronx, or key leader versus regular member, as is done in the remaining three case studies. Indeed, SBU had been working toward such an internal system, and Mothers on the Move was also working toward a more uniform matrix of what it means to be a "key leader." At the same time, these Freirean category SCOs wanted to maintain their overall cultural practices of deep participation by all—or almost all—of their members.

Substantively, the case studies here suggest that there are concrete means of honing cultural practices toward more flexible political strategies. In contrasting Saul Alinsky's and Paulo Freire's approaches, Miller (1993) writes, "Organizing often has been criticized for focusing on winning rather than on educating. But the dichotomy is a false one" (section 2, para. 6). The extent that the groups' political strategies are shaped by embedded preferences suggests that rupturing this dichotomy is no easy task. There are certainly moments when organizers go for the short-term win and put leaders' opportunities for learning and collective reflection on the side. Because the pull of existing cultural scripts can be strong, it is only possible to combine different traditions if organizers and leaders collectively make a concerted effort to do so. There are specific changes that SCOs can try to make to their tool kits, in order to pursue more successful political strategies.

First, the careful and appropriate use of social activities or services such as peer tutoring, musical events, and job training can be complementary rather than antithetical to political organizing. In addition to building capacity, these cultural practices can harness empowerment and a sense of obligation. The use of services offers a model of fostering commitment that does not rely on high dues, as in the case of ACORN Bronx, or more traditional notions of self-interest, as in some Alinskyite organizations. The use of spoken word, musical workshops, and political theater not only made policy analysis more fun for many leaders, but it also allowed them to engage in critical reflection, and to connect to one another, the campaign issues, and the organizations in new ways. Rather than distracting the leaders from the work at hand, it further fueled the leaders' enthusiasm and commitment to the cause. This might help SCOs to build unlikely constituencies and alliances in their political campaigns.

The strong upsurge in the number of social services agencies and settlement houses in the Bronx that have ventured into organizing is an important phenomenon, one that could influence both organizing movements and community-based organizations.[4] Approximately half of the organizations working on education organizing in the Bronx started as social services agencies.[5] This is not to say that social services agencies have all transitioned into organizing with ease. One organizer complained that her supervisor did not feel that rallies were a "legitimate use" of her time.

The inclusion of services in a growing organizing model is significant both empirically and theoretically, for little current research examines how the nature, effectiveness, and quantity of the services influence political mobilization, and how different sectors of the organization—like that of pure social services versus that of organizing, or that of management versus that of the street-level workers—shape the organizational culture. A combination of the literature on organizational studies with that on social and political mobilization may shed further insight on the power of SCOs' tool kits.[6]

Second, the flip side of the first lesson also applies. Specifically, Freirean SCOs must address the issue of recruitment in their cultural practices. While SBU and MOM had begun to make recruitment one of the centers of their attention, they might go further in incorporating recruitment as an organic, consistent component of their tool kits. They might do this by emphasizing networking in their workshops as more Alinskyite SCOs do, or more likely, they might more greatly emphasize the importance of recruitment in existing activities and rituals as part of the process of becoming a peer leader. Leaders and organizers could jointly underscore the need to bring friends and recruits to meetings by acting as exemplars rather than giving instructions. Freirean leaders will be more satisfied with large-scale or confrontational strategies if they have the opportunity to demonstrate their in-depth knowledge of policy proposals and do more than ask bluntly worded questions. Together, all of the SCOs need to strike a balance between wide, conspicuous publics and narrower, well-informed ones.

Third, the experience of SBU suggests that making room for youth-based organizations will do more than bring new constituents into the organization. High school students have the potential of representing grassroots interests at a level of schooling with traditionally low levels of parent involvement.[7] To the extent that students are well versed in deliberation and have even more of an "insider" perspective on schools than parents do, they are more likely to bring with them the traditional benefits of participatory democracy: a keen sense of real-life, street-level problems and school strengths, the ability to help with the execution and the monitoring of implementation, and a stamp of stakeholder legitimacy.[8]

The students who do participate tend to be highly active, so that they are *all* key leaders. In addition, and more relevant to the core of this book, is the fact that youth might bring new tool kits, new cultural practices, and, in turn, new political strategies to the organization. This is what SBU has done with the NWBCCC, and as Youth on the Move appeared to be doing in Mothers on the Move. In this study, some of the most innovative policy proposals came from SBU.

More difficult are the remaining suggestions for potential practice, such as a greater focus on the needs of individual leaders and subgroups in Alinskyite SCOs. Such a focus might, at first, seem to highlight differences among members, but work at the NWBCCC showed that it could be done, that it revealed overlapping concerns among leaders, and that it helped organizers and leader to explicitly address and bridge racial divides.

An activity that more easily fits with other Alinskyite cultural practices involves the introduction of workshops on the issue of race; such workshops, however, might have facilitators or include lectures from "experts" on race, and would continue leadership development practices with organizers as teachers rather than partners. In the end, there may be irreconcilable differences in opinion, for community organizers wedded to a Freirean tool kit believe that as long as organizers are teachers rather than partners, members will not feel comfortable or competent enough to critically analyze issues of race.

Pragmatic Applications

In addition to lessons on capacities and embedded preferences, more ho-listic themes also emerged from the two tool kits. Specifically, the Alinskyite SCOs excelled in politics as is, and in personal empowerment and civic capacity. In a way, they served as intermediary organizations between schools on one side, and students and parents on the other, arming the latter with the knowledge and skills to enhance their family involvement.[9] Even their language was reminiscent of Alinskyite maxims to deal with the world as it is rather than as it should be. This worked well with bread-and-butter issues, such as overcrowding in the schools and facilities repairs. It helped the otherwise disenfranchised to gain policy wins and funding for programs that are known to work. In sum, it got them a bigger slice of the pie.

Still, the Freirean tool kit allows leaders to tackle bigger, more complex problems, even if a campaign win is not at hand, a week or especially a year from now. As Fung (2003) has observed, "If Warren, Wood, and Osterman correctly describe the [primarily Alinskyite, faith-based] organizing logic of the IAF and PICO, they would likely resist deploying their considerable networks and influence around issues such as an unjust war in the Middle East or national health care policy" (2003, section 2, para. 8)—or, perhaps, issues of diversity in education, or racial and economic segregation in tracked curricula and guidance counseling. Left unaddressed, these challenges will continue to undermine the promise of American public education as the Great Equalizer.

The Freirean category is about personal and social transformation, rather than civic capacity per se. The interviewees at MOM and SBU were the ones who spoke most passionately about how they had become lifetime activists rather than trying to distance themselves from the label, asserting instead that they were "just" trying to attain decent schools. Such Freirean SCOs strove for education reform, but they also attempted to restructure the policy-making structures that determine which policies "are known to work." By allowing leaders to become steeped and conversant in policy, they altered policy-making relations by challenging technocratic or political elite domination of policy proposals, especially in education, and especially in the recentralized New York City school system. For them, democracy was not just about choosing the right representatives but about participating in policy-making themselves.

Too often, social transformation and legitimacy are rendered as contradictory goals. It is true that the line between legitimacy and co-optation is often as fine as leaders agonize it to be. As discussions in chapter 7 showed,

SCOs want to challenge policy makers, be taken seriously by them, and never be dismissed outright. When they do have the ears of policy makers, they want to make sure that they are not being taken for a ride. Because education reform campaigns tend to have long time horizons, it is impossible to make substantive deals without collaboration, so finding a good balance between cooperation and confrontation is especially tricky. Still, it should be possible for an SCO to advocate for social change and act as legitimate policy makers. Indeed, the cases of SBU and MOM suggest that SCOs can introduce and realize *their* visions of good schooling, as potential models for more widespread implementation, via smart collaboration.

The task is especially tricky because legitimacy is itself socially constructed; grassroots efforts that seem radical at first, like MOM's small school, can later be seen as common sense. While the Alinskyite category helps to mobilize citizens to win the policy debate, the Freirean category aims to help citizens reframe the debate as a whole. When we reconsider the context of local school reform, we see that reforms rarely come in obvious, watershed moments. When they do take place, they often no longer seemed radical. If one takes the Freirean category seriously, one predicts a time when policies advocated by groups like MOM and SBU—even ones that may seem a bit offbeat, like school safety protocols primarily based on student-generated maps of school violence—will appear as "rational" as adequate school construction and overall notions of teacher quality, issues marking the other case study SCOs' signature campaigns.

Therefore, such SCOs do not have to be relegated to alternative institution making, whereby organizations run their own small programs and hope these programs will become models, but often claim few allies in the mainstream political system.[10] Freire himself explicitly rejected "armchair revolutions," stating that campaigns "cannot be purely intellectual but must involve action" (1972, 52). In a more contemporary twist, Polletta writes of how leaders in some social change organizations deem too much navelgazing as "Californian"—that is, "more concerned with self-liberation than with political change and more interested in how things 'feel' than what they can accomplish" (2002, 198). One SBU leader notes that he sometimes gives the following speech to folks who either dismiss his efforts or fail to appreciate the consequences at stake: "I'm not trying to discredit your viewpoint. It's valid. But when it comes down to it, social justice for you is a hobby. For me, it's my life. For you, it's a good idea. For me, it's survival. I have a stake in these campaigns. If they don't work out for you, you have the privilege to go somewhere else." For activists in the case study SCOs, "Californian" personal liberation is solidly a sociopolitical playground of the privileged.

It remains significant that the Freirean case study SCOs were bound not only by personal transformation but by school reform. Their emphasis on critical analysis made it easier for leaders to interpret patterns in school conditions within and across districts. It also helped them to theorize about the causal mechanisms of education inequalities in the U.S.

MOM and SBU endeavored to create a whole new kind and shape of pie, rather than capturing a greater slice, by challenging the policy makers (the bakers, in this metaphor) head on, and by gaining entrance to the back kitchen. However, the shape of this new pie is not predetermined; it is not necessarily anticapitalist or ideologically driven. In keeping with Freirean category practices, it will instead grow out of collaborative research and policy making. New parent involvement protocols and new school safety and counseling standards, as developed by MOM and SBU, helped to address socially embedded, behavior-dependent issues like high dropout rates and patterns of violence in the schools. In the meantime, while Freirean SCOs have greater potential for innovative repertoires and strategies, Alinskyite SCOs exhibited a narrower but more reliable repertoire of strategies for certain types of policy adoption campaign wins, especially in the short term.

Another related, important question is that of scale. Conventional wisdom holds that large organizations have to become hierarchical at some point, and that antihierarchical organizations end up being structureless or lacking direction.[11] The Freirean organizations in the present study are anything but structureless, if such a thing as structurelessness can exist in real life. The Freirean case study SCOs suggest that a middle ground can be struck. They did not rely upon passive consensus or wait for leaders to volunteer for specific tasks. They very consciously assigned tasks to leaders on a rotating basis, systematically recorded everyone's opinion, and built kinship networks based on interest and capacity rather than the other way around—providing training to certain individuals, according to their social networks. Along the way these SCOs also allowed individual leaders to hone strengths and certain skills over others. Nevertheless, some of the same questions rightfully lobbed at "structureless" women's liberation groups from the 1970s have been raised regarding Freirean category SCOs: Can these organizations mount national campaigns? Put bluntly, can they achieve campaign successes on a greater scale?[12]

First, there is no reason to presume that it is impossible for Freirean SCOs to operate on a large scale. On the one hand, the Freirean focus on individuals suggests that large-scale work will be slow going for these SCOs. On the other hand, once these individuals are committed to the work, they are more likely to stay so. Freirean organizations leaders suffer from much lower rates of burnout. Further, both SBU and MOM have mounted large efforts to train leaders themselves to recruit and organize. These two organizations are also more likely to run orientation and send delegations without staff present, and to be already reliant on and prefer peer networks, so expansion will not necessarily lead individual members to lose focus. It does appear that Freirean SCOs can succeed on a large scale.

Second, drawing upon empirical evidence, both SBU and MOM were growing quickly; they were the two case study SCOs with rising membership rolls. MOM's annual budget also almost doubled in the eighteen months of my fieldwork, from approximately $250,000 to over $450,000. Since the increase in funds has gone toward capacity building, in the form of a full-time fundraiser as well as expanded campaigns, this growth can be seen as part of a pattern rather than a fluke or outlier. Further, it is also worth repeating that both ACORN and the NWBCCC, to a smaller extent, are federation-style SCOs. The last *C* in *NWBCCC* does stand, after all, for "Coalition."

Another possible step for Freirean SCOs is to join forces with like-minded organizations. This is indeed what SBU sometimes did with the NWBCCC, judiciously flaunting their affiliation when needed, minimizing it when it could be potentially damaging. In 2004, SBU, Youth on the Move, and Brooklyn-based Make the Road by Walking—itself an SCO that draws its name from Freire's writings and appears to follow Freirean cultural practices (at least according to the literature available)—formed the Urban Youth Collaborative (UYC). While coalitions are sometimes mere information exchange networks rather than alliances in political strategies, the UYC quickly launched campaigns and engaged in issue selection, press conferences, and deliveries of grievance letters.[13]

After this book's fieldwork period ended, events, protests, and collaborations created by youth organizations citywide lent further proof that Freirean SCOs can scale up, even if it takes them some time to do so in a substantive way. By 2008, the UYC included more than a dozen other organizations. Together these groups achieved the scale necessary to be a citywide presence. Their alliance respects the work of individual organizations and yet is sustainable enough to outlast specific campaigns. In one protest at DeWitt Clinton High School in the Bronx, over fifteen hundred students walked out in protest of the metal detectors and oppressive security measures at the school.[14]

The alliance also articulated its top priorities—namely, forced exit from high schools and the oppressive policing of the schools. The students delivered a letter to Chancellor Joel Klein protesting the illegal steering of older or academically struggling students into specious alternative programs in order to open up space for more small schools (and elicit more favorable statistics for the schools, since these students would be counted as "transfers" rather than de facto dropouts). Around this time, the Department of Education also began to widely implement a "broken windows" theory–inspired policy of security in certain high schools, several of which were in the Bronx; students were disciplined for small infractions, such as showing up to school late. According to the controversial "broken windows" theory,[15] these students were assumed to be troublemakers, regardless of the conditions in which they lived and attended school, so that the earlier the system caught and disciplined them the better.

When the Department of Education refused to collaborate seriously with the UYC, the alliance held a widely publicized press conference and a series of attempted negotiations. Then, the citywide alliance strengthened their position by formalizing their collaboration, just as SBU leaders had done among themselves and with teachers and counselors. The UYC accomplished this via intensive, bonding activities over a three-day retreat, where students tackled strategic questions regarding their larger visions for social change. Again, such a retreat suggests that the alliance's emerging tool kit had at least some elements that fit well with the Freirean category—student leaders spent time sharing meals and hanging out as well as working on campaigns, and much of their campaign work focused more on individual concerns and overlapping interests than on existing campaigns per se. A year after its formation, the UYC hosted a conference that drew over eight hundred students from over forty schools and ten different youth organizations, the largest such meeting in New York City's history.[16]

This strong showing suggests that the youth population remains a relatively untapped source of stakeholder power, and one that is capable of implementing and utilizing substantive, in-depth tool kits for larger social change. Indeed, the UYC's main struggle thus far has not been a lack of mobilization but a lack of understanding on the part of administrators and policy makers, many of whom do not feel comfortable with youth-led organizing. The key message sent by policy makers is often "You're students, you have no place in the system." Even when policy makers are well-intentioned, it is only via careful, challenging collaboration that students can overcome the negative troublemaker stereotypes so often projected onto them and contribute to the thoughtful, innovative policies that well-executed grassroots organizing facilitates.[17]

Further, the UYC students have used their work not to just express dissent for existing policies but to come up with both broad goals and specific policy proposals to guide policy makers instead. If SBU's leaders are any indication, these students are committed to school reform efforts that will benefit future generations, even if they themselves do not reap the rewards. They are lifelong activists, passionate about social justice and committed to long-term justice as well as short-term campaigns or medium-term organizations.

Tying together overall themes like social transformation and practical considerations such as scale, one of the strengths of the Freirean category is its capacity to build unifying interests among members, when and where none were apparent before. A remaining niche for Freirean SCOs is organizing those who are left behind, who do not already belong to any conspicuous community. This helps to reveal new, cross-cutting denominators among social groups. By building these ties that bind, Freirean SCOs can rely on committed members even when obstacles seem daunting and wins seem anything but imminent. With time, Freirean SCOs can concurrently build larger constituencies, tackle controversial issues not pursued by others, and strengthen collaborative relationships and social bonds.

In an increasingly complex, globalized, and unequal world, we cannot take current systems of power for granted. What if, in the coming years, there are genuine opportunities for large-scale social change? Grassroots organizations will need resources and coordination, for sure, but they should not be held back by their own lack of imagination. All of the SCOs in this study have been working for power, but they must also ask the question, "Power for what?" In a context of what has been called a "diminished democracy" and record low levels of domestic political involvement, these groups are performing great feats by engaging the most marginalized.[18] It behooves them to take advantage of this substantive participation, to not just react to current inequalities but also to articulate the kind of world they wish to create.

Regime Change Begins at Home

The explanatory power of key practices partly stems from the fact that they do not appear at random; rather, they are fairly stable, and they can be categories and analyzed according to their themes. When desired, how can change take place? Or do organizations just die, as ones with different cultures develop? To the extent that a good tool kit can lead to more balanced and flexible sets of political strategies, how does an SCO adopt a different set of cultural practices? Can an SCO simply adopt an activity in an official capacity, or must it be implemented in specific ways? In this book, a one-on-one meeting in an Alinskyite organization does not necessarily look anything like a one-on-one meeting in a Freirean one. The default script differs, both in the content of the likely lines and in the stage directions for organizer and leader.

While changing the habits of a group of organizers and leaders is difficult, it is not impossible. Changes can be generally initiated in two ways: through top-down introduction of new cultural practices, and through the adoption of cultural practices already existent in a subgroup, as was the case in SBU and the NWBCCC. In that case, SBU developed its own tool kit, pursued successful political strategies, earned the respect of leaders and organizers at the NWBCCC, and introduced cultural practices to be adopted, slowly, by the NWBCCC.

The most obvious way to initiate change may be to change the official messages used in recruitment and espoused by organizers and key leaders. This is a limited means of changing cultural practices, however. Even if the organizers and key leaders espoused a new recruitment message in a coordinated way, this new model would do little to counter or reinforce other components and consequences of the existing tool kit, such as underlying messages between the lines, intermember trust, default preferences, and strengths and weaknesses formed by existing practices.

While severe crises tend to encourage change, there is unfortunately less existing theory on how change might take place in such noncrisis situations.[19] In the SBU/NWBCCC model, transition is slow, but leaders often initiate new cultural practices themselves. In all of these organizations, cultural practices of self-evaluation, accountability, and introspection also create opportunities for smoother, more organic initiations of new cultural practices or suggestions for different sets of rituals, activities, and messages.

When there exists internal division within an SCO, severe rifts can lead to compromise or to a new set of goals being adopted. Incremental bottom-up changes within the organization can especially occur when members do not suggest a whole set of new values but instead a series of new rituals that become popular or valued through repetition.

To facilitate organizational learning, SCOs must also make greater efforts to both prevent and prepare for organizer "churning" and high turnover. Trusting relationships between organizers and leaders are sometimes simply dependent on the amount of time spent or passed; when an organizer does leave, lessons and skills learned are frequently lost. This is not just wasteful; this pattern also angers many key leaders, who do not want to see organically developed vision statements lost or old victories forgotten. Well-documented archives of case histories, lessons, and leadership development models can help both leaders and new staff to draw upon organizational traditions and cultural practices. What made MOM's documentation system stand out is that it was designed not for occasional audits but for everyday, recurrent use. To a certain extent, this cut down on the amount of time organizers spent explaining the history of the SCO to new members. It helped new leaders to more quickly draw upon a tradition and legacy of cultural practices, and it helped older leaders to explain themselves and to express pride in the knowledge they have acquired over the years. There appears to be no substitute, however, for hands-on experience in policy analysis, research, and brainstorming about social change.

Start Spreading the News

Examining four case studies helps us to flesh out whether and how culture matters, but not to what extent, and how often. Although the case study SCOs were selected so as to hold several factors constant—including overall mission, education campaign staffing levels, political context, and overall ideology—there is no guarantee that these SCOs are representative of the entire field of education organizing. While the Alinskyite and Freirean tool kits developed in this study are helpful, institutional field-level studies can more readily gauge the prevalence of each type of tool kit. Such studies can also measure the level, shape, and extent of isomorphism that takes place among social change organizations.

Do SCOs adopt cultural practices that appear to be effective in peer SCOs? Are these adoptions substantive, or do they, as predicted by researchers of new institutionalism, lead to loose coupling, superficial conformity for the sake of legitimacy?[20] What cultural practices are more adaptable across space as well as time? By bringing the world back in, so to speak, such research can highlight the ways in which an SCO's cultural practices are constructed and interpreted by outsiders as well as insiders, synthesizing the dynamics of both structural and cultural factors without conflating them.

An Elliptical Ending

As Hart (2001), Wood (2002), and others have described, articulated moral values, such as those found in faith-based organizing, make a difference in binding people together and giving them the cultural tools necessary to build power and engage in education organizing. Further, many of these tools are more about walking the walk than talking the talk. That is, all the groups might claim to be fighting City Hall, but a closer inspection reveals that such a feat is not so easy, and that the groups are actually pursuing their campaigns in different ways. In the long struggles toward sustainable school reform, the present study tells not only that tool kits matter, but that there is no monolithic model. Each tool kit comes with its own strengths and weaknesses, and social change organizations must make difficult choices in developing the tool kits that lend them greatest dexterity and flexibility.

A final lesson lies in the fact that leaders and organizers at all of the case study SCOs emphasized the importance of being "real." This authenticity lends not only legitimacy but substance and emotional commitment to their cultural practices and, in turn, to their political strategies. The parents and high school students are not only fighting politically on behalf of younger students; they are also teaching future leaders how empowerment takes place.

A MOM leader spoke of how her son, Eddie, had just gone on a class trip to Albany. He wandered off and got lost, and, according to his mother,

> They thought they would have to leave without him. But he went into the legislature building, and he passed [the legislator's] office. He had come just for one action with me, against her in [the city], and I didn't know that he even remembered the name, but he passed by her office, and he asked to speak to her. And she wasn't there, but he spoke to her secretary. And he asked to leave a message, that she needs to give more funding to the schools in the city. And he was speaking about it, and the class teachers, they said that they didn't even know he was into this, and they didn't even know he knew what he was talking about!...He got to make a speech about it, on the steps of the legislature. Everybody was impressed!

If this anecdote is any indication, political engagement can be as infectious and gratifying as, well, the opportunity to attend well-funded, caring, challenging, and intellectually invigorating schools. At a time when scholars and pundits alike lament the decline of democratic practices in the United States, this is no small feat. Ultimately, the source of frustration in education organizing is also the root of its hope. School reform seems at once insurmountable and infinite, and so the horizon lies taunting, in wait. Across the country, teachers, parents, students, and others are ready for the struggle. They are mounting campaigns to make a meaningful, well-resourced, high-quality public education available to everyone. They are whispering, pleading, and screaming to be heard.

POUNDING THE PAVEMENT

Research Methods

The key question in this book concerns how cultures of participation in social change organizations (SCOs)—leadership development activities, explicit and implicit missions, decision-making processes, and their informal practices—influence or shape the external political strategies pursued by these organizations. I was interested in this because I wanted to credit organizers and member leaders for their creativity and ingenuity amid formidable political and resource constraints. Over the course of two years, I both explored the cultures inside SCOs and tracked how they approached external targets and public officials in their campaigns.

Over time, I came to realize the utility of examining these organizational cultures as *tool kits,* as I describe in chapter 1. I simultaneously conducted data collection and developed my book's theoretical framework, following an iterative case study process presented by Yin (1984), which allows the researcher to utilize multiple research methods, such as documentary analysis, interviews, and observation.

Much of the required data could not be elicited through survey, since the risk of social desirability bias was rather high. Observation in a real-life context was necessary. In fact, many of the observed protocols and practices contradicted stated principles, and comments made during meetings often belied those made during interviews, and vice versa. As I conducted preliminary interviews, archival research, and literature reviews, I honed in on meaningful variables and exploring theories that appeared to be applicable. In keeping with Miles and Huberman (1994), I refined the theoretical framework as the "current version of the researcher's map of the territory being investigated" (20) until its delineated concepts, and the directional arrows between them, made sense.

Validity and Reliability

Specifically, I focused on the notions of validity that are appropriate for each phase,[1] especially construct validity of measures toward the beginning, external and internal validity during analysis, and reliability throughout. I chose ways of evaluating culture that were both established in the literature and could be measured in the actual fieldwork. I chose a setting where there were many cases so as to hold the political context as constant as possible, and chose cases as to hold other potential confounding variables, especially high variance of resources, constant. In its analysis, this book relies upon "thick description" of the South Bronx context of my book in order to allow limited, nuanced generalizability and transferability to other settings.[2] Each of the stages of my research, as well as the accompanying issues regarding validity, is described below.

Stages of Case Selection and Data Collection

I first conducted a literature review of grassroots organizing groups, especially those working on education issues, as well as the larger context of grassroots movements and democracy. I focused on the theoretical frameworks described in chapter 1—namely, that of social change organizations and their cultures. Concurrently, I spoke with experts (both academics and practitioners) in order to share and examine my research question, the robustness of my theoretical frameworks, and the rigor and practicalities of my methodology.

In case selection, I followed a stratified strategy whereby case studies were purposive and reflected the required diversity of organizational tool kits among school reform SCOs in the Bronx.[3] The participants recruited for each case were snowballed and triangulated, to gain data that was as in-depth and complete as possible. I held constant the time period of the investigation, the local political context, the overall type of organization, and the campaign issue. In addition, all of the organizations work with predominantly poor households. Partly because of the high poverty and school enrollment rates in the South Bronx, there are many groups working on education organizing in a small area, and the potential for rich, comparative case studies was great. By constraining the organizations' geographical area, I was able to investigate how organizational practices differed when dealing with similar populations, demographic characteristics, and political context. While some variance exists, all of the organizations work with primarily Latino, African American, and African populations, in descending order by percentage.

The South Bronx boasts of a relatively high concentration of grassroots organizations in a small geographical area. While all have initiatives for school improvement, the groups vary according to affiliations, ideologies, and length of experience. I attempted to control for these variations and selected cases based on their activities and rituals, rather than on ideology per se.[4]

Several organizations in the South Bronx were eliminated as potential cases because their ideologies correlated highly with certain political strategies. For example, one potential case study was a race-based organization with a strong anticapitalist ideology, and it has explicitly admitted to an aversion to some collaborative strategies. This means that its cultural practices are less likely to be independent of its ideology. Another was also eliminated because its ideology diverges greatly from those of the other groups. Another prominent organization was not organizing around education but solely around sanitation and housing during the fieldwork period; it was therefore also eliminated as a case study. Finally, some of the organizations had been organizing for fewer than five years.

The remaining organizations were contacted with letters of introduction, and they all agreed to become part of this study. At each organization, I first approached an organizer, conducted a preliminary interview, and then formally requested permission to observe the organization. When it existed, the social change organization's board, rather than the organizer, made the decision. The organizations were not offered monetary payment in return for participation, although I offered to share research findings and to write relevant reports that they might find useful. In addition, I conducted some basic quantitative data analysis on area demographics and student achievement scores when requested.

The selected SCOs were chosen according to the independent variable: their different activities, rituals, and other potential components of cultural tool kits. None of them appears to have predetermined political strategies. All of these community organizations are so-called power organizations in that they all attempt to work through traditional channels of politics, such as the New York City Council, and to influence policy making by gathering residents to work on a single education campaign.[5] They all operate with the notion that there is "power in numbers," and that, overall, current political institutions respond to social change organizations. This differentiates them from groups ideologically opposed to the current political economy as inherently unjust and classist, as well as those that aim to improve the community via "social control" mechanisms rather than changing policies or getting involved in politics.

The four organizations in this study are the Bronx chapter of the Association of Community Organizations for Reform Now (ACORN), the

Northwest Bronx Community and Clergy Coalition (NWBCCC), Sistas and Brothas United (SBU), and Mothers on the Move (MOM). All of these organizations have been working on education campaigns for seven or more years; none has worked with a large group of parents for more than twelve years. As the NWBCCC's name suggests, it is actually a coalition of small organizations, including nine neighborhood associations and SBU, a coalitionwide youth group.

I investigated the four organizations for the 2002–4 time period. Because finding former staff is difficult, a longer investigation period without concurrent fieldwork might have introduced selection and recall bias into the interviews. Although such bias cannot be completely eliminated, the two-year time frame allowed me to capture data that were both comprehensive and sufficient. These data included several key campaign initiatives and decision-making protocols, as well as some potential cultural changes, in each organization.

I anticipated most of my research to be qualitative in order to observe abstract variables such as "experience," norms, and culture that are not easily quantifiable. Via my case studies I hoped to glean the immediate causes and effects of these variables, since "culture" itself is not easily encapsulated or captured, in order to construct narratives and provide a "thick description" for each case study (Stinchcombe 1968, 42).[6] Given my research question, I was especially interested in the multiple layers of interpretation of the same situation, and in the different perspectives of multiple actors.

Prior to actual fieldwork, I completed and submitted an approved Human Subjects Review in order to conduct interviews and direct observation. I then began a four-pronged plan of data collection: archival research and documentary analysis, direct observation, interviews, and triangulation.

First, I studied documents such as meeting minutes, newsletters, flyers, websites, official mission statements, memoranda, public correspondence, and relevant legislation or reforms enacted. I also gathered quantitative data on the funding and personnel aspects of each organization's capacity, and on public school system data—for example, school, district, and new regional level dropout rates, achievement test scores, reduced or free lunch eligibility, and the like, as well as basic demographic data on race, gender, and income in the Bronx and New York City.

The bulk of my research, however, took place in the form of fieldwork. I attended education committee meetings, accountability sessions, and rallies, and spent time, over repeated visits, with each organization. As part of my research into the organizations' cultural practices, I paid particular attention to formal and informal rules and routines in their decision-making processes, and to protocols during meetings, training sessions, and other events or conversations. I also observed their interaction with other organizations and public officials as part of the investigation into the political strategies chosen. I attended as many events as I could; when events conflicted, I chose to attend special rallies or retreats rather than regularly scheduled meetings.

Toward the latter third of my fieldwork period, I conducted semistructured interviews with organizing directors, leaders, and parents in each of the organizations, and with public officials and other third parties. I interviewed at least five people at each of the organizations in my study (See appendix B). I did not begin this immediately, but instead spent some time focusing on participant observation. This is partly because many of the organizations' members did not trust new outsiders, and because I wanted to ensure that all questions stemmed from the data. This adheres to an "evolving theory" process in qualitative studies, where beginning stages of data collection are designed to be open to all observations and discovery, and later stages place gradually greater emphasis on theoretical relevance.[7]

For each interviewee, I explained the goals and nature of my study. Participants had the opportunity to ask questions about my study and signed consent forms with the understanding that their participation was voluntary, that they would have the opportunity to review notes and transcripts, and that any comments they made could be held confidential or anonymous upon request. Each interview followed a protocol of ten questions (see appendix B), which served as starting points for in-depth discussions on the interviewees' roles in the organizations, the activities and practices of the organizations, and the political strategies of the organizations. To this end, I conducted very open-ended interviews and conversations, whereby I mostly asked follow-up questions such as, "What you mean by that?" "How so?" and "Can you think of an example or story?" I also asked participants to explain their stance and the rationales of their opinions to me as best they could, so that I could better understand underlying assumptions of different viewpoints, as well as better articulate my own. Most of the interviews were audiotaped and transcribed. In some cases, the interviewee felt more comfortable with notes as the primary record. For the purposes of this book, the names of all interviewees from the four case study organizations have been changed.

I also combined the above methods to conduct triangulation in order to glean multiple perspectives on each event and theory. For instance,

I interviewed public officials who were targets of education campaigns, as well as people who collaborated with the organizations.

In all, I attended approximately 150 events, ranging from two-hour meetings to three-day retreats, primarily over the fifteen-month period of May 2003 to July 2004. I eventually interviewed approximately fifty participants, some several times; each interview took place over one to three hours, occasionally longer.

As far as I could tell, my relationship with the organizers and leaders defied categorization. For the original fieldwork, I simply told them that I was finishing a Ph.D. at the Massachusetts Institute of Technology, and that this research was part of my final dissertation project. Later, I said that I was working on transforming my dissertation into a book, and that I wanted to conduct additional interviews to further explore some issues raised. This information appeared to impress teachers and some policy makers during campaign meetings, but the leaders themselves did not seem to respond in any patterned ways. Further, the racial sociopolitical context in which the organizations operated was largely that of an African American and Latino versus white binary. As an Asian American who was born in Brazil, I had no obvious role in this binary.

At first, I felt self-conscious about the invisible racial, geographic, and socioeconomic divide between us. I felt uncomfortable about the fact that I did not live in the Bronx, and I wanted to ensure that I did not carry out a bizarre sort of "mini-orientalism,"[8] taking the subway to study "those people" in "that borough." A mentor of mine had suggested that I emphasize my developing world roots as a means of connecting with the SBU leaders. In the end, I felt that this was unnecessary. The leaders were incredibly personable, well-spoken, and friendly, and they opened up easily when I asked them questions about their backgrounds and their lives as activists. They were passionate about the topics at hand, and did not show much interest in my personal background.

I suspect that the organizations' leaders became used to my presence as a friendly outsider, one who was keenly interested in and sincerely cared about their opinions and thoughts. I chanted with them and held up placards at rallies, as I sympathized with their goals (and it would have been conspicuously awkward not to), but I was not consistently present at meetings, especially when they conflicted with events at other case study organizations. I certainly did not offer ideas for campaigns or vision statements. These leaders regularly spoke with media reporters and public officials, so they were used to speaking about their work. My interviews kept going as long as they wanted them to.

Analysis

In my analysis, I followed a five-stage model outlined by Sarantakos (1998) in which I transcribed the data from the original audiotape form to paper, as well as organized transcripts and notes; reviewed transcripts, organized the data, and prepared them for interpretive analysis; tabulated all quantitative data and further organized the qualitative data, focusing on patterns that emerged, and the evolving theoretical frameworks in my study. Finally, I verified and revised my analysis after reviewing data, sharing some of my analysis with participants and receiving their feedback, conducting further triangulation by checking my data for bias, and employing a "cross-site analysis" as suggested by Miles and Huberman (1994). If a single campaign, event, or situation was described by multiple interviewees, I tried to get as many perspectives as possible, acknowledging that there might not be any single version of the "facts." Indeed, how each version came to be was part of the crux of my analysis.

In my analysis, I acknowledged that few, if any, "facts" exist outside of socially embedded relations. I believe that the data in my fieldwork are "real," but that they are nevertheless socially constructed and mediated by each actor's (the participant's, the researcher's) viewpoint. Therefore, I tried to contextualize each piece of data (participant observation, interview, document) as much as possible, jotting down who was involved, what stakes each person might have had, what the relationships between the different actors were, what my relationship with each person was like, and so on. To the extent that I attempted to examine what the different grassroots groups' organizational cultures were like, I compared them to (1) how each participant conceived of and described these cultural tool kits and (2) how one group's tool kit compared to that of another case study group. Therefore, I did not analyze these organizational cultures as entities that could be simply picked up and plopped down elsewhere. I concluded the data collection and analysis stages of my book when new data confirmed—rather than added new themes to—previously obtained data, thus signaling "saturation."[9]

Appendix B

Interview Protocol and List of Interviewees

Interview Protocol

1 How did you get started with [name of organization]?
2 How long have you been involved?
3 How do you feel about the school system (teachers, board of education, chancellor, mayor)?
4 Do you think of yourself as an activist?
5 Has your experience with [name of organization] changed you?
6 What strategies or tactics were used?
7 How did your organization decide upon those strategies?
8 Has your personal experience influenced your thinking about education reform?
9 What keeps you going here, at [name of organization]?
10 Are there other unexplored topics or questions?

List of Interviewees

All names, except those of elected officials and public administrators, have been changed. Here, both organizers and other staff members are called "staff."

ACORN Bronx

1 Angela   Leader
2 Carol   Organizer
3 Edgar   Organizer
4 Helen   Leader
5 Melissa   Organizer
6 Paula   Organizer
7 Sylvia   Leader
8 Tara   Organizer

Northwest Bronx Community and Clergy Coalition

1 Mark   Leader
2 Monica   Leader, Organizer

3 Rachel   Organizer
4 Sam   Organizer
5 Yonathan   Organizer

Sistas and Brothas United

1 Daniel   Staff
2 Elena   Staff
3 Ernest   Staff
4 Jeremy   Leader
5 Lisa   Leader
6 Michael   Staff
7 Nathaniel   Leader
8 Nicole   Staff
9 Rosalinda   Leader

Mothers on the Move

1 Diana   Leader
2 George   Leader
3 Isabela   Leader
4 Katerina   Organizer
5 Michele   Leader
6 Stephen   Organizer

Other Institutions

1   Altagracia   Leader, Bronx organization X
2   Anthony   Staff, Bronx organization X
3   Daniela   Leader, Bronx organization X
4   Gabriela   Leader, organizer, Bronx organization X
5   Hector   Organizer, Bronx organization X
6   Leander   Leader, Bronx organization X
7   Victoria   Leader, Bronx organization X
8   Isabela   Organizer, Bronx organization Y
9   Jeannie   Campaign coordinator, education alliance Z
10 Adolfo Carrion   Bronx borough president
11 Fernando Ferrer   Researcher, former Bronx borough president
12 Elaine Frazier   Chief of staff, Bronx Borough President's Office

Notes

Chapter 1. A Kaleidoscope of People Power

1. For a fuller description and analysis of social change organizations in the United States see Chetkovich and Kunreuther (2006). I discuss why I decided to call the four case studies social change organizations later in this chapter.

2. A large body of work critiques the ways in which color-blind policies in fact perpetuate existing inequalities in American society. In real life, after all, people are not racially color-blind in the way that some are medically color-blind, and color-blind policies can therefore work to mask and exacerbate racist practices in everyday life as well as structural racism. See Crenshaw et al. (1995), Carr (1997), Bonilla-Silva (2003), Doane and Bonilla-Silva (2003), and Wang (2006). Nevertheless, community activists legitimately debate the respective strengths and weaknesses of different policies and political strategies.

3. Mediratta and Fruchter (2003) argue that the Children First reforms were unlikely to substantially improve schools if the Bloomberg administration did not implement better institutional channels for bottom-up participation by parents and communities.

4. In addition to fieldwork for this book, a plethora of newspaper articles and policy reports have documented the efforts of parents and community groups to gain substantive policy-making and advisory roles in the city school system. See, for example, Herszenhorn (2005), Simpson (2006), and the Annenberg Institute for School Reform publications (available at http://www.annenberginstitute.org/CIP/publications.html (accessed May 2, 2008).

5. Macedo et al. (2005) provide an excellent and up-to-date overview of national trends on civic participation, different types of existing barriers to participation, and proposals on what can be done. While Putnam's seminal works (1995, 2000) sounded alarms on declining social capital in the United States as a whole, Verba, Schlozman, and Brady (1995) trace the income and gender inequalities in American political participation.

6. Here, political strategies are defined as the systematic plans of action meant to elicit a political position for the organization or policy change. They involve a series of decisions and events, as well as overall motivating factors and an overarching vision of the plan. For example, while the events described at the beginning of the chapter on their own describe tactics and not strategies per se, they still hint at the overall political strategies in which they are embedded, at whether they are meant to be part of continued pressure, persuasion, or bargaining, for example. Tactics are the modes of action chosen for specific events or actions. See Mondros and Wilson (1994), especially chapter 6, for definitions of tactics and strategies in a community organizing context.

7. Tarrow (1998) and McAdam, Tarrow, and Tilly (2001) analyze the roles of political opportunities, resource mobilization, and cultural frames in social movements and social movement organizations. McAdam cites four key dimensions of political opportunity structures: (1) the relative openness or closure of the institutionalized political

system; (2) the stability or instability of that broad set of elite alignments that typically undergird a polity; (3) the presence or absence of elite allies; and (4) the state's capacity and propensity for repression (1996, 27).

8. See McCarthy and Zald (1977), Klandermans (1991), and Mayer (1991). McAdam's political process model (1982) and Morris (1984) demonstrate that resources do not just come from external elites but also from indigenous organizations, such as black churches during the civil rights movement.

9. See Chetkovich and Kunreuther (2006), especially chapter 5.

10. For discussions of loose coupling, especially as applied to educational organizations, and other applications of the concept, see Weick (1976) and Orton and Weick (1990).

11. Alonso et al. (2009) present case studies from Los Angeles and New York that highlight the aspirations and frustrations of young African American and Latino students in inner-city schools. Dyson's analysis (2005) takes apart Cosby's arguments, while Carter (2005) draws upon original data on so-called "street cultures" of urban youth. Jencks and Phillips (1998) present macrolevel, quantitative data to provide contextual evidence on associations among income, school funding, demographics, and school achievement.

12. Emirbayer and Mische define agency as "the temporally constructed engagement of actors of different structural environments—the temporal-relational contexts of action—which, through the interplay of habit, imagination, and judgment, both reproduces and transforms those structures in interactive response to the problems posed by changing historical situations" (1998, 970). This working definition suggests that culture matters, but that it is both enabling and constraining.

13. See also Mondros and Wilson (1994), Gamson (1995), Robnett (1997), and Wood (2002) on the many ways in which community organizers or social movement activists mobilize constituents. Johnston and Klandermans (1995), Snow and Benford (1988), Meyer, Whittier, and Robnett (2002), and Foldy, Goldman, and Ospina (2004) focus on cultural framing, sense-making, and sense-giving processes in mobilization. Morris and Mueller (1992) and Mansbridge and Morris (2001) specifically focus on the construction of oppositional consciousness in social movements work.

14. Lichterman (1996) and Wood (2002) make especially compelling cases about the need for in-depth, ethnographic research on grassroots organizations.

15. A large, robust literature exists on organizational culture; see, for example, Frost et al. (1985). I have chosen to draw my definition of culture from the literature on social change organizations, however, because traditional organizational culture research primarily focuses on what happens inside for-profit firms and workplaces rather than social change organizations. For example, the collective goals of education organizing groups are much more similar to those of social change organizations, and organizer-leader relations are quite different from manager-employee ones. Since social change organizations are dependent upon voluntary action, dissent and coercion are often expressed very differently in social change organizations than they are in paid workplace situations. See also Johnston and Klandermans (1995) and Hall et al. (1996) for discussion on culture, its dominant definitions, and how it might be measured in research.

16. Prominent examples include Delgado (1986), Rogers (1990), Russell (1990), Rooney (1995), Gecan (2002), and Jonnes (2002).

17. Fisher (1984) provides a definition and analysis of neighborhood-based community organizing.

18. Wood argues that the race-based organization held steadfastly to a more extremist class-based ideology, which helped it to excel on controversial issues such as police brutality, but impeded its progress on issues that demanded collaboration or the planning and development of new policies or programs such as the creation of new schools; ultimately, OCO was more successful in its campaigns. I wondered whether I could make similar arguments because, at first glance, the more campaign-oriented Alinskyite organizations in the present study (including the NWBCCC) were more successful. Certainly, they were more adept at gaining immediate wins within the school system.

19. Osterman (2002), Wood (2002), Hart (2001), and Warren (2001) all include fine-grained descriptions of religious rituals, homilies, and the like in faith-based organizing.

20. Hyde (1986) provides another exploration of the women-centered model.

21. This is not to say that organizers or researchers blithely place Freire and Alinsky together. Mondros and Wilson (1994), Kroeker (1995), and Zachary and olatoye (2001) discuss the influence of both on community organizing work.

22. Key readings on critical race theory are presented in Crenshaw et al. (1995), while Delgado and Stefancic (2001) provide a nice introduction. Yosso (2005) discusses some implications of critical race theory in a community context, especially in the ways in which the strengths and resources of nonwhite communities can be devalued by falsely, facially neutral "white" criteria.

23. Warren (2001), Wood (2002), and Osterman (2002) all present such dramatic processes of personal transformation in their case study organizations' leaders.

24. See Goodwin, Jasper, and Polletta (2000, 2001) on the role of emotions in social movements, especially framing processes, identity formation, and repertoires of protest. Rogers (1990) talks about a sense of controlled and directed outrage, or "cold anger," in the context of grassroots organizing.

25. See Mediratta and Fruchter (2001).

26. This range of political tactics and campaign activities is presented in Burghardt (1982), Delgado (1986), Warren (2001), Russell (1990), and Mediratta and Karp (2003).

27. Chetkovich and Kunreuther (2006) make this point. They also state that practitioners are much more likely to talk about "social change organizations" than academics; in this case, research has not kept up with practice.

28. For example, while Anyon (2005) and Oakes and Rogers (2006) are more hopeful about education organizing as a social movement, Schutz (2007) is less so. It is interesting to note that Swarts (2007) examines national networks of community organizing groups via the lens of social movement theory.

29. Ospina and Foldy (2005) discuss similar dynamics in the data on social change organizations drawn from the Leadership for a Changing World program.

30. Here I am again drawing from parameters set forth by Chetkovich and Kunreuther (2006).

Chapter 2. Public Education and Organizing in the Bronx

1. More recent analyses of the Ocean Hill–Brownsville story include Stafford (2000), Back (2001), and Podair (2003).

2. This argument was laid out in Gordon (1968).

3. Gittell (1969), Ravitch (1974, 1978), and Katz (1987) present different perspectives of the debate; Naples (2002) analyses the debate itself via the lens of discourse analysis. Barrett (2002, 2003) talks about the legacy of the debate and its impact on the Bloomberg administration.

4. See Ravitch (1978), Barrett (2002), and Kay (2003). While Podair (2003) would probably agree that popular media outlets distorted the parents' claims, he ultimately points to seemingly unbridgeable cultural divides between blacks and whites. Yet, as Wilder (2001) writes, "The furor of the 1960s campaign can obscure its primary cause. Black and Latino residents were not just fighting about the quality of education and the condition of the schools at that moment, rather they were engaged in a broader conflict over the inability of communities of color to secure the children's future given ghettoization...[and lack of] control of educational resources" (223–24).

5. Detailed descriptions of the lawsuit, as well as full transcripts of court orders, can be found via the Campaign for Fiscal Equity website, http://www.cfequity.org/ (accessed July 1, 2004).

6. See Winter (2004).

7. See Herszenhorn (2006).

8. The entire No Child Left Behind legislation is available via its website, http://www.ed.gov/nclb/landing.jhtml?src=pb (accessed August 5, 2004).

9. See Gootman (2004a).

10. Indeed, Stone et al. (2001) contend that long-term reform requires a "community synergy" of the kind that Gold et al. (2004) might claim community organizing facilitates. Henig et al. (2001) argue that, at least in the case study cities of Atlanta, Baltimore, Detroit, and Washington, D.C., well-intentioned African American leadership was not a force powerful enough to bring about school reform; this was partly because organizational and curricular innovations are not adequate replacements for the accountability that comes with civic capacity and collective action.

11. Mediratta (2001) provides an excellent overview of New York City community organizing, especially on education reform.

12. See Jacobson and Kasinitz (1986).

13. Jonnes (2002), for example, writes about the NWBCCC's campaigns to stop banks from granting loans to abusive or negligent landlords.

14. Tyack and Cuban (1995) and Meier (1996) tackle the ways in which the American educational system has or has not changed over the years, and the ways in which *A Nation at Risk* led some policy makers to fuel hysteria about American public schools and popular support for the standards reform movement.

15. See Mediratta (2001).

16. See Herszenhorn (2007).

17. Jonnes (2002) describes these events in her history of the Bronx.

18. These statistics were applicable during the book's fieldwork period and were drawn from Advocates for Children (2004).

19. I compiled these statistics at http://www.infoshare.org (Community Studies of New York, 2004).

20. See Gootman (2003).

21. I used data relevant to the fieldwork period of the present study, 2003–4; all of the data were drawn from census, state, and city surveys and then tabulated using the Infoshare website (Community Studies of New York, 2004).

22. According to the U.S. Census, a Hispanic/Latino background is one of ethnicity rather than race per se; for instance, a person can be both if he is an African descendant who hails from Puerto Rico.

23. O'Connell (1991) provides a nice history of the grassroots campaigns (and the alliances with business groups) that led to the Chicago reforms.

24. Bryk et al. (1998a) and Fung (2004) discuss the history and efficacy of local school councils.

25. An interesting, concurrent debate surrounds the changing legacy of "community control." Margonis and Parker (1999) analyze how the same term has been adopted by groups with ideologies quite incongruous with those of 1960s community control activists. Specifically, voucher proponents view community control as a means for fiscal control, to promote school choice and other marketlike mechanisms in the school system; with this, an unlikely alliance was struck between neoconservative policy makers and the African American community in Milwaukee, Wisconsin. Hess (1999) writes about the ways in which, after a few years, the alliance soured when African American leaders felt that policy makers were not addressing their goal of racial justice. Naples (2002) dissects how community control, originally used to lend power to disenfranchised, inner-city minority populations, was transformed by groups of suburban social conservatives in a way unimaginable to those who coined the term. Specifically, these conservative groups have used the community control frame to successfully ban textbooks that do not reflect their community values, such as New York City's Rainbow Curriculum literature about gay and lesbian families. In New York, the Forest Hills (Queens) and Canarsie (Brooklyn) neighborhoods took community control to mean that they could block housing projects or busing programs that would have brought African Americans into their neighborhoods (Podair, 2001).

Chapter 3. Organizing the Organizations: The Alinskyite Tool Kit

1. Warren (2001) and Osterman (2002), for instance, examine the evolution of Alinskyite principles in contemporary IAF affiliates.

2. Fisher and Kling (1990) present an analysis of the role of ideology in community organizing. They argue that organizing without the "conscious use of ideology" often leads to reactionary politics, and a failure to place issues within a larger political context.

3. Both Warren (2001) and Osterman (2002) include quotes by Ernie Cortes on this subject.

4. All names have been changed to ensure confidentiality. See appendix A for a more thorough overview of the study's methods.

5. This point is based on the observations and comments made during meetings associated with the Northwest Bronx Clergy and Community Coalition (http://www. northwestbronx.org; accessed September 30, 2008). See also Dunlap (1982) and Lewine (1995) for more contemporaneous documentation of the fluctuating "northernmost" boundaries of the South Bronx.

6. Delgado (1986), Warren (2001), and Wood (2002) discuss the diversity of faiths and denominations represented in other faith-based networks and organizations.

7. Such official tiers of leadership are reminiscent of IAF categories of leadership described in Warren (2001) and Osterman (2002).

Chapter 4. Friends Forever: The Freirean Tool Kit

1. Facundo (1985) discusses interpretations of Freire's books, especially as applied in community organizing, in the United States. Heaney (1996) and Schugurensky (2000) focus on the impact of Freire's legacy on adult popular education, while Carroll and Minkler (2000) look at public health campaigns through a Freirean lens.

2. Isaksen (2003) is but one work that draws upon Freire's work in a critical analysis of issues of race.

3. See, for example, Minkler (1997).

4. See Trebay (2000).

5. This is cited in Mediratta and Karp (2003, 3).

6. See, for example, Guishard et al. (2003).

7. See Rooney (1995), Jonnes (2002), and Harris (2003).

8. An important exception is Goodwin, Jasper, and Polletta (2001), who themselves make this assertion. Some of the key dynamics examined in their edited collection are not applicable to social change organizations that operate outside of social movements, but others are. For instance, case studies dissect how participants articulate shared emotions, such as shock or betrayal, in mobilization and how they control fear in high-risk situations, as well as how emotional benefits, such as solidarity and self-respect, sustain activists or insurgents, especially when more "concrete" gains might take a while.

9. Schutz (2007, 2008) forcefully asserts that social inquiry is often not what it's cracked up to be.

Chapter 5. Off the Charts: Tackling Issues of Race in SCOs

1. This is a crucial assertion in critical race theory. See Crenshaw et al. (1995) and Delgado and Stefancic (2001).

2. Although Agocs (2004) focuses on workplaces as a whole and not on social change organizations, I found her heuristic to be quite helpful.

3. Mansbridge (1983) writes about the ways in which, even in town hall meetings or consensus proceedings that appear to be more egalitarian, better-trained or more eloquent parties can dominate discussions.

4. Both Russell (1992) and Delgado (1986) raise concerns about the racial demographic composition of ACORN staff, especially in the upper ranks.

5. Guinier and Torres (2002), for instance, write about race as "political race," as a means with which our society as a whole can talk about issues that will ultimately plague us all, but are first most explicit among the most marginalized. See also Center for Reflective Community Practice (2004).

6. A similar dynamic is described by Delgado (1994, 2003) and Wood (2002).

7. One version of the debate on whether different identities (those of class, race, gender, sexual orientation, etc.) have to be placed on a hierarchy, and how they should be addressed in grassroots organizing is Mike Miller, "Critique of Delgado, Beyond the Politics of Place,'" available at http://comm-org.wisc.edu/papers96/Millerindex.html (accessed September 1, 2007).

8. Ostrander (1999) analyzes tensions surrounding race and gender in the context of a progressive foundation. She writes that in her case study organization, people

"modified their structure for a variety of reasons that were often race and gender based. While conflict did occur, people created some measure of organizational solidarity across gender and race around their agreement on the modifications, an agreement that sometimes seemed unstable and transitory" (640). She is cautiously optimistic about the organization's ability to tackle issues of race: "It is possible to create...organizing across the intersections of gender, race, ethnicity...solidarity, but most probably in the form of continued struggles...and active ongoing efforts to repeatedly resist and challenge them...[constitute] an ongoing and unstable project" (641).

9. Delgado (1998) uses the phrase "lowest possible denominator."

10. Evans (1979) and Evans and Boyte (1986) provide discussions of the importance and implications of "free spaces," while Polletta (1999) problematizes indiscriminate and wide-ranging use of the concept.

11. While no single study combines analyses of social capital with the notion of organizational spaces in community organizing, Woolcock (1998) provides an incredibly helpful framework of analysis on the definitions, sources, and implications of different types of social capital, especially in the context of economic development; Warren (2001) articulates the ways in which the Texas branch of the Industrial Areas Foundation was especially adept at building bridging capital; and Fabricant and Fisher (2002) specifically examine the role of social capital in community organizing work.

12. See Woolcock (1998) and Warren (2001).

13. Also see Sen (2003) about working across differences in community organizing.

14. Delgado (1998) also makes this assertion.

15. A key criticism of "cultural work" and "subjective consciousness" approaches is that they consist of idealistic, pie-in-the-sky calls to an abstract common humanity and ignore important power inequalities within the coalition (see Carmichael and Hamilton 1967, Chung and Chang 1998, Sonenshein 2001). Nevertheless, more contemporary approaches to coalition-building suggest that cultural work by social change organizations has become more sophisticated (Bernstein 2005), and my own research with data from the Leadership for a Changing World program (http://www.leadershipforchange.org/) suggests that many social change organizations highlight multiple, cross-cutting identities held by any individual rather than a superordinate "human" one.

16. Collins (2004) further scrutinizes the dynamics of intersectionality.

17. Santow (2007) looks back upon Alinsky's Chicago organizing in the 1960s through a social geography lens—what he defines as the "relationship between place, identity, and social structure"—and concludes that purely local, place-based organizing was not equipped to battle metropolitanwide, institutional and social forces like redlining, "white flight," and segregation (29).

18. One interviewee, drawing upon his previous experiences working as an ACORN organizer in the Midwest, spoke about being at a loss for words when the undocumented Latino workers he was helping to organize insisted that they wanted their next campaign to oust sex workers from the local area, even though many of these sex workers were themselves undocumented or trying to escape abject poverty. For this organizer, the nonideological Alinskyite framework, with its emphasis on winnable issues, did not equip him with the reflection, issue-selection processes, and dialogue needed to engage his constituents in ways that did not pit them against, rather than with, another marginalized group.

Chapter 6. What These Tools Can Build: Developing Capacities for Policy Making

1. This is an iteration of the policy-making process presented by Lindblom (1968).

2. Kingdon's (1984) multiple streams approach or garbage can theory provides a helpful alternative perspective.

3. Miller (1996) and Osterman (2002) are two of the authors that discuss this, especially in the context of the IAF.

4. Conyers (2004).

5. Fung (2004) and Polletta (2002) disentangle the benefits and complications of decisions made in a participatory or deliberative democratic context. While Fung focuses on governmental institutions such as local school councils, Polletta focuses on social movement organizations.

6. This exercise is akin to "cognitive mapping" of one's environment in Freirean participatory action research models, as explored in Romero González et al. (2007).

7. In a review of Warren (2001), Ganz analyzes division of labor at the Texas IAF and concludes that "IAF organizations do develop local leadership, but the authority remains in the hands of professional organizers, who serve as the hubs linking part-time efforts of volunteer leaders. However, democracy promises the opportunity not only to participate but also to exercise control" (2002, 63). To Ganz, this system helps organizers to represent grassroots interests at the local level, but it conflicts with democratic principles at the state or national levels.

Chapter 7. Favorite Hits: Embedded Preferences for Confrontation or Collaboration

1. The issue of nonmaterial rewards, such as pride from fulfilled obligations or close friendships, is closely linked to that of emotions in social change work; see Goodwin, Jasper, and Polletta (2001).

2. Those involved in Freirean SCOs might argue that "social activities" help organizers and leaders to look beyond "self-interest," cultivate friendships, and, collectively, expand their notions of "community" and the "public good." In a discussion of self-interest in public life, Eliasoph writes, "Self-interest is not always the only thing that matters to people, anyway. Citizens forfeit their own power when *any* preconceived definition of public life systematically filters some valuable kinds of speech out of the public forum" (1998, 17, emphasis in the original). In such a scenario, engaging in challenging discussions about "what we really want" is as important as getting it.

3. According to this leader, this remark's conscious use of arguable diction is meant to act as a rhetorical weapon, as a means of forcing issues of gender, sexuality, and race to be contested. Other leaders and organizers at the same organization might have objected to the language used, and upon reading this quote, one organizer adamantly stated that such language was not representative of the NWBCCC. The fact that others might disagree, then, is indicative of some of the embedded issues toward gender and race discussed in chapter 5.

4. Indeed, Piven and Cloward (1977) might argue that disruption is the only true weapon of social change organizations with few resources.

Chapter 8. Commitment and Commencement

1. See Association of Community Organizations for Reform Now (2004) and the ACORN website as a whole (http://www.acorn.org) for documentation. While ACORN's voter registration record in impressive, the results of the 2004 presidential election have prompted progressive organizations to debate the effectiveness of their political strategies in the early 2000s. In the 2008 presidential election, Republican politicians accused ACORN of engaging in a voter fraud "scandal" because some of its voter registration cards were clearly false. In 2008's last presidential debate, Senator John McCain stated that ACORN "may be destroying the fabric of democracy." As this book goes into press, however, inquiries into ACORN's voter registration efforts have failed to find any large-scale irregularities. Meanwhile, pundits also expressed concern over voter roll purges and stated that voter suppression constituted a much larger threat to the legitimacy of election results than ACORN's alleged voter fraud. See, for example, Herbert (2008). At the same time, the organization has been working to sever all ties with founder Wade Rathke, whose brother Dale Rathke embezzled nearly $1 million from organizational coffers in 2000, and named the New York chapter's executive director, Bertha Lewis, as ACORN's national chief organizer (Strom 2008). These developments fueled larger discussions among organizers on (1) whether these incidents, so emphasized in the mainstream media, would overshadow ACORN's 38 years of work and campaign wins on behalf of and by working-class Americans, and (2) the extent to which ACORN's troubles reflect endemic structural inequalities and challenges that plague all social movements and SCOs. See Dreier and Atlas (2008) and discussions from July 2008 at http://comm-org.wisc.edu (accessed October 23, 2008).

2. Kugel (2004) and Gonzalez (2005) are two examples.

3. See, for instance, Gootman, 2004b.

4. Minkoff (1994, 2002) examines trends in national women's and minority organizations since 1955, noting a rise in a hybrid advocacy-and-services form that helped the organizations to tap additional resources and build legitimacy, but only for a while. Her findings emphasize the need for constant adaptation by social change organizations to changing institutional contexts.

5. See Mediratta and Fruchter (2001).

6. See Davis et al. (2005).

7. Bryk et al. (1998a, 1998b) discuss this in the context of Chicago school reform.

8. These are some of the strengths of participatory democracy articulated by Fung and Wright (2003), Fung (2004), and Polletta (2002).

9. Lopez, Kreider, and Coffman (2005) specifically emphasize the role of such social change organizations as "intermediaries" at what they describe as individual, organizational, and relational levels.

10. As discussed in chapter 4, Schutz (2007) is wary about the potential of certain models of action (such as those forwarded by John Dewey and, perhaps, Freire) to move beyond critique and enact concrete change.

11. Osterman (2007) writes about the ways in which community organizing groups might evade the "iron law of oligarchy" forwarded by Michels (1915).

12. See Freeman (1973).

13. For more information, see Urban Youth Collaborative (2007) and their website at http://www.urbanyouthcollaborative.org.

14. This episode is documented in Mediratta (2006).

15. Harcourt (2002) examines the assumptions embedded in, as well as the political uses of, the "broken windows" theory.

16. See Mediratta (2006).

17. Alonso, Anderson, Su, and Theoharis (2009) argue that meaningful, effective school reform is unlikely to be developed without the participation of the youth who are most affected in the policy-making process.

18. Skocpol (2004) analyzes the contours and potential remedies for our "diminished democracy."

19. Swidler (1986) argues that there are actually two models of cultural action and tool kits, one for settled cultural periods and one for unsettled cultural periods. In unsettled periods, change is more likely to occur; new, coherent ideologies can be presented to give individuals and SCOs a full set of instructions, thereby guiding direct lines of action, instead of just producing potential tool kits. Still, it remains unclear whether this requisite "unsettling" of the culture is one that occurs in the society at large, within a social change organization, or both. Also, since "unsettled periods" are usually euphemisms for crises, they do not exactly sound pleasant. Hopefully, organizers and leaders at SCOs can think about improving their tool kits even when they are not in crisis. See also Lichterman (1996) and Steinberg (2002).

20. These arguments are outlined in Weick (1976) and DiMaggio and Powell (1983).

Appendix A. Pounding the Pavement: Research Methods

1. According to Mason, a work of research's validity is measured by "how well matched...the logic of the method [is] to the kinds of research questions you are asking and the kind of social explanation you are intending to develop" (1996, 147).

2. See Guba and Lincoln (1981).

3. This method was informed by Ragin (1992).

4. See King, Keohane, and Verba (1994) and Collier and Mahoney (1996).

5. I use the definition of "power organizations" forwarded by Smock (2003), as discussed in chapter 1.

6. See Geertz (1983, 1973).

7. See Strauss and Corbin (1998).

8. I am using, in a rather loose way, the term forwarded by Said (1979) to highlight the impossibility of being a "neutral" participant observer in my research, as well as the many complications of conducting research with people from different backgrounds (defined in a variety of ways) and occupying different social positions than myself.

9. See Morse (1994, 1995).

References

Association of Community Organizations for Reform Now. 2004. "Over 1 Million Voters Registered!" http://www.acorn.org/index.php?id=2724 (accessed November 15, 2004).

Advocates for Children. 2004. "The New York City School System." http://www.advocatesforchildren.org/resource/nycfactsheet.php3 (accessed August 15, 2004).

Agocs, Carol. 2004. *Surfacing Racism in the Workplace: Qualitative and Quantitative Evidence of Systemic Discrimination.* Toronto, ON: Ontario Human Rights Commission.

Alinsky, Saul. 1946. *Reveille for Radicals.* New York: Vintage.

———. 1971. *Rules for Radicals.* New York: Random House.

Alonso, Gaston, Noel Anderson, Celina Su, and Jeanne Theoharis. 2009. *Our Schools Suck: Young People Talk Back to a Segregated Nation on the Failures of Public Education.* New York: New York University Press.

Anyon, Jean. 2005. *Radical Possibilities: Public Policy, Urban Education, and a New Social Movement.* New York: Routledge.

Back, Adina. 2001. "Blacks, Jews, and the Struggle to Integrate Brooklyn's High School 258: A Cold War Story." *Journal of American Ethnic History* 20:38–69.

Badillo, Herman. 2006. *One Nation, One Standard: An Ex-Liberal on How Hispanics Can Succeed Just Like Other Immigrant Groups.* New York: Sentinel.

Barrett, Wayne. 2002. "Déjà Vu All Over Again: Echoes from the '60s Haunt Bloomberg's School Reform." *Village Voice,* June 11. http://www.villagevoice.com/news/0223,170262,35580,5.html (accessed August 1, 2004).

———. 2003. "The Underside of Bloomberg's School Reform." *Village Voice,* October 22–28. http://www.villagevoice.com/issues/0343/barrett.php (accessed August 1, 2004).

Bernstein, Mary. 2005. "Identity Politics." *Annual Review of Sociology* 31:47–74.

Berry, Jeffrey. 1999. "The Rise of Citizen Groups." In *Civic Engagement in American Democracy,* edited by Theda Skocpol and Morris P. Fiorina. Washington, DC: Brookings Institution Press.

Bonilla-Silva, Eduardo. 2003. *Racism without Racists: Color-blind Racism and the Persistence of Racial Inequality in the United States.* Lanham, MD: Rowman and Littlefield.

Bryk, Anthony, Penny Bebring, David Kerbow, Sharon Rollow, and John Q. Easton. 1998a. *Charting Chicago School Reform: Democratic Localism as a Lever for Change.* Boulder, CO: Westview.

Bryk, Anthony, Yeow Meng Thum, John Q. Easton, and Stuart Luppescu. 1998b. *Academic Productivity of the Chicago Public Elementary Schools: A Technical*

Report Sponsored by the Consortium on Chicago School Research. Chicago: Consortium on Chicago School Research. http://www.consortium-chicago.org/ac robat/Technical%20Report.pdf (accessed December 1, 2003).

Burghardt, Stephen. 1982. *The Other Side of Organizing.* Cambridge, MA: Schenckman.

Calpotura, Francis, and Kim Fellner. 1996. "The Square Pegs Find their Groove: Reshaping the Organizing Circle." Washington, DC: National Organizing Alliance.

Carlo, Fernando, Antoine Powell, Laura Vazquez, Shoshana Daniels, and Clay Smith, with Kavitha Mediratta and Amy Zimmer. 2005. "Youth Take the Lead on High School Reform Issues." *Rethinking Schools* 19. http://www.rethinking-schools.org/archive/19_04/yout194.shtml (accessed March 2, 2006).

Carmichael, Stokely, and Charles V. Hamilton. 1967. *Black Power: The Politics of Liberation in America.* New York: Vintage.

Carr, Leslie G. 1997. *"Colorblind" Racism.* Thousand Oaks, CA: Sage.

Carroll, Julie, and Meredith Minkler. 2000. "Freire's Message to Social Workers: Looking Backward, Looking Ahead." *Journal of Community Practice* 8:21–36.

Carter, Prudence. 2005. *Keepin' It Real: School Success Beyond Black and White.* New York: Oxford University Press.

Center for Reflective Community Practice. 2004. *Vital Difference: The Role of Race in Building Community.* Cambridge, MA: Massachusetts Institute of Technology. http://web.mit.edu/crcp/vitaldiffi/ (accessed December 7, 2004).

Check, Joseph W. 2002. *Politics, Language, and Culture: A Critical Look at Urban School Reform.* Westport, CT: Praeger.

Chetkovich, Carol, and Frances Kuneuther. 2006. *From the Ground Up: Grassroots Organizations Making Social Change.* Ithaca, NY: Cornell University Press.

Chung, Angie, and Edward Chang. 1998. "From Third World Liberation to Multiple Oppression Politics: A Contemporary Approach to Interethnic Coalitions." *Social Justice* 25:80–100.

Collier, David, and James Malloney. 1996. "Insights and Pitfalls: Selection Bias in Qualitative Research." *World Politics* 49:56–91.

Collins, Patricia Hill. 2004. *Black Sexual Politics: African Americans, Gender, and the New Racism.* New York: Routledge.

Community Studies of New York, Inc./Infoshare. 2004. *Area Profiles.* [Tabulated data.] http://www.infoshare.org (accessed August 2, 2004).

Conyers, Allison. 2004. "ACORN Members in 48 Cities Rally for Education Funding and Civic Participation." http://www.acorn.org/index.php?id=2088andtx_ ttnews[tt_news]=3795andtx_ttnews[backPid]=43andcHash=d85b0a0165 (accessed December 1, 2004).

Crenshaw, Kimberlé, Neil Gotanda, Gary Peller, and Kendall Thomas, eds. 1995. *Critical Race Theory: The Key Writings that Formed the Movement.* New York: New Press.

Davis, Gerald F., Doug McAdam, W. Richard Scott, and Mayer N. Zald, eds. 2005. *Social Movements and Organization Theory.* New York: Cambridge University Press.

Delgado, Gary. 1985. *Organizing the Movement: The Roots and Growth of ACORN.* Philadelphia: Temple University Press.

———. 1994. *Beyond the Politics of Place: New Directions in Community Organizing in the 1990s.* Oakland: Applied Research Center.

———. 1998, November–December. "The Last Stop Sign." *Shelterforce.* http://www.nhi.org/online/issues/102/stopsign.html (accessed July 1, 2004).

———. 2003. *Multiracial Formations: New Instruments for Social Change.* Oakland, CA: Applied Research Center.

Delgado, Richard, and Jean Stefancic. 2001. *Critical Race Theory.* New York: New York University Press.

DiMaggio, Paul, and Walter Powell. 1983. "The Iron Cage Revisited: Institutional Isomorphism and Collective Rationality in Organizational Fields." *American Sociological Review* 48:147–60.

Doane, Ashley, and Eduardo Bonilla-Silva, eds. 2003. *White Out: The Continuing Significance of Racism.* New York: Routledge.

Dreier, Peter. 1996. "Community Empowerment Strategies: The Limits and Potential of Community Organizing in Urban Neighborhoods." *Cityscape: A Journal of Policy Development and Research* 2:121–59.

———. 2005. "ACORN and Progressive Politics in America"; http://comm-org.wisc.edu/papers.htm (accessed November 1, 2007).

Dreier, Peter, and John Atlas. 2008. "ACORN under the Microscope." *The Huffington Post,* July 14. http://www.huffingtonpost.com/peter-dreier/acorn-under-the-microscop_b_112491.html (accessed July 29, 2008).

Dunlap, David W. 1982. "Bronx Housing Devastation Found Slowing Substantially." *New York Times,* March 22.

Dyson, Michael Eric. 2005. *Is Bill Cosby Right? Or Has the Black Middle Class Lost Its Mind?* New York: Basic Civitas Books.

Eliasoph, Nina. 1998. *Avoiding Politics: How Americans Produce Apathy in Everyday Life.* New York: Cambridge University Press.

Emirbayer, Mustafa, and Ann Mische. 1998. "What is Agency?" *American Journal of Sociology* 103:962–1023.

Evans, Sara. 1979. *Personal Politics: The Roots of Women's Liberation in the Civil Rights Movement and the New Left.* New York: Alfred A. Knopf.

Evans, Sara, and Harry Boyte. 1986. *Free Spaces: The Sources of Democratic Change in America.* Chicago: University of Chicago Press.

Fabricant, Michael, and Robert Fisher. 2002. "Agency-Based Community Building in Low-Income Neighborhoods: A Praxis Framework." *Journal of Community Practice* 10:1–21.

Facundo, Blanca. 1985. "How is Freire Seen in the United States?" http://www.uow.edu.au/arts/sts/bmartin/dissent/documents/Facundo/Facundo.html (accessed February 1, 2004).

Fernandez, Manny. 2006. "Memories Fade, as do Some Bronx Boundary Lines." *New York Times,* September 16.

Ferree, Myra and David A. Merrill. 2000. "Hot Movements, Cold Cognition: Thinking about Social Movements in Gendered Frames." *Contemporary Sociology* 29:454–62.

Fisher, Dana. 2006. *Activism, Inc.* Palo Alto, CA: Stanford University Press.

Fisher, Robert. 1984. *Let the People Decide: Neighborhood Organizing in America.* New York: Twayne.

Fisher, Robert, and Joseph Kling. 1990. "Leading the People: Two Approaches to the Role of Ideology in Community Organizing." In *Dilemmas of Activism,* edited by Prudence Posner and Joseph Kling. Philadelphia: Temple University Press.

Foldy, Erica, Laurie Goldman, and Sonia Ospina. 2004. "Shaping Policy, Making History: The Role of Cognitive Shifts in Social Change Leadership." Paper presented at the 26th Annual Research Conference Association for Public Policy Analysis and Management, October 28–30, Atlanta, Georgia.

Freire, Paulo. 1972. *Pedagogy of the Oppressed.* Translated by Myra Bergman Ramos New York: Herder and Herder.

———. 1985. *The Politics of Education: Culture, Power, and Liberation.* Translated by Donaldo Macedo New York: Bergin and Garvey.

Freeman, Jo. 1973. "The Tyranny of Structurelessness." *Berkeley Journal of Sociology* 17:151–65.

Frost, Peter J., Larry F. Moore, Meryl Reis Louis, Craig C. Lundberg, and Joanne Martin. 1985. *Organizational Culture.* Beverly Hills, CA: Sage.

Fung, Archon. 2004. *Empowered Participation: Reinventing Urban Democracy.* Princeton, NJ: Princeton University Press.

———. 2003. "Can Social Movements Save Democracy?" *Boston Review* 28(1). http://www.bostonreview.net/BR28.1/fung.html (accessed December 1, 2005).

Fung, Archon, and Erik Olin Wright, eds. 2003. *Deepening Democracy: Institutional Innovations in Empowered Participatory Governance.* London: Verso.

Gamson, William. 1995. "Constructing Social Protest." In *Social Movements and Culture,* edited by Hank Johnston and Bert Klandermans. Minneapolis: University of Minnesota Press.

Ganz, Marshall. 2002. "Making Democracy Work?" *Contexts,* Fall, 62–63.

Gecan, Michael. 2002. *Going Public: An Organizer's Guide to Citizen Action.* Boston: Beacon Press.

Geertz, Clifford. 1973. "Thick Description: Toward an Interpretive Theory of Culture." In *The Interpretation of Cultures: Selected Essays.* New York: Basic Books.

———. 1983. *Local Knowledge: Further Essays in Interpretive Anthropology.* New York: Basic Books.

Gittell, Marilyn. 1969. "Professionalism and Public Participation." In *The Politics of Urban Education,* edited by Marilyn Gittell and Alan G. Hevesi. New York: Praeger.

Gold, Eva, Elaine Simon, Leah Mundell, and Chris Brown. "Bringing Community Organizing into the School Reform Picture." *Nonprofit and Voluntary Sector Quarterly,* supplement 33:54S–76S.

Gonzalez, David. 2005. "Yesterday's Tenant Activist, Today's Landlord." *New York Times,* January 11.

Goodwin, Jeff, James Jasper, and Francesca Polletta. 2000. "The Return of the Repressed: The Fall and Rise of Emotions in Social Movement Theory." *Mobilization: An International Journal* 5: 65–83.

———. 2001. *Passionate Politics: Emotions and Social Movements.* Chicago: University of Chicago Press.

Gootman, Elissa. 2003. "Lunch at 9:21, and the Students Are the Sardines." *New York Times,* October 14.

———. 2004a. "Schools Are Breaking Law on Transfers, Suit Charges." *New York Times,* October 16.

———. 2004b. "More Police, but Halls Are Still Jammed at Unruly School." *New York Times,* December 15.

Gordon, Sol. 1968. "The Community School and Decentralization: Dilemma or Opportunity for Planners?" *Pratt Planning Papers* 51:31–36.

Granovetter, Mark. 1973. "The Strength of Weak Ties." *American Journal of Sociology* 78:1360–80.

Guba, Egon G., and Yvonna S. Lincoln. 1981. *Effective Evaluation: Improving the Usefulness of Evaluation Results through Responsive and Naturalistic Approaches.* San Francisco: Jossey-Bass.

Guinier, Lani, and Gerald Torres. 2002. *The Miner's Canary: Enlisting Race, Resisting Power, Transforming Democracy.* Cambridge, MA: Harvard University Press.

Guishard, Monique, Michele Fine, Christine Doyle, Jeunesse Jackson, Rosemarie Roberts, Sati Singleton, Travis Staten, and Ashley Webb. 2003. "'As Long as I Got Breath, I'll Fight': Participatory Action Research for Educational Justice." [Research digest.] Cambridge, MA: Harvard Graduate School of Education, Harvard Family Research Project. http://www.gse.harvard.edu/hfrp/projects/fine/resources/digest/par.html (accessed September 1, 2003).

Hall, Stuart, David Held, Don Hubert, and Kenneth Thompson, eds. 1996. *Modernity: An Introduction to Modern Societies.* Cambridge: Open University Press.

Harcourt, Bernard. 2002. "Policing Disorder." *Boston Review* 27. http://bostonreview.net/BR27.2/harcourt.html (accessed April 4, 2007).

Harris, Lis. 2003. *Tilting at Mills: Green Dreams, Dirty Dealings, and the Corporate Squeeze.* Boston: Houghton Mifflin.

Hart, Stephen. 2001. *Cultural Dilemmas of Progressive Politics: Styles of Engagement among Grassroots Activists.* Chicago: University of Chicago Press.

Heaney, Tom. 1996. "Adult Education for Social Change." ERIC Monograph. http://www3.nl.edu/academics/cas/ace/resources/TomHeaney_Insight.cfm (accessed July 1, 2004).

Henig, Jeffrey R., Richard C. Hula, Marion Orr, and Desiree S. Pedescleaux. 1999. *The Color of School Reform: Race, Politics and the Challenge of Urban Education.* Princeton, NJ: Princeton University Press.

Herbert, Bob. 2008. "The Real Scandal." *New York Times,* October 21.

Herszenhorn, David. 2005. "Parents Seek Greater Voice in Schools from Chancellor." *New York Times,* December 12.

———. 2006. "New York Court Cuts Aid Sought for City Schools." *New York Times,* November 21.

———. 2007. "Restructuring of Schools Is Detailed by Chancellor." *New York Times,* April 17.

Hess, G. Alfred. 1999. "Community Participation or Control? From New York to Chicago." *Theory into practice* 38:216–24.

Hirschmann, Albert O. 1970. *Exit, Voice, and Loyalty: Responses to Decline in Firms, Organizations, and States.* Cambridge, MA: Harvard University Press.

Hyde, Cheryl. 1986. "Experiences of Women Activists: Implications for Community Organizing Theory and Practice." *Journal of Sociology and Social Welfare* 13:545–62.

Isaksen, Judy L. 2003. "From Critical Race Theory to Composition Studies: Pedagogy and Theory Building." *Legal Studies Forum* 24:695–711.

Jacobson, Michael, and Philip Kasinitz. 1986. "Burning the Bronx for Profit." *Nation,* November 15.

Jasper, James. 1997. *The Art of Moral Protest: Culture, Biography, and Creativity in Social Movements.* Chicago: University of Chicago Press.

Jencks, Christopher, and Meredith Phillips. 1998. *The Black-White Test Score Gap.* Washington, DC: Brookings Institution Press.

Johnston, Hank, and Bert Klandermans, eds. 1995. *Social Movements and Culture.* Minneapolis: University of Minnesota Press.

Jonnes, Jill. 2002. *South Bronx Rising: The Rise, Fall, and Resurrection of an American City.* Bronx, NY: Fordham University Press.

Katz, Michael B. 1987. *Reconstructing American Education.* Cambridge, MA: Harvard University Press.

Kay, Philip. 2003. "Striking Differences." *City Limits,* April.

King, Gary, Robert O. Keohane, and Sidney Verba. 1994. *Designing Social Inquiry.* Princeton, NJ: Princeton University Press.

Kingdon, John. 1984. *Agendas, Alternatives, and Public Policies.* Boston: Little, Brown.

Klandermans, Bert. 1991. "New Social Movements and Resource Mobilization: The European and the American Approach Revisited." In *Research on Social Movements: The State of the Art in Western Europe and the USA,* edited by Dieter Rucht. Boulder, CO: Westview Press.

Kroeker, Caroline J. 1995. "Individual, Organizational, and Societal Empowerment: A Study of the Processes in a Nicaraguan Agricultural Cooperative." *American Journal of Community Psychology* 235:749–64.

Kugel, Seth. 2004. "Down at the Grass Roots, an Emotional Fight over Turf." *New York Times,* December 5.

Lewine, Edward. 1995. "The South Bronx? It's a State of Mind." *Bronx Beat,* March 13. http://www.columbia.edu/cu/bb/oldstuff/bb0313.35.html (accessed September 1, 2007).

Lichterman, Paul. 1996. *The Search for Political Community: American Activists Reinventing Commitment.* New York: Cambridge University Press.

——. 1999. "Talking Identity in the Public Sphere: Broad Visions and Small Spaces in Identity Politics." *Theory and Society* 28:101–40.

Lindblom, Charles E. 1968. *The Policy-Making Process.* Englewood Cliffs, NJ: Prentice-Hall.

Lopez, M. Elena, Holly Kreider, and Julia Coffman. 2005. "Intermediary Organizations as Capacity Builders in Family Educational Involvement." *Urban Education* 40:78–105.

Macedo, Stephen, Yvette Alex-Assensoh, Jeffrey M. Berry, Michael Brintnall, David E. Campbell, Luis Ricardo Fraga, Archon Fung, William A. Galston, Christopher F. Karpowitz, Margaret Levi, Meira Levinson, et al. 2005. *Democracy at Risk: How Political Choices Undermine Citizen Participation, and What We Can Do about It*. Washington, DC: Brookings Institution Press.

Mansbridge, Jane. 1983. *Beyond Adversary Democracy*. Chicago: University of Chicago Press.

Mansbridge, Jane, and Aldon Morris. 2001. *Oppositional Consciousness: The Subjective Roots of Social Protest*. Chicago: University of Chicago Press.

Margonis, Frank, and Laurence Parker. 1999. "Choice: The Route to Community Control?" *Theory into practice* 38:203–8.

Mason, Jennifer. 1996. *Qualitative Researching*. London: Sage.

Mayer, Margit. 1991. "Social Movement Research and Social Movement Practice: The U.S. Pattern." In *Research on Social Movements: The State of the Art in Western Europe and the USA*, edited by Dieter Rucht. Boulder, CO: Westview Press.

McAdam, Doug. 1982. *Political Process and the Development of Black Insurgency, 1930–1970*. Chicago: University of Chicago Press.

———. 1996. "Conceptual Origins, Current Problems, Future Directions." In *Comparative Perspectives on Social Movements*, edited by Doug McAdam, John D. McCarthy, and Mayer N. Zald. New York: Cambridge University Press.

McAdam, Doug, Sidney Tarrow, and Charles Tilly. 2001. *Dynamics of Contention*. New York: Cambridge University Press.

McCarthy, John, and Mayer Zald. 1977. "Resource Mobilization and Social Movements." *American Journal of Sociology* 82:1212–41.

Mediratta, Kavitha. 2001. *Community Organizing for School Reform in New York City*. New York: Institute for Education and Social Policy, New York University.

———. 2006. "A Rising Movement." *National Civic Review*, Spring, 15–22.

Mediratta, Kavitha, and Norm Fruchter. 2001. *Mapping the Field of Organizing for School Improvement*. New York: Institute for Education and Social Policy, New York University.

———. 2003. "From Governance to Accountability: Building Relationships that Make Schools Work." New York: Drum Major Institute for Public Policy.

Mediratta, Kavitha, and Jessica Karp. 2003. *Parent Power and Urban School Reform: The Story of Mothers on the Move*. New York: Institute for Education and Social Policy, New York University.

Ment, David. 1995. "Board of Education." In *The Encyclopedia of New York City*, edited by Kenneth T. Jackson. New Haven, CT: Yale University Press.

Meier, Deborah. 1996. *The Power of Their Ideas: Lessons for America from a Small School in Harlem*. Boston: Beacon Press.

Meyer, David S., Nancy Whittier, and Belinda Robnett, eds. 2002. *Social Movements: Identity, Culture, and the State*. New York: Oxford University Press.

Michels, Robert. 1915. *Political Parties: A Sociological Study of the Oligarchical Tendencies of Modern Democracy.* Translated by Eden Paul and Cedar Paul. New York: Free Press.

Miles, Mathew B. and Michael Huberman. 1994. *Qualitative Data Analysis: An Expanded Sourcebook.* Thousand Oaks, CA: Sage.

Miller, Mike. 1993. "Organizing and Education." *Social Policy* 24:51–63.

———. 1996. *"Beyond the Politics of Place:* A Critical Review." San Francisco: ORGANIZE Training Center. http://comm-org.wisc.edu/papers96/miller.html (accessed January 20, 2004).

Minkler, Meredith, ed. 1997. *Community Organizing and Community Building for Health.* New Brunswick, NJ: Rutgers University Press.

Minkoff, Debra. 1994. "From Service Provision to Advocacy: The Shifting Legitimacy of Organizational Forms." *Social Forces* 72:943–69.

———. 2002. "The Emergence of Hybrid Organizational Forms: Combining Identity-Based Service Provision and Political Action." *Nonprofit and Voluntary Sector Quarterly* 31:377–401.

Mondros, Jacqueline, and Scott Wilson. 1994. *Organizing for Power and Empowerment.* New York: Columbia University Press.

Morris, Aldon. 1984. *The Origins of the Civil Rights Movement: Black Communities Organizing for Change.* New York: Free Press.

Morris, Aldon, and Carol Mueller, eds. 1992. *Frontiers in Social Movement Theory.* New Haven, CT: Yale University Press.

Morse, Janice M. 1994. "Designing Funded Qualitative Research." In *Handbook of Qualitative Research,* edited by Norman K. Denzin and Yvonna S. Lincoln. Thousand Oaks, CA: Sage.

———. 1995. "The Significance of Saturation." *Qualitative Health Research* 5:147–49.

Mumm, James. 2003. "Grounding Transcendence: New Additions to the Literature of Faith-Based Community Organizing." *Social Policy,* Fall. http://www.social policy.org/index.php?id=813 (accessed January 2, 2005).

Naples, Nancy A. 2002. "Materialist Feminist Discourse Analysis and Social Movement Research: Mapping the Changing Context for 'Community Control.'" In *Social Movements: Identity, Culture, and the State,* edited by David S. Meyer, Nancy Whittier, and Belinda Robnett. New York: Oxford University Press.

New York ACORN Schools Office. 1996. *Secret Apartheid: A Report on Discrimination against Black and Latino Parents and Children in the New York City Public Schools.* New York: Association of Community Organizations for Reform Now. http://www.acorn.org/index.php?id=547 (accessed September 30, 2008).

New York City Department of Education. 2003. "$51 Million Grant from Gates Foundation to Support Small, Dynamic High Schools to Boost Student Achievement." http://www.nycenet.edu/Administration/mediarelations/PressReleases/2003-2004/9-18-2003-9-36-51-337.htm (accessed May 1, 2004).

Oakes, Jeannie, and John Rogers with Martin Lipton. 2006. *Learning Power: Organizing for Education and Justice.* New York: Teachers College Press.

O'Connell, Mary. 1991. *School Reform Chicago Style: How Citizens Organized to Change Public Policy.* Chicago: Center for Neighborhood Technology.

Orr, Marion, ed. 2007. *Transforming the City: Community Organizing and Challenge of Political Change.* Lawrence: University Press of Kansas.

Orton, J. Douglas, and Karl E. Weick. 1990. "Loosely Coupled Systems: A Reconceptualization." *Academy of Management Review* 152:203–23.

Ospina, Sonia, and Erica Foldy. 2005. "Toward a Framework of Social Change Leadership." Paper presented at the Annual Meeting of the Public Management Research Association, September 30–October 1, Los Angeles.

Osterman, Paul. 2002. *Gathering Power: The Future of Progressive Politics in America.* Boston: Beacon Press.

——. 2007. "Evading the Iron Law of Oligarchy: Culture and Ritual in Social Movement Organizations." *Administrative Science Quarterly* 514:622–49.

Ostrander, Susan A. 1999. "Gender and Race in a Pro-Feminist, Progressive, Mixed-Gender, Mixed-Race Organization." *Gender and Society,* 13:628–42.

Piven, Frances Fox, and Richard A. Cloward. 1977. *Poor People's Movements: Why They Succeed, How They Fail.* New York: Vintage.

Podair, Jerald E. 2001. "The Ocean Hill–Brownsville Crisis: New York's *Antigone.*" New York: Gotham History Conference, October 6. http://www.gothamcenter. org/festival/2001/confpapers/podair.pdf (accessed September 1, 2003).

——. 2003. *The Strike that Changed New York: Blacks, Whites, and the Ocean Hill–Brownsville Crisis.* New Haven, CT: Yale University Press.

Polletta, Francesca. 1999. "'Free Spaces' in Collective Action." *Theory and Society* 28:1–38.

——. 2002. *Freedom Is an Endless Meeting.* Chicago: University of Chicago Press.

Putnam, Robert D. 1995. "Bowling Alone: America's Declining Social Capital." *Journal of Democracy* 6:65–78.

——. 2000. *Bowling Alone: The Collapse and Revival of American Community.* New York: Simon and Schuster.

Ragin, Charles C. 1992. *What Is a Case?: Exploring the Foundations of Social Inquiry.* New York: Cambridge University Press.

Ravitch, Diane. 1974. *The Great School Wars.* New York: Basic Books.

——. 1978. *The Revisionists Revised: A Critique of the Radical Attack on the Schools.* New York: Basic Books.

Robnett, Belinda. 2002. "External Political Change, Collective Identities, and Participation in Social Movement Organizations." In *Social Movements: Identity, Culture, and the State,* edited by David S. Meyer, Nancy Whittier, and Belinda Robnett. New York: Oxford University Press.

Rogers, Mary Beth. 1990. *Cold Anger: A Story of Faith and Power in Action.* College Station: University of North Texas Press.

Romero González, Erualdo, Raul Lejano, Guadalupe Vidales, Ross F. Conner, Yuki Kidokoro, Bahram Fazeli, and Robert Cabrales. 2007. "Participatory Action Research for Environmental Health: Encountering Freire in the Urban Barrio." *Journal of Urban Affairs* 29:77–100.

Rooney, Jim. 1995. *Organizing the South Bronx.* Albany: State University of New York Press.

Russell, Daniel M. 1990. *Political Organizing in Grassroots Politics.* New York: University Press of America.

———. 2003. "Detailed History of ACORN." http://www.acorn.org/index.php?id=51 (accessed October 15, 2003).

Said, Edward. 1979. *Orientalism.* New York: Vintage.

Santow, Mark. 2007. "Running in Place: Saul Alinsky, Race, and Community Organizing." In *Transforming the City: Community Organizing and Challenge of Political Change,* edited by Marion Orr. Lawrence: University Press of Kansas.

Sarantakos, Sotirios. 1998. *Social Research,* 2nd ed. London: Macmillan.

Schugurensky, Daniel. 2000. "Adult Education and Social Transformation: On Gramsci, Freire and the Challenge of Comparing Comparisons." *Comparative Education Review* 44:515–22.

Schutz, Aaron. 2007. Educators Have Much to Learn about Social Action." *Education Review* 103. http://edrev.asu.edu/essays/v10n3index.html (accessed March 17, 2007).

———. 2008. "Social Class and Social Action: The Middle-Class Bias of Democratic Theory in Education." *Teachers College Record* 110:405–42.

Skocpol, Theda. 2004. *Diminished Democracy: From Membership to Management in American Civic Life.* Norman: University of Oklahoma Press.

Sen, Rinku. 2003. *Stir It Up: Lessons in Community Organizing and Advocacy.* San Francisco: Jossey-Bass.

Shirley, Dennis. 1997. *Community Organizing for Urban School Reform.* Austin: University of Texas Press.

———. 2002. *Valley Interfaith and School Reform: Organizing for Power in South Texas.* Austin: University of Texas Press.

Shirley, Dennis, and Michael Evans. 2007. "Community Organizing and No Child Left Behind." In *Transforming the City: Community Organizing and Challenge of Political Change,* edited by Marion Orr. Lawrence: University Press of Kansas.

Sonenshein, Raphael. 2001. "When Ideologies Agree and Interests Collide, What's a Leader to Do? The Prospects for Latino-Jewish Coalition in Los Angeles." In *Governing American Cities: Inter-Ethnic Coalitions, Competition, and Conflict,* edited by Michael Jones-Correa. New York: Russell Sage.

Simpson, April. 2006. "City Parents Don't Like New Councils, Report Finds." *New York Times,* June 14.

Smock, Kristina. 2003. *Democracy in Action: Community Organizing and Urban Change.* New York: Columbia University Press.

Snow, David, and Robert Benford. 1988. "Ideology, Frame Resonance, and Participant Mobilization." *International Social Movement Research* 1:197–218.

Stafford, Walter. 2000. "The Struggle of New York City's Black Civil Society to Include Its Narrative in the Educational Policy Domain." Brighton, England: Institute for Development Studies. http://www.ids.ac.uk/ids/civsoc/final/usa/USA16.doc (accessed May 1, 2004).

Stall, Susan, and Randy Stoecker. 1998. "Community Organizing or Organizing Community? Gender and the Crafts of Empowerment." *Gender and Society* 12:729–56.

Steinberg, Marc. 2002. "Toward a More Dialogic Analysis of Social Movement Culture." In *Social Movements: Identity, Culture, and the State,* edited by David S. Meyer, Nancy Whittier, and Belinda Robnett. New York: Oxford University Press.

Stinchcombe, Arthur. 1968. *Constructing Social Theories.* Chicago: University of Chicago Press.

Stone, Clarence N., Jeffrey R. Henig, Bryan D. Jones, and Carol Pierannunzi. 2001. *Building Civic Capacity: The Politics of Reforming Urban Schools.* Lawrence: University Press of Kansas.

Strauss, Anselm, and Juliet Corbin. 1998. *Basics of Qualitative Research: Techniques and Procedures for Developing Grounded Theory,* 2nd ed. Thousand Oaks, CA: Sage.

Strom, Stephanie. 2008. "Acorn Working on Deal to Sever Ties with Founder." *New York Times,* October 16.

Swarts, Heidi. 2007. "Political Opportunity, Venue Shopping, and Strategic Innovation: ACORN's National Organizing." In *Transforming the City: Community Organizing and Challenge of Political Change,* edited by Marion Orr. Lawrence: University Press of Kansas.

Swidler, Ann. 1986. "Culture in Action: Symbols and Strategies." *American Sociological Review* 51:273–86.

———. 1995. "Cultural Power and Social Movements." In *Social Movements and Culture,* edited by Hank Johnston and Bert Klandermans. Minneapolis: University of Minnesota Press.

Tarrow, Sidney. 1998. *Power in Movement: Social Movements and Contentious Politics.* New York: Cambridge University Press.

Traub, James. 2002. "A Lesson in Unintended Consequences." *New York Times Magazine,* October 6.

Trebay, Guy. 2000. "Alternating Currents." *Village Voice,* January 19–25. http://www.villagevoice.com/issues/0003/trebay.php (accessed September 1, 2003).

Tyack, David, and Larry Cuban. 1995. *Tinkering toward Utopia: A Century of Public School Reform.* Cambridge, MA: Harvard University Press.

Urban Youth Collective. 2007. "What We Do." http://www.urbanyouthcollabora tive.org/page/what-we-do (accessed December 1, 2007).

Verba, Sidney, Kay Lehman Schlozman, and Henry E. Brady. 1995. *Voice and Equality: Civic Voluntarism in American Politics.* Cambridge, MA: Harvard University Press.

Wang, Lu-In. 2006. *Discrimination by Default: How Racism Becomes Routine.* New York: New York University Press.

Warren, Mark. 2001. *Dry Bones Rattling: Community Building to Revitalize American Democracy.* Princeton, NJ: Princeton University Press.

Weick, Karl. 1976. "Educational Organizations as Loosely Coupled Systems." *Administrative Science Quarterly* 21:1–19.

Wilder, Craig. 2001. *A Covenant with Color: Race and Social Power in Brooklyn.* New York: Columbia University Press.

Winter, Greg. 2004. "City Schools Need $5.6 Billion More, Court Panel Says." *New York Times,* December 1.

Wood, Richard. 2002. *Faith in Action: Religion, Race, and Democratic Organizing in America.* Chicago: University of Chicago Press.

Woolcock, Michael. 1998. "Social Capital and Economic Development: Toward a Theoretical Synthesis and Policy Framework." *Theory and Society* 27: 151–208.

Yin, Robert K. 1984. *Case Study Research: Design and Methods.* Beverly Hills, CA: Sage.

Yosso, Tara J. 2005. "Whose Culture Has Capital? A Critical Race Theory Discussion of Community Cultural Wealth." *Race Ethnicity and Education* 81:69–91.

Zachary, Eric, and shola olatoye. 2001. *Community Organizing for School Improvement in the Bronx.* New York: Institute for Education and Social Policy, New York University.

INDEX